Copyright and Course Reserves

Copyright and Course Reserves

Legal Issues and Best Practices for Academic Libraries

Carla S. Myers

Foreword by Kyle K. Courtney

LIBRARIES UNLIMITED®
An Imprint of ABC-CLIO, LLC
Santa Barbara, California • Denver, Colorado

Library of Congress Cataloging-in-Publication Data

Names: Myers, Carla S., author.
Title: Copyright and course reserves : legal issues and best practices for academic libraries / Carla S. Myers ; foreword by Kyle K. Courtney.
Description: Santa Barbara, California : Libraries Unlimited, an Imprint of ABC-CLIO, LLC, [2022] | Includes bibliographical references and index.
Identifiers: LCCN 2022019822 (print) | LCCN 2022019823 (ebook) | ISBN 9781440862038 (paperback) | ISBN 9781440862045 (ebook)
Subjects: LCSH: Fair use (Copyright)—United States. | Academic libraries—Law and legislation—United States. | Library copyright policies—United States. | Academic libraries—Reserve collections—United States.
Classification: LCC KF3030.1 .M94 2022 (print) | LCC KF3030.1 (ebook) | DDC 346.7304/82—dc23/eng/20220519
LC record available at https://lccn.loc.gov/2022019822
LC ebook record available at https://lccn.loc.gov/2022019823

ISBN: 978-1-4408-6203-8 (paperback)
978-1-4408-6204-5 (ebook)

26 25 24 23 22 1 2 3 4 5

This book is also available as an eBook.

Libraries Unlimited
An Imprint of ABC-CLIO, LLC

ABC-CLIO, LLC
147 Castilian Drive
Santa Barbara, California 93117
www.abc-clio.com

This book is printed on acid-free paper ∞

Manufactured in the United States of America

Samuel Clemens (also known as Mark Twain) wrote, "Only one thing is impossible for God: to find any sense in any copyright law on the planet." I respectfully disagree! While U.S. copyright law may seem overwhelming at first, it's really not so intimidating once you have mastered a few basics. So, to all of you working in libraries who are eager to learn about U.S. copyright law and ensure your reserve service policies and practices fall within the scope of the law . . .
I hope this book helps.

Contents

Foreword ix
Kyle K. Courtney

Acknowledgments xiii

Introduction xv

Part I Reserve Administrative Considerations **1**

Chapter 1 Course Reserves: An Overview 3

Chapter 2 Print Reserve Administration and Management 13

Chapter 3 Electronic and Media Reserves Administration and Management 55

Part II Copyright and Course Reserves **81**

Chapter 4 An Introduction to U.S. Copyright Law 83

Chapter 5 Determining the Copyright Status of a Work 109

Chapter 6 Section 107: Fair Use 119

Chapter 7 Section 108: Reproduction by Libraries and Archives 137

Chapter 8 Section 109: The First Sale Doctrine 149

Chapter 9 Section 110(2): The Technology, Education, and Copyright Harmonization Act 161

Chapter 10 Section 1201: The Digital Millennium Copyright Act 171

Chapter 11 Permissions and Licensing 181

Part III Additional Legal Considerations for Reserve Services **197**

Chapter 12 A Copyright Workflow for Reserve Services 199

Chapter 13 Accessibility Considerations Related to Reserve Services 211

Chapter 14 Mitigating Legal Risk 235

Appendix A: Copyright Term and the Public Domain in the United States Charts 259

Appendix B: Copyright Checklist: Fair Use 273

References 275

Index 287

Foreword

Welcome to the fold! I can't think of a more exciting, controversial, and essential topic than the book you currently have in your hand, *Copyright and Course Reserves: Legal Issues and Best Practices for Academic Libraries.*

There is certainty a great deal of concern over the "reserves conundrum" that is occurring in modern academic libraries today. High-level negotiations, 12+ years of electronic reserves litigation, and failed attempts at national community norms have led to a mass of confusion surrounding this topic. However, at its core, reserves are very much part of the fundamental mission of libraries: providing open, free, nondiscriminatory access to materials. Technology and the advent of what we call "e-reserves" shouldn't limit our service—in fact, it should improve it. We should be utilizing technology to enhance access to our collections. It's as if we have forgotten the real purpose of reserves, and that, as legally authorized purchasers of said works, we can make the works available to our patrons for as many times as they care to use the material, electronic, print, or otherwise.

Libraries have been managing reserve collections for hundreds of years. Want to see an original reserves collection? Have a look at the image of the Chained Library, Hereford Cathedral, in England.

The books are available to the patrons, but they literally can't leave with them because they are chained to a desk. Hundreds of books chained to desks in a library. These books are, therefore "reserved" for all patrons who need to use the book, but they will always be available because you can't check the book out. I know a lot of you are thinking that this would certainly solve a great deal of our concerns if we went back to this method!

In the modern context of e-reserves, aren't we doing the same thing? Of course, the chains have been replaced by a password or paywall, and the digital copies are not subject to the same wear-and-tear, but yes, in many ways we are providing the same service. Our patrons can't take these works without being duly authorized for access, and then we put them on notice

Chained Library. Used with the permission of Hereford Cathedral

that they should not distribute these materials any further. The chained library of the past is our e-reserves of today.

But what is a reserve collection? It certainly is the result of a pedagogical demand, not one invented by libraries, but requested by instructors and students. We created reserves as a result of our close relationship with the pedagogy surrounding classical educational needs.

The concept was simple: these reserve collections featured volumes with a short, restricted borrowing period subsequently these materials could serve more patrons. Cost certainly was a factor as well. Over time, instructors began to request that books and periodical volumes be placed on course reserves. These activities raised no copyright concerns because the library was not reproducing the works. With the advent of the photocopier, libraries had the ability to substitute photocopies of book chapters and articles for the original book or journal volume in the reserve collection. This raised copyright issues because now the library was reproducing materials for course reserves.

In a series of cases in the 1990s, we started to flesh out the difference between reserves and "course packs." As it turns out, these categories of works are different. Course packs are collections of print or electronic readings assembled by teachers to supplement college and university courses. They are often housed for purchase at institutional bookstores, copy shops, or outsourced course pack companies. As decided by the courts, the "law of course packs" is permission based.

Reserves are different, but still true to their original purpose. They are supplementary print or electronic course materials that instructors and staff put on hold, with limited circulation periods, for patrons to use. These materials are housed at the circulation and service desks at libraries, and are also similarly available online through an e-reserve system. The "law of reserves or e-reserves" is based on fair use and first sale. Both of these laws, which are important exceptions to copyright, allow the limited, educational uses—and the ability to purchase and granted unlimited loans to patron. Just because we put an "e" in front of the reserve word does not mean it should upend the purpose or the law behind the acquisition and use of e-reserves. Technology gives us the ability to enhance access to reserves, but it doesn't change the purpose of the reserves or the legal analysis that can be applied to them!

Kyle K. Courtney
Copyright Advisor
Harvard Library Office for Scholarly Communication

Acknowledgments

I wish to thank my editor, Jessica Gribble, for her guidance, encouragement, and support throughout the writing and publication process. I would also like to thank Dr. Kenneth D. Crews, Donna Ferullo, and Kevin L. Smith for their tireless patience in answering my many questions when I began learning about U.S. copyright law and for their continued friendship and support over the years. There are many wonderful copyright librarians I have come to know throughout my career who have generously shared their knowledge with me and who work diligently to help educate our professional community and patrons about the law. They are too numerous to list here, but they know who they are. Thank you.

A special thanks to those colleagues who reviewed my manuscript and provided feedback on it. They include Brandon Butler, Director of Information Policy at the University of Virginia Library; Sara Benson, Copyright Librarian for the University of Illinois Library; Carrie Russell, Director of Public Policy and Advocacy for the American Library Association; Tom Lipinski, Dean and Professor, School of Information Studies, University of Wisconsin—Milwaukee; and Donna Ferullo, Interim Associate Dean for Academic Affairs and Director, University Copyright Office. A special thanks to Ana Enriquez, Scholarly Communications Outreach Librarian for Penn State University Libraries, for reviewing my final drafts. This book benefitted tremendously from their thoughtful suggestions and recommendations!

Professionally, I would not be where I am today without the guidance and mentorship of some fabulous folks, including Phyllis O'Connor, Kyle Passmore, Melanie Smith, Christina Martinez, Teri Switzer, Elias Tzoc, and Jerome Conley. I thank them all for taking a chance on me. I draw so much strength and inspiration from my family and am always grateful for their love and support.

Introduction

About 15 years ago, when I accepted a professional staff position that included managing reserve services, I was charged by my supervisor to learn about copyright to ensure our reserve practices fell within the scope of the law. As I began researching the law, especially topics like fair use, I was surprised by the sheer volume of information to be found. Unfortunately, it took me a while to realize that much of the information being disseminated about copyright, especially copyright and course reserves, was propagating myths and misconceptions about the law and limiting the ways academic libraries provided reserve services. When the opportunity to write this book presented itself, I was excited by the idea of sharing the knowledge I have gained regarding the legal issues associated with course reserves with others, and it is my sincere hope that I can help colleagues avoid some of the frustrations I encountered as I struggled to sort copyright facts from fiction. The legal information you find here is based on the law, relevant court cases, and information shared by fellow copyright librarians who, like me, seek to help others understand the ways the law empowers libraries in providing services and resources to patrons. I truly hope it will be helpful to you. However, the information I provide about the law should not be seen as a substitute for legal advice obtained from a licensed attorney. I strongly encourage you to develop a relationship with your institution's legal counsel and collaborate with them to ensure your library's reserve practices comply with the law.

In regards to the administrative side of course reserves, it is my hope that this book will serve as a useful guide for academic libraries looking to launch or to expand the reserve services they offer to their campus communities. As each academic institution, academic library, and branch library within a college or university library system is a bit different, I have tried to include recommendations and best practices for the development and management of reserve services that are functional, flexible, and adaptable based on the resources a library may have available. This is a bit different from the information presented here about copyright considerations associated with course reserve services, as the application of the law will be the same for libraries in the United States, regardless of size.

I welcome and encourage readers to contact me with questions they may have regarding the information found in this book. The views and opinions expressed in this book are my own and do not necessarily reflect those of my current or previous employers.

PART I

Reserve Administrative Considerations

CHAPTER ONE

Course Reserves: An Overview

Academic library course reserve services provide instructors and students with short-term access to required and supplementary course learning materials in support of the educational mission of the institution, including teaching, research, and the creation of new scholarship. McCaslin (2001, 53) tells us that reserve services draw their name from the fact that libraries set aside or 'reserve' certain materials from the general library collection to help ensure students can access them for use in their courses. Reserve materials can include books; book chapters; articles from newspapers, magazines, and scholarly periodicals; motion pictures and audiovisual works; sound recordings; and music.

Types of Reserve Services

Presently, there are three primary types of reserve services offered by academic libraries: (1) print reserves, (2) electronic reserves, and (3) media reserves.

Print Reserves

Also known as hard copy reserves or just course reserves, this service provides instructors and students with access to physical copies of works such as books, Digital Video Discs (DVDs), and compact discs (CDs), usually from a designated area within the library (e.g., a reserve room) or at a specific service point (e.g., the circulation or reference desk).

Electronic Reserves

Frequently referred to as e-reserves, this service provides instructors and students with online access to digital copies of textual learning materials, including newspaper and journal articles; book chapters; and instructor generated content such as notes, study guides, and practice tests.

Media Reserves

Media reserve services make digital copies of motion pictures, audiovisual works, sound recordings, and music available online for student and instructor use.

Why Offer Reserve Services?

Providing reserve services offers the library an opportunity to ensure that students can readily access learning materials that can help them succeed academically. In a time when many people believe they can find all the information and resources they need using Google, reserve services provide libraries an opportunity to showcase their collections and help reinforce their usefulness and relevancy to students and instructors. Reserve services can also help address affordability issues in higher education by providing students with access to works they may not be able to afford otherwise, such as copies of textbooks. Libraries can also play an important role in helping to mitigate legal risk for their academic institution by having policies and procedures that ensure works are made available via reserve services in a way that is compliant with U.S. copyright law.

As beneficial as reserve services may be, a substantial investment of library resources is needed to launch, administer, and maintain them, including staffing, technology, space, and funding.

Staffing

Employee responsibilities associated with providing reserve services include accepting reserve requests; reviewing requested items for availability; reviewing requests for compliance with U.S. copyright law; processing items to be placed on reserve; and, where applicable, removing items from reserve when they are no longer needed by instructors and students.

Technology

Technologies needed to manage reserve services include software and hardware. Many integrated library systems offer print or electronic reserves modules that can be used to administer these services. Electronic and media reserve services can also be administered through other platforms, including homegrown systems, the academic institution's learning management system (LMS), or commercial platforms. In terms of hardware, computer workstations are required for the processing of all types of reserve items. Scanners, scanning software, duplication equipment, and software for digitizing music and video may also be needed depending on which reserve services the library offers.

Space

Physical space must be provided for processing all types of reserve requests. When offering print reserve services, the physical space needed to house these collections must be made available. Digital space provided by cloud-based or in-house server infrastructure will be needed to host the platforms and software that support print, electronic, and media reserve services and to store the associated digital documents and media files.

Funding

Funds will need to be allocated from the library's budget to pay staff supporting reserve services, to acquire print and digital items instructors wish to place on reserve, and, when applicable, to pay permission fees for the use of certain copyrighted works. Other expenses associated with providing reserve services can include purchasing supplies and materials for processing items (e.g., barcodes, labels, and tattle-tape) and covering the costs of the hardware and software needed to operate reserve services.

Should Academic Libraries Offer Course Reserve Services?

Libraries are constantly being asked to provide more services and resources for patrons, yet library budgets often remain stagnant for years on end or are in decline. Given the substantial investment of resources required to support reserve services, academic libraries must carefully consider if offering them is in their best interests, and if it is in the best interest of their patrons. This can be done by assessing instructor and student need for these services. Academic libraries should also perform an institutional scan to determine whether they can meet the required investment of resources needed to launch or expand reserve services.

Assessing Instructor Need

For reserve services to be functional and beneficial they must be supportive of instructors' pedagogical practices. To better understand these practices staff can use surveys, focus groups, and one-on-one discussions to find answers to the following questions.

What Types of Materials Are Instructors Using?

Instructors should be asked what types of learning materials they are assigning to students as required or supplementary resources as their answers would help the library identify which reserve services are most beneficial to the campus community. For example, if instructors say that much of their content is made up of electronic resources such as electronic books (ebooks) and articles, this may signify a need for e-reserve services. If instructors are using video, music, or sound recordings as part of class instruction, the library may need to consider investing resources to make DVDs or CDs available via print reserves services, or in streaming these works via media reserve services.

Staff should also inquire how instructors are currently having students find and access learning materials. Are they making a copy of the course textbook available to students through their department or campus tutoring services? Are they providing students with a reading list that contains citations for required and supplementary readings, or are they posting copies of reading materials to their LMS course page? Are they directing students to find and engage with video through YouTube, Netflix, or similar commercial streaming services? Do they have a Spotify or iTunes playlist for students to listen to? If instructors are successfully connecting students with required and supplementary learning materials on their own, then library reserve services may not be needed. However, if instructors are seeing students struggle to find and access learning materials, this may indicate there is a need to provide access to them with these resources through reserve services.

Course Structure

Today, higher education institutions offer three primary types of course instruction: (1) face-to-face instruction, (2) hybrid learning, and (3) fully online courses.

Face-to-face instruction. Students enrolled in face-to-face instruction courses will be on campus frequently, and so it may seem that print reserves are a convenient option for them. However, these types of courses still often require students to engage with an online course page within the institution's LMS, especially when a flipped method of instruction is being used. In a flipped classroom "students gain first exposure to new material outside of class, usually via reading or lecture videos, and then use class time to do the harder work of assimilating that knowledge, perhaps through problem-solving, discussion, or debates" (Brame 2013). Whether the class uses a traditional instruction model of instruction or the flipped model, having convenient access to learning materials outside of class time so they can be fully prepared to engage in class activities can be critically important for busy students. Therefore, there may be a need for e-reserves and media reserves for these types of classes in addition to print reserves.

Hybrid learning. With hybrid courses, a portion of the instruction is conducted in a traditional classroom instruction setting while the remaining instruction time is done through web-based learning, usually via the institution's LMS. When students are on campus for instruction sessions they can access and use print reserves, but during the online instruction days having access to works through e-reserves or media reserves will likely be preferable.

Distance education. Distance education occurs when instructors and students do not meet in a traditional classroom setting. Instead, all instruction, discussion, assignment submission, and testing are conducted online. According to the *Digital Learning Compass: Distance Education Enrollment Report*, 29.7 percent of the students enrolled in institutes of higher education are taking at least one distance education course (Allen and Seaman 2017, 4). Of this percentage, 14.3 percent of students were enrolled exclusively in distance education courses and 15.4 percent were enrolled in a combination of distance and in-person courses (4). Students enrolled in online courses may be living in the same city as the college or university where they are enrolled, but often they are spread out across the state, the country, or even the world. As colleges and universities increase the number of distance learning courses they offer to meet student demand for online education, the library can become a key ally and partner in helping students find and access learning materials via electronic and media reserves.

Instructor Needs

Instructors have a myriad of professional duties, such as teaching, grading papers, advising students, serving on committees, and conducting research. If the process for placing works on reserve is time consuming or cumbersome, they may forgo using these services. Staff should therefore ask instructors what types of training and support they might require to ensure they can take full advantage of reserve services. For example, if the library does not own items instructors are interested in placing on reserve, are they aware of the procedures for requesting that the library purchase a copy? Will instructors need assistance from staff in reviewing the copyright considerations associated with items they wish to place on reserve? Will those instructors who are not comfortable with technology require training and assistance in completing online forms or making digital copies of works—for example, scanning a print copy of an article to a digital file? Staff should also ask about the ways instructors would like to have training and support materials regarding reserve services made available to them (e.g., online video tutorials and resources, workshop sessions, one-on-one consultations, or email or chat assistance). In asking instructors about their training and support expectations, the library can determine how much staff time may need to be dedicated to assisting them with reserve requests and prepare accordingly.

Assessing Student Need

Staff should also speak with students to determine their needs and their potential interest in accessing course materials through reserve services.

Preferences Regarding Material Type

To determine which type of reserve service students may be most likely to use, staff should try to determine whether students have a general overall preference for print or digital learning materials. For example, research conducted by the Pew Research Center in 2017 found that "61 percent of adults ages 18 to 29 say the primary way they watch television now is with streaming services on the Internet" (Rainie 2017). Given this preference for engaging with video online, students may prefer to access video through media reserve services rather than checking out a DVD through a print reserve service. Alternately, the *2018 Academic Student Ebook Experience Survey* compiled by *Library Journal* found that 68 percent of students said they preferred print books for assigned narrative reading, compared with 23 percent who expressed a preference for ebooks (Enis 2018, 4). Given this, there may be certain situations where students prefer to access physical copies of learning materials through print reserves rather than online via e-reserves.

Barriers in Accessing Learning Materials

Students should be asked about barriers they face in finding and accessing learning materials so the library can consider if reserve services may remove these barriers or compound them. There are several common challenges students may identify:

Affordability issues. Many students struggle financially. In 2016 in the United States, 42 percent of independent students (those "assumed to be receiving little or no financial support from their parents") and 20 percent of dependent students (those "assumed to be receiving financial support from their family) were living in poverty (Fry and Cilluffo 2019). Given their financial constraints, students may struggle to afford copies of learning materials, such as the course textbook, and this can have a negative impact on their educational experience. For example, a recent survey of students conducted by the Florida Virtual Campus Office of Distance Learning and Student Services found that 35.6 percent of respondents earned a poor grade in a course and approximately 17 percent of students reported that they had failed a course because they could not afford to purchase a copy of the course textbook (Donaldson et al. 2019, 14). In these situations having copies of textbooks on reserve may make the difference between students succeeding in a course or failing it.

The digital divide. Students who are struggling with their finances may not be able to afford technology that others take for granted, such as owning a computer and having access to broadband internet at home. The Pew Research Center found that "as of early 2021, 27% of adults living in households earning less than $30,000 a year are smartphone-only internet users—meaning they own a smartphone but do not have broadband internet at home" (Vogels 2021a). In these situations, students may struggle to engage with course readings and other learning materials made available through e-reserves or media reserves on their phone screen.

Geography can also affect students' ability to engage with online learning materials made available through e-reserves or media reserves. Research conducted by the Pew Research Center in 2021 found that approximately 30 percent of rural households did not have access to broadband internet, and "though rural areas are more wired today than in the past, current infrastructure does not support consistently dependable broadband access in many rural areas" (Vogels 2021b). Slow internet connections can cause problems for students when downloading files from e-reserve or when trying to stream video or music made available through media reserves.

Technology can also pose a problem if users are not familiar with or comfortable using the platforms used to provide access to reserves, such as the library's online public access catalog (OPAC) or the discovery layer and navigating platforms used by the library to provide access to electronic and media reserves.

In situations where access to items made available via reserves may be hindered by technological barriers, libraries can consider making additional resources available for students to access through reserve services that can remove them. For example, the library could make laptop computers and wireless internet hotspots available for check-out through print reserve for those students who may not have a computer or high-speed internet access at home. To help those students who are uncomfortable navigating online platforms, staff can offer workshops or one-on-one instruction to students on how to search the OPAC or use the discovery layer to find reserve items.

Time. Students often have obligations aside from their studies. Many students work to pay for tuition and living expenses. Students may also be caring for children or other family members in addition to working and going to school. For this portion of the student population accessing works through electronic or media reserves may be ideal, as finding time to come to campus to check out print reserve items could be a barrier to access, especially as these items usually have short-term loan periods and are restricted to being used in the library. Electronic and media reserve services may also be appealing for commuter students who may not be looking to spend time on campus outside of that spent in the classroom.

Accessibility considerations. Students who have physical disabilities (e.g., who are blind, deaf, or have mobility issues) or cognitive disabilities (e.g., dyslexia) may have difficulties accessing and engaging with learning materials in their original formats. Because of this, academic libraries must have a plan in place to ensure that print, electronic, and media reserve materials can be made available in accessible formats so the benefits afforded by these services will not be lost to these students.

Performing an Institutional Scan of the Library

Libraries should not implement reserve services that are being offered by peer institutions because it seems like the right or trendy thing to do, nor should they offer them because a few instructors and students have requested that they do so. Reserve services require too much of an investment of library resources to be offered incidentally or on a whim. For this reason, while obtaining information from students and instructors about their needs and interests in reserve services, the library should also determine if reserve services align with their own goals and priorities. Questions to consider include:

- Is there a need for reserve services on campus?
- In what ways can the library support reserve services?
- How will they be marketed to students and instructors?

Is There Truly a Need for These Services?

As part of an institutional scan libraries should determine if similar services are being offered by other campus departments. For example, are there tutoring centers on campus that make copies of textbooks or other learning materials such as study guides, practice tests, or class notes available for students? Does the department that supports and maintains the institution's LMS aid instructors looking to post copies of readings to their course pages? Is there a department on campus that is already assisting instructors with digitizing music, sound recordings, and audiovisual works to post to their LMS course page? If these services are being offered by other departments on campus and are meeting the needs of instructors and students looking to connect with course learning materials, then there may not be a need for the library to duplicate efforts by offering reserve services. Instead, the library can refer instructors to these departments for assistance in connecting students with materials. However, if services similar to reserves are not being offered by other departments on campus, are being offered in a way that does not meet user demand, or offered in a way that increases institutional risk for claims of infringement, then an opportunity may exist for the library to launch and grow reserve services to address these needs.

To What Extent Can the Library Support Reserve Services?

Libraries must consider what resources they have available to implement new reserve services or expand existing ones. For example, will new staff have to be hired to coordinate and maintain the services, or can these responsibilities be taken on by a current employee? Is there a staff member knowledgeable about U.S. copyright law who can aid in policy development and making copyright determinations, or will training in the law need to be provided to staff supporting these services? Does the library currently have access to the technology and platforms needed to support reserve services, or will these need to be acquired? Is there funding in the library's budget to appropriately support reserve services? If not, will the funds be made available by eliminating other services or through the cancellation of resources, or can funds be added to the library's budget by the academic institution to cover these expenses? Logistics must also be considered. For example, if there are multiple libraries on a campus, will each library offer each type of reserve service? Will the services all be run out of one library, or could it be a combination (e.g., each library has its own print reserve collection, but one library administers electronic and media reserves)? If an institution has multiple campuses, will each campus that has its own library be responsible for operating reserve services for that location?

Putting It All Together

To be successful, library reserve services must balance the needs of instructors and students with the library's ability to effectively support and administer them (see Figure 1.1).

Many of the questions regarding instructor, student, and institutional needs will be addressed in depth as each specific reserve service is explored in subsequent chapters of Part One, but the issues outlined in this chapter should be considered by the library before deciding to offer a new reserve

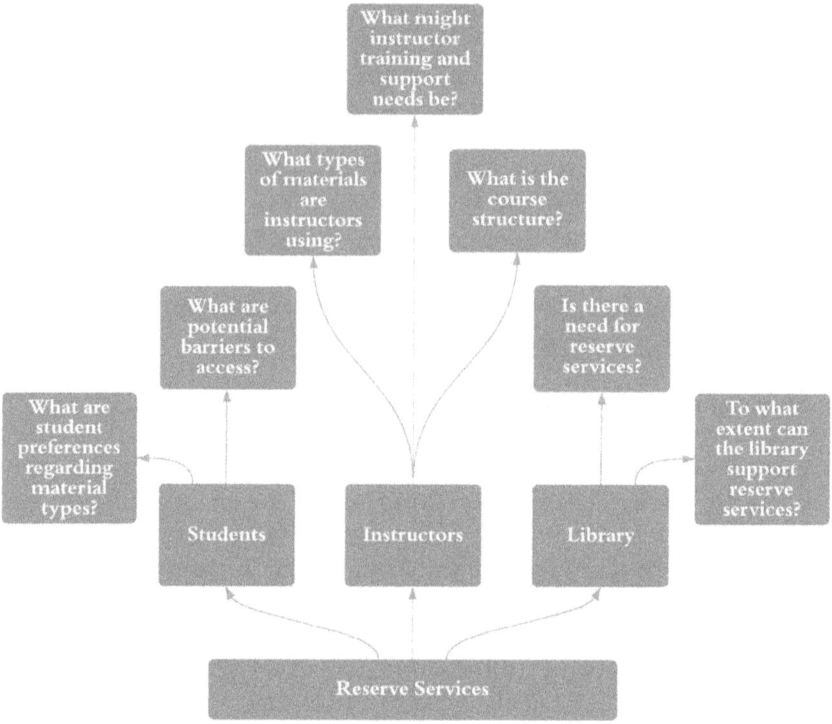

Figure 1.1 Relationships between instructor and student needs and library considerations

service or expand an existing one. Savvy readers will have noticed that the copyright considerations associated with offering reserves services were not explored in this chapter. U.S. copyright law permeates almost every facet of print, electronic, and media reserve services, including:

- The circulation of physical copies of works through print reserve services
- Making copies of works to be placed on print, electronic, or media reserve
- Uploading copies of works to e-reserve and media reserve platforms
- Making accessible copies of reserve items available for patrons with disabilities

Copyright considerations associated with reserve services, obtaining permission and licensing issues, and workflows for navigating them will be addressed in Part Two of this book. The discussion will be rounded out in Part Three, which explores copyright law as it applies to accessibility issues and best practices for mitigating legal risk when offering reserve services. Together, this book should help prepare staff to provide efficiently operated and legally compliant reserve services to patrons.

CHAPTER TWO

Print Reserve Administration and Management

Print reserve services provide students with short-term access to physical copies of learning material. Examples of materials made available via this service include:

- Books, magazines, newspapers, and scholarly periodicals
- Photocopies of book chapters, articles, poems, and short stories
- Video home system (VHS) tapes, Digital Video Discs (DVDs), and Blu-ray discs
- Compact discs (CDs) of music and sound recordings

Print reserve services can play a key role in supporting the educational mission of the institution, including teaching, research, and the creation of new scholarship.

A library's ability to offer print reserve services will be dictated by the availability of resources such as staffing, space, hours of operation, and access to technology and equipment. Service parameters will also need to be established to guide staff in administering print reserves and students and instructors in utilizing the service.

Resource Requirements

Before launching or expanding print reserve services, staff should determine if they have the resources need to support and maintain them.

Staffing

Staff will need to engage with requested materials in many ways, including:

- Accepting requests to place materials on print reserve and answering questions instructors may have about the process
- Reviewing submitted requests for completeness and, if needed, following up with the requestor to obtain supplementary information
- Searching the catalog to see if requested items are owned by the library and, if so, pulling them from the collection or, if the items are currently checked out, placing a hold on them or recalling them
- If the requested items are not currently owned by the library, working with staff to see if they can be acquired and made available via print reserve
- Reviewing requests to determine whether they fall within the scope of one of the options for making works lawfully available under the law
- When appropriate, obtaining permission or a license to make works available via print reserve
- Processing the item for circulation via print reserves and, if needed, attaching barcodes, spine labels, or other identifying information to the resource being circulated
- Shelving the resource for use on the reserve stacks
- Engaging with patrons wishing to check out items
- Locating items in the reserve stacks and checking them out to patrons
- Checking in items upon return and inspecting them for wear and damage
- If needed, performing repairs on items or working with staff in the acquisitions department to purchase replacement copies
- Processing fines for overdue reserve materials and preparing bills for reserve materials that are lost or damaged by students or those not returned
- Removing items from print reserve at the time designated by the instructor

Frequently, additional staff support is needed at the beginning of each semester and several weeks leading up to its start to process the influx of reserve requests submitted by instructors and to help students determine if items they are looking for are available via print reserve. As many items come off reserve at the end of each semester, additional staff time should also be allotted then to help support the service.

When launching or expanding print reserve services, library administration will need to decide:

- Whether a dedicated position is required to support the service or if these responsibilities will be added to the workload of individuals already employed by the library
- Whether current employees will be reassigned to new positions associated with the service
- Whether new staff needs to be hired to help manage the workload

If new employees are being hired, administrators will need to determine whether they will be librarians, support staff, student employees, or a combination of the three and how much money is available to fund these positions.

Staffing may also vary by campus library or location. Smaller libraries on a campus (or at regional campus libraries) may not have staff needed to fully support print reserve services. In these situations these libraries may forgo offering print reserves services and, instead, direct patrons looking for reserve items to a location that does offer them. Alternately, if minimal staffing at one of these locations prevents staff from being able to process reserve requests, items to be placed on reserve could be processed at another campus library and then sent to these locations so that staff there only need to circulate them.

Library Location

If a campus has more than one library then administrators of these libraries will need to decide whether print reserve services will be offered at each location, some of the locations, or only at one location. If a college or university campus is spread out over a significant area and has multiple libraries across campus, then as a matter of convenience it may make sense for multiple campus libraries to offer print reserve services. On larger campuses it can also make sense to house print reserve materials in the libraries that are closest to where the students using them will be taking classes. For example, if there is a fine arts library located in or near the buildings where the majority of the fine arts classes are being taught, then for students' convenience it would make sense to house the items on reserve for these classes at that library rather than in one that is farther away.

Available Space

Print reserve items can take up a lot of space. Staff and administrators should tour the library (or libraries) where reserve services will be offered to identify available spaces where print reserve items can be processed and housed. As part of this assessment process administrators will need to decide whether reserve stacks will be closed or open. For closed stacks, access to the reserve stacks is restricted to staff only. This is usually accomplished by placing the collection behind a service desk such as the circulation desk or reference desk. With closed stacks, patrons must ask staff to pull items for them by providing the title, call number, associated course name and number, or other identifying information about the work. Closed print reserve stacks provide a certain level of security for items as they are generally not allowed to be removed from the service desk area without first being checked out to a patron, but this type of set-up prevents patrons from browsing the collection. With open print reserve collections, stacks housing these materials are located in a public area where patrons can freely browse items and locate resources themselves. However, this ease of access is not without risks. It can create an opportunity for theft. Similarly, when reserve items are removed from the area without being checked out or are misshelved by patrons, it can be difficult for other patrons to locate them. Libraries can balance these two models by having a room in the building with open stacks that houses the reserve collection (a 'reserves room'), but not allow patrons to remove items from the room without first checking them out. Alternately, some libraries have both closed and open print reserve stacks (see Pitts-Noggle and Rafferty 2017).

When dealing with space considerations, costs may be incurred if new shelving needs to be installed to accommodate the print reserve service, or if a service desk needs to be constructed, or if area needs to be constructed to accommodate them.

Library Hours of Operation

If a campus had multiple libraries, administrators will want to consider the hours of operation at each location when deciding where they will house the print reserve collections. Locations that have the longest hours of operation may be the ideal place to house the print reserve items with the highest circulation so that students have as much access to them as possible, especially during periods of high demand like before an assignment is due or exams.

Technology and Equipment

Many integrated library systems (ILS) have a reserve module that can be used to circulate items via print reserve. Libraries wishing to launch a print reserve service should speak with their ILS vendor to learn more about what features are available through their system. Libraries looking to expand their current print reserve services should also speak with their ILS vendor to see if there are any features of their reserve module that are not currently being utilized that can be turned on to help enhance the service.

Equipment the library will need to administer print reserves, aside from computers running the ILS, can include scanning equipment and software that can be used to make photocopies of works to circulate on print reserve (e.g., selections from books or journal articles). If the library is circulating VHS tapes, DVDs, Blu-rays, or audio CDs, they should ensure equipment is available in the library to play them. These can be provided as stand-alone stations, may be integrated into computers available for public use, or portable DVD or CD players can be placed on print reserves and be checked out to patrons.

Service Parameters

The following questions are ones that libraries should consider when developing service parameters for print reserves.

Who Can Place Items on Print Reserve?

At most institutions only instructors and teaching assistants (TAs) have the authority to place items on reserve. However, Hoppenfeld and Arant-Kaspar (2010) argue that students should also be allowed to request that items be placed on reserve for a course, stating that "since the primary users of course reserves are students" (355) they can be well positioned to identify items that might be helpful to classmates. The Oregon State University Libraries also support this practice, allowing students to "make requests and suggestions for books that should be purchased in future semesters" that will then be placed on print reserve (McElroy et al. 2017, 85). If libraries are not comfortable extending this privilege to students, they can advise students to share with their instructor the list of items they would like to see made available through print reserve that they can submit to the library on their behalf.

What Types of Items Can Be Placed on Print Reserve?

Items circulated via print reserves often include scholarly monographs, works of fiction, DVDs, and CDs. Other items that can be made available for check-out through this service include copies of textbooks; journal issues; photocopies of book chapters or articles from journals, newspapers, and magazines; and photocopies of instructor-generated materials such as study guides, notes, and practice tests. When deciding what types of materials will be circulated through print reserve libraries will need to consider several factors outlined in the following sections.

Challenges with Circulating Photocopies

Photocopies of works, such as a selection from a book, will require special care and attention from staff managing reserves, as:

- Many will end up with bent or ripped pages due to frequent use. Pages from these documents will also turn up missing. Staff time will need to be allotted to review these documents each time they are returned and, when needed, recopy pages from the original to replace the damaged or missing ones.
- Often these documents will be kept in folders or envelopes that are labeled with the class name, number, or other identifying information used for classification. When a student checks out multiple readings at a time it is not unusual for documents to be placed back into the wrong folder or envelope. Staff will have to review each folder or envelope as it is returned to ensure that each document is in its correct folder or envelope.
- The folders or envelopes containing the copies of readings will often be placed in file organizers on the reserve stacks or in file cabinets. It not uncommon to find a course reading in its correct folder or envelope but filed incorrectly in the organizer or cabinet. Staff may need to check the organization of the file organizers or file cabinets on a regular basis to ensure that files or envelopes are in the correct location.

In an effort to negate the challenges circulating photocopies of works may present, some libraries that offer both print and electronic reserve services no longer permit photocopies to be placed on print reserve. Instead, they make digital copies available through their e-reserve service.

Circulating Unique Items

Print reserves need not to be limited to traditional items like books and films. Libraries should consider the benefits of circulating nontraditional items through print reserve that may support learning. Examples include molecular model sets that can be used by students studying chemistry, puppets that can be utilized by students studying early childhood education, mineral and rock collections that can be used by students studying geology, and piano keyboards that can be used by music majors. Circulating these unique items via print reserve provides an opportunity for the library to partner with other departments and centers on campus to help make items more broadly available to students. For example, an anatomy and physiology lab on campus may only be open from 8:00 a.m. to 5:00 p.m. Monday through Friday, making it impossible for students who wish to use the models for study in the evenings and on weekends to access them. If the lab can provide skeletons and anatomical models for the library to circulate through print reserve, then students will be able to engage with them after-hours. Libraries can also make equipment such as digital cameras, camcorders, and audio recorders available to students via print reserve. Some libraries also choose to make certain types of supplies available for check-out through reserve. Examples include dry erase markers and white board erasers, art supplies such as markers and colored pencils, headphones, and even umbrellas.

Case Study: Textbooks on Reserve

Making textbooks available for students to check out through print reserves may be one of the more controversial aspects of this service. Some libraries have strict collection development policies that prohibit or discourage the library from actively purchasing textbooks. Some librarians believe that students should plan for and fully bear the costs of their own education, including textbook costs, and so have no duty or obligation to make copies available for check-out. Some librarians are not opposed to purchasing copies of textbooks but are concerned about how quickly new editions of textbooks are released and the potential drain on library resources in having to purchase them on a regular basis. For most libraries, hesitancy to acquire copies of textbooks stems from the realization that it will not be practical or feasible to purchase a copy of every textbook being used on campus. Not only will most library budgets not be able to support this practice, but also "in an era when allocation of space is so closely scrutinized, locating shelving for collection of that size would provide challenging" (MacKay Snowman 2017, 43).

Despite these considerations, many libraries do circulate textbooks via print reserve. For these libraries, addressing textbook affordability issues in higher education is one of the primary motivators. The College Board estimates that college students will spend approximately $1,240 on course materials and other supplies in the 2021–2022 academic year (Ma 2021, 11). For many students, this price point poses a challenge that can negatively affect their ability to succeed academically. For example, a recent survey of students conducted by Donaldson et al. (2019, 14) found that

- Approximately 64 percent of students have not purchased a textbook needed for class due to high costs.
- Almost 23 percent of students surveyed have dropped a course they had enrolled in due to high textbook costs.
- Eighteen percent of students have withdrawn from a course they had enrolled in due to their inability to purchase the course text.

A textbooks on reserve program can help students struggling to afford their textbooks by providing a way to access them freely through the library. These programs can also benefit those students who can afford their textbooks but who have delayed access in getting them. This could include students who ordered their textbook online but who have not received them in time for the first week of classes, or those who go to the campus bookstore to purchase a copy but find they are sold out. Having a copy of their textbook on print reserve can help keep these students from falling behind on their assignments while they are waiting for copies of their books to arrive. Some students may "rely on the library's reserve textbooks while waiting for their financial aid to come through so they can buy books" (McElfresh 2009, 4). In a survey conducted by Pitts-Noggle and Rafferty about reserve services, students stated that "when [students] forgot their textbook, the library's [print reserve] copy served as a backup" (2017, 71). Circulation statistics reflect the popularity of this service with students. For example, a textbooks on reserve program implemented by Portland Community College resulted in an increase in their reserve circulation by 35 percent (Greiner 2012, 1), and a textbooks on reserve program at the University of California Los Angeles saw "circulation statistics for course reserves across eight libraries . . . steadily increase from 19% in 2009–2010 to 25% in the 2013–2014 fiscal year" (Celik and Peck 2016, 275). In counter to the argument that students should be expected to purchase and budget for their own textbooks, McDonald and Burke (2010, 25) argue that it is "part of [libraries] mission to make materials for learning as widely available as possible" and that staff "should reasonably respond to expressed needs for [textbooks] as we develop our collections." In response to concerns expressed by library staff that the frequency with which textbooks may be updated have the potential to render them obsolete, McDonald and Burke argue that often "that these quickly 'obsolete' [textbooks] see more checkouts in their short lives than items that stay on our shelves for a decade" (25).

Identifying Textbooks Already in the Library's Collections

Staff may be surprised to find that they frequently have many resources being used as textbooks in their collection. Some of these works will be traditional textbooks and others may be works of fiction or nonfiction, poetry, anthologies, and so on that are being used as required reading for courses. Staff can obtain a list of the textbooks being used in a given semester from the campus bookstore and compare the titles found there to those found in the library's collection. As textbooks are identified, staff can make a proactive decision to add them to the print reserve collection. This can ensure that all students enrolled in a class have access to the library's copy of the textbook rather than just one student getting to check it out. It can also help prevent the library's copies of textbooks from going out to students at other institutions via consortium lending or interlibrary loan (ILL).

Deciding What Textbooks to Purchase

When purchasing textbooks to circulate through print reserves staff can utilize some strategies for prioritizing their spending so that the collection will do the most good for the largest number of users. For example, McElroy et al. (2017, 84) worked with their institution's Office of Admissions "to identify the 90 courses each year with the highest percentage of Pell-eligible first-year students [as] Pell-eligible students have the highest need for financial aid, as defined by data gathered through the Free Application for Federal Student Aid (FAFSA)." Based upon this information, they spent $9,700 on 168 textbooks to circulate on reserve "to support about 30 of these courses" (84). Their strategy involved, among other things, targeting purchases that would benefit students who may have a demonstrated financial need. Other libraries choose to target high-enrollment classes that have high-priced textbooks. Examples of these courses could be introductory psychology, biology, and chemistry courses that undergraduate students are often required to take. Research performed by Murphy (2013, 148) found that some libraries choose only to purchase undergraduate textbooks, refusing requests that they receive for graduate texts, while other libraries consider purchasing any level textbook but set a minimum on the cost of these resources (e.g., $90). Some libraries will purchase required textbooks only, not recommended texts, or vice versa (Pollitz, Christie, and Middleton 2009, 467). Some libraries will only purchase textbooks that are specifically requested by an instructor. Other libraries also let their staff identify titles to purchase, which can be done by keeping a list of textbook titles students have been requesting. Whatever collection development practices the library establishes for the acquisition of textbooks, it will likely need to be made clear to both instructors and students that they cannot afford to purchase every copy of every text being used on campus. However, allowing instructors and students to have some say in the identifying and selecting what textbooks will be acquired and placed on print reserve may help assuage concerns they may have about access to them. Instructors and students can also be enlisted to help increase the number of textbooks on reserve through alternate means.

Alternate Means of Textbook Acquisition and Funding

Staff should actively reach out to instructors to see if they have copies of textbooks they can donate to the library or lend to the library temporarily (e.g., for a semester or an academic year) to place on print reserve (the section *Circulating Instructor's Personal Copies*, found in this chapter, provides suggestions and recommendations for this option). Doing so can exponentially expanded the size of a library's print reserve textbook collection. For example, in the 2017–2018 academic year 63.5 percent of the items in the print reserve collection (1,145 titles out of 3,561) at the California

Polytechnic State University' in San Luis Obispo's Robert E. Kennedy Library were instructor's personal copies (Nichols 2019, 520). Academic departments may also be willing to purchase and provide the library with copies if textbooks for students to use, or the academic institution may also be able to provide funds to support these collections. For example, students from the University of Oklahoma's Student Congress Association brought their concerns regarding textbook affordability to the President's office, resulting in the University President providing the library with funding of $200,000 per year to purchase textbooks to circulate on print reserve (Murphy 2013, 146). Students can be encouraged to donate copies of their textbook to the library at the conclusion of a course. If a library decides to run a textbook donation campaign, they can ask instructors to help by mentioning this option to students at the end of the course. Nichols (2019, 522) highlights a campaign coordinated by the Robert E. Kennedy Library and their Student Library Association Counsel they branded as the Textbook GIVEback program and that, in fall and spring semesters of 2018, "received donations of hundreds of textbooks" that were added to their reserve collection. As libraries coordinate fundraising campaigns a fund can be established to allow donors to contribute to the library's efforts to acquire and circulate textbooks on reserve. The Miami University Libraries (Ohio) has such a fund that, in a 1-day fundraising campaign, received "$3,400 from 33 donors—the equivalent of more than 28 new textbooks, at an average cost of $120" (Miami University Libraries, n.d.). There are also opportunities for student to get involved in this philanthropy. For example, "Penn State's Class of 2018 selected the University Libraries' Textbook and Educational Resources Fund as one of three options for their legacy through Penn State's Class Gift Campaign. [This] endowed fund exists to provide required textbooks on reserve to help lower students' cost of attendance" (Penn State University, 2017).

Keeping Older Editions of Textbooks on Reserve

Reserve textbooks frequently receive a lot of wear-and-tear and may need to be replaced from use before a new edition comes out. However, if older editions of textbooks are still in serviceable condition, the library may wish to leave them on print reserve. This is because many textbooks, especially introductory textbooks in areas like history, psychology, chemistry, or biology, usually do not change much between editions. Sometimes new chapters are added or the order of chapters is changed, but often, aside from updates, there is not a tremendous amount of difference between two sequential editions. Staff can ask instructors to review the older edition and see if it would still be serviceable, from a content perspective, as a reserve resource. If so, leaving it on print reserve alongside the newer edition means there will be more copies available for students to use.

Making a Decision Regarding Textbooks on Reserve

MacKay Snowman (2017, 44) tells us that "there is no single successful methods, no single effective tactic" libraries can pursue to address textbook affordability issues in their entirety. However, "textbooks in libraries, no matter what format, is one way" to do so (44). At minimum, placing textbooks the library already has in its collection on print reserve is one thing staff can do to ensure equitable access to textbooks it owns. Beyond this, staff can consider the solicitation of instructor copies of textbooks, accepting student donations of their old textbooks, or implement textbook collection development practices for print reserve as time, administrative support, and student demand for access to textbooks via print reserve requires.

What Types of Items Can Not Be Placed on Print Reserve?

The library may wish to designate specific types of works that will not circulate on print reserve. For example, libraries will generally not circulate materials borrowed from other libraries (e.g., those borrowed through a consortium) as the ILS will usually not allow these items to be checked out by anyone other than the patron who requested them. The library's own barcodes could be attached to such items in order to allow the check-out to individuals other than the person who requested them, but, in addition to ethical considerations in doing this, the library would have to contend with returning the item to the lending library at the end of its loan period, which may expire before the end of the semester or the date the item will be used as part of course instruction. Instead, if the library does not own a copy of a work an instructor is interested in placing on print reserve, staff should determine if a copy could be purchased for the library's collection. In these situations, the instructor will need to ensure that their request is submitted in a timely manner, allowing the library time to order, receive, and process the item in time for the start of the semester.

Sometimes an instructor may wish to have an item from the noncirculating collection placed on print reserve. For example, a reference item or a special collections item. If the instructor has other items on print reserve then an advantage to agreeing to such requests is that students can check out materials they may need to access for their course from one central location rather than having to visit multiple service desks. For reference items, another advantage to agreeing to these requests includes being able to better track who has the item and identify when it might be returned. For example, if a reference item that is being used for a course is left in the reference stacks any patron could pull it off the shelf at any time and, when they are done with it, could leave it anywhere in the library, making it difficult or impossible for other students to find. The student could also choose to hide the book somewhere in the library, retrieving it when they return to study and then hiding it again before they leave, which would prevent all other patrons from accessing it. However, if the reference item in question is placed on print reserve then students must check it out and return it when they are done to clear it from their record. If they do not return it, at least staff will know which patron has the resource and can ask them to do so. Circulating the item from print reserve will also allow staff to tell patrons who inquire about the item when it is due back.

In the case of special collections items, many special collections departments have hours of operation that align with a normal business day (e.g., 9:00 a.m. to 5:00 p.m., Monday through Friday). Circulating these items on print reserve will allow students to have access to them after-hours. Of course, especially with special collections items, these resources may be more susceptible to wear-and-tear due to high reserve use, so the library will need to carefully determine what policies they wish to put into place when requests are received from instructors to place such items on print reserve.

How Many Copies of an Item Can Be Placed on Print Reserve?

Instructors may inquire about placing multiple copies of a work on print reserve. Sometimes libraries choose to limit the number of copies of a particular item that may be placed on reserve for a course. This may have to do with how many copies of the work the library actually owns, or due to the availability of shelf space. Some libraries place limits on the number of copies of a work that can be placed on reserve, thinking this is a requirement of U.S. copyright law. Generally, this is not the case, and this misconception will be explored further in Chapter 8, which explores the first sale doctrine.

How Long Will Items Circulate For?

To ensure that print reserve items are made available to a broad range of users it is common for these items to circulate for short periods of time, often anywhere from a few hours to a few days. To maintain consistency, it is best to have a standard set of reserve circulation periods for instructor to choose from—for example, 2 hours, 3 hours, or 4 hours, or 1 day, 3 days, or 7 days. Items used in high-enrollment courses will usually only circulate to for a few hours at a time, while items placed on reserve for graduate courses that have fewer students enrolled in them may check-out for several days. Staff should be open and amendable to changing circulation periods of items if patron use demands it. For example, an instructor may ask that a textbook circulate for 1 day, but due to high patron demand for the item staff may elect to change this circulation period to 4 hours. Staff should decide ahead of time whether decisions to change the circulation period of a reserve items will be made at their discretion; whether proposed changes to the circulation period will be shared with the instructor who requested that the item be placed on reserve, and made at their discretion; or whether such decisions will be made by the library staff and instructor in consultation together. If an item is on reserve for multiple courses, it may be best to have a shorter circulation period to ensure that students across all sections are able to access it. When in doubt, it is better to start with a shorter circulation period that can later be extended, as few students will complain about being granted extra time with an item, whereas students who are used to checking out a reserve item for 1 day could become quite upset when they are told that they will now only have 4 hours with it.

Some libraries that are not open 24 hours a day, 7 days a week allow students to keep reserve items that normally circulate for only a few hours overnight. This option allows students to have after-hours access to these items and can be especially convenient for students looking to have additional time with a print reserve resource prior to a text or class project being due. If libraries are interested in offering this option, they should first check to ensure that their ILS offers this functionality. Staff will also have to decide under what circumstances they will allow overnight check-outs. For example, they may only allow students to take advantage of the overnight check-out option if the check-out occurs an hour or two before the library closes. When allowing overnight check-outs, libraries may also require that patrons return the materials expeditiously the next day (e.g., within an hour or two of when the library opens). If staff make the decision to offer overnight circulation for reserve items, they should make clear to students the policies associated with this special check-out option and any fines that may be assessed if the item is not returned in a timely manner.

Case Study: When Items Fly Off the Shelves

Every print reserve collection will have several items that are constantly being checked out by students. Some libraries put into place a first-come-first-served model through which the first patron to ask for the item after it is returned gets to check it out next. Some libraries do allow holds to be placed on reserve items, and most ILS will have a hold function for items in the library's collection. Libraries will need to identify if this feature is available for items placed on reserve and, if so, whether they wish to activate it and how long items will be held for patrons before the hold is canceled and the item is made available to others (e.g., 15 or 30 minutes). Goodson et al. (2009, 117) outline a novel system developed for using "restaurant-style pagers to notify patrons that reserve collection material for which they were waiting had been returned and was available" for check-out. If a student askes for a print reserve items that is checked out,

> a staff member asks the patron if they have time to wait until the item is returned. If they do, a fully charged pager is checked-out to the patron . . . [and] when the requested item is returned, a circulation desk staff member pages the next patron in line [for the item] and records the time of the transmission on the pager board. The patron has fifteen minutes to return to the service desk and pick up the item. If a student takes longer than fifteen minutes to return, the item is released to the next patron. (Goodson et al. 2009, 120)

For popular reserve items, the library may need to investigate purchasing multiple copies of a work, especially when items have been placed on print reserve for those courses that have hundreds of students enrolled across multiple sections. In these situations, having only one copy of a resource on reserve will likely not meet student demand for access to it. Staff who check out reserve items to patrons can help identify the high-demand titles. Most ILS will allow staff to run reports that can be used to identify high-circulating reserve items. Policies regarding the purchase of multiple copies of works by the library for reserves should be put into place before these situations arise so that the additional copies can be ordered in a timely manner, keeping in mind that the circulation of multiple copies is not prohibited by copyright law. Alternately, the library can reach out to the instructor who is using the item to see if they can donate a personal copy of the work to place on reserve alongside library's copies.

Who Can Check-Out Reserve Items?

Administrators will need to decide whether all patrons, including public patrons, will be able to check out any reserve item, or if some items, like those placed on reserve for a specific course, will be available for check-out by students and instructors only. Options for limiting the check-out of reserve items by patron type may be limited by the functionality of the ILS, so the ILS user manual or the ILS vendor should be consulted to see what the system supports.

Occasionally an instructor will ask that items they place on print reserve only be checked out to students enrolled in their course. While their intent may be to ensure that their students have priority access to the item, this request can be difficult to accommodate for several reasons. The library's ILS may be able to limit the check-out of certain items to certain patron types, but unique patron types or designators would have to be created for each course where an instructor has asked for this limitation and then these patron types or designators will have to be added to the patron record for each student enrolled in each course. This process will involve a lot of time and effort from staff, which could quickly get out of hand if multiple instructors request this service. If students add one of these courses to their schedule a few weeks into the semester, the library will have to be notified so they can add the specific designator to the students account. Likewise, should a student drop one of these courses, the library would have to be notified so they can remove the designator from that patrons account. All of these special patron types or designators would then need to be removed from all patron's accounts at the end of the semester.

Alternately, some instructors will offer to give the library a list of students currently enrolled in their course and ask that staff check a student's name against this list before checking a reserve item out to them. This is a simpler way of limiting check-outs to only a certain group of students but can be time consuming for staff. If the list is not kept up to date throughout the semester, the items may be checked out to those who should not have access to them (e.g., students who have dropped the course) or someone who should have access to them but whose name has not been added to the list (e.g., students who have added the course to their schedule). There are ethical considerations for libraries to consider in denying access to works in these situations. Whether they wish to access it out of interest (e.g., perhaps it is a popular movie) or out of need (e.g., they are studying the same topic and it is a work of critical importance in the field), if the item in question was purchased with library funds then it can be argued that all patrons should be able to access it, not just a select few enrolled in a specific course. If libraries are going to offer the option to limit check-out of a reserve item to students enrolled in a specific course, they may wish to do so only in those situations where an instructor is lending the library a personal copy of the work to place on reserve for their course.

Can Reserve Items Leave the Building?

As an added security measure, some libraries do not allow patrons to take print reserve items from the building and enforce this policy by tattle-taping reserve items and not desensitizing the tape upon check-out. However, determined patrons will find ways to evade this rule. It could include desensitizing the tape on their own or removing the tape, which often damages the book in the process, or it could also be that they keep on walking after setting the alarm gates off, ignoring staff requests to stop and return to the service desk. Students may have good reasons for wanting to leave the building with reserve items—taking them back to a dorm room to study, wishing to take the item to class, looking to use items for study while also grabbing a bite to eat in a campus café or dining hall, or wanting to take items home or to work to use during downtime. Before deciding to require that print reserve items be used in the library only, staff should speak with the patrons who will be using the reserve items to gain an understanding of how they hope to engage with the materials and where they envision using them.

Renewals

Libraries will have to decide whether they will allow reserve items to be renewed by patrons and, if so, under what circumstances. Some libraries allow print reserve items to be renewed under any circumstances. As print reserve items tend to be in high demand, some libraries choose not to allow the renewal of reserve items at all. When renewals are not allowed, patrons may ask if they can return a print reserve item and then check it back out again immediately. In these situations, some libraries will allow patrons to do so, while others will allow the same patron to check the book back out only after a period of time (e.g., 15 or 30 minutes), allowing other students the opportunity to ask for the item. When deciding whether to allow for the renewal of reserve items libraries should first check to see what renewal options are available through their ILS and also speak with instructors and students to see what their preference may be regarding renewals.

Assessing Overdue Fines

Print reserve items will be returned late. Sometimes patrons simply lose track of time when using the items, while other times they intentionally keep them past the time they are due. Whatever the reason, libraries will need to determine whether they will charge fines for overdue print reserve items and, if so, how much those fines will be. The fines should be reflective of the in-demand nature of reserve items and be high enough to disincentives patrons from intentionally returning items late. Staff will also need to determine whether fines will begin to accrue immediately after the item is due or if any type of grace period will be provided (e.g., 15 minutes). If overdue fines are assessed information regarding the overdue policy and associated, fines should be made available on the library's website, be posted where reserve items are checked out, and perhaps even printed on bookmarks or similar handouts that so the information can be readily shared with patrons should they ask about it.

Sometimes students make the conscious decision to keep a reserve item for an extended period, ranging from weeks to the entire semester, especially when they realize that it is cheaper for them to pay a fine at the end of the semester for keeping the item then it is to purchase a copy for themselves (especially in the case of textbooks). In these situations, it is beneficial to have expedited billing policies in place that allowed the library to quickly address the issue and, if needed, replace the item. For items in the regular circulating collection, many libraries will not bill patrons for the replacement of the item until it has been overdue for an extended period of time (e.g., 30 days). If the library waits 30 days to bill a student for an in-demand reserve item, then almost a quarter of the semester could pass before the billing process commences, meaning that during this time other students in the class who needed access to the item in order to complete coursework do not have access to it. In having expedited billing procedures for reserve items (e.g., students are billed for the replacement of the item 3 days after it is overdue), the library can quickly begin the replacement process to ensure that a new copy is made available as soon as possible. In many of these situations, once a student receives a substantial bill for the replacement cost of the item and the associated overdue fines and processing charges, they quickly return the item.

There will be situations where students keep print reserve items beyond their due date due to circumstances beyond their control or because they simple do forget to return it on time. Staff should always be willing to reduce or waive fines, when appropriate, or make arrangements with the student for a repayment schedule. Some libraries have the ability to transfer student fines over to the student's account with the Bursar's office so that they are paid as part of the student's bill.

Replacing Damaged, Lost, or Stolen Items

Print reserve items can easily become damaged from frequent use and staff overseeing print reserve services will need to constantly be checking items for signs of wear-and-tear. This can include reviewing books, magazines, and photocopies for torn or missing pages and checking CDs, DVDs, and Blu-rays for scratches that may cause them to skip or stick. Inevitably, print reserve items will be lost by patrons, may be stolen by a patron or from a patron, or they may be damaged (accidently or otherwise) by a patron. Libraries will need to have policies and procedures in place for replacing these items. It is likely that these procedures will be the same for replacing any item in the library's collection that has been damaged, lost, or stolen (though some replacement copies can be made under Section 108, a topic discussed in depth in Chapter 7). However, reserve items may need to be replaced in and expedited manner, especially if the item is required for use in the course, such as a textbook or other work that students must engage with in order to complete class assignments. When a reserve item has been lost, stolen, or damaged beyond repair staff should:

1. Reach out to the instructor who placed the item on reserve and inform them of the situation. At this time, staff can ask if the instructor has a personal copy of the item they can place on reserve for students to use until a replacement can be obtained by the library. The instructor can also notify their students of the situation.
2. Immediately order a replacement copy of the work, requesting priority shipping from the vendor (when possible) and asking that staff responsible for processing and cataloging the item move the work to the front of the processing queue after it arrives. When it comes to textbooks, staff can also explore options for purchasing copies from the campus bookstore, allowing for same day acquisition and processing of the replacement copy.
3. Once the library has an idea of how long it will take to replace the item, staff should follow up with the instructor to let them know when the item will likely be available for check-out again. Staff should contact the instructor when the replacement item is available for check-out so they can convey this information to their students.

If the item that has been lost, stolen, or damaged is a supplementary resource rather than a required one, then there may not be the same sense of urgency in replacing it, or the instructor may be fine with using an alternate resource from the library's collection in its place. Staff managing print reserves can have this conversation with the instructor when they reach out to inform them the item was lost, stolen, or damaged.

It should be made clear to students what the replacement costs for lost, stolen, and damaged reserve materials will be. Some libraries charge a flat fee for any item in their collection, while others charge the true replacement cost of the item. Processing fees are also often charged as well. All charges for lost, damaged, and stolen reserve materials should be made available for patrons to view on the library's website. Some libraries also post notices of overdue and replacement charges where reserve materials are checked out.

Case Study: Info Labels on Print Reserve Items

Some libraries have found success in placing labels on items on print reserve that identify:

- The circulation period of the item
- Overdue fines assessed for items that are returned late
- Replacement charges for lost, stolen, or damaged items

- Contact information for the library—for example, a phone number for the service desk that manages print reserves
- Other special instructions, such as a statement that reserve items should not be placed in a book drop

Removable labels are available for purchase that can be placed on the front of books, DVD cases, and CD cases. These labels adhere well to these items yet remove easily from the item when it is time for it to be removed from reserve. These types of labels are available in a multitude of sizes and colors. Many label companies offer free, downloadable label templates online that can be used to design the label. Programs like Microsoft Word also have features that allow users to design their own labels. Before ordering labels, staff should:

1. Decide what information they wish to include on the label.
2. Sketch what they would like the label to look like: for example, will it be purely textual, or will it include library branding?
3. Use a free label template to determine what size of label would be best to incorporate the desired text in a font size that is easily readable.
4. Determine whether more than one sized label will be needed to accommodate various sized items (e.g., books vs. CDs) that may be circulating on print reserve.

A label could look like this:

PRINT RESERVES CIRCULATION INFORMATION

This item Circulates for **2 HOURS**
Overnight check-out allowed 2 hours before closing, with item due back
1 hour after the library opens the next day.
Inquire about renewals at the Circulation Desk.
Overdue Reserve items incur heavy fines. Be sure to return items on time!
DO NOT place reserve items in the book drop. Return them directly to the service desk you checked them out from.

Questions? Contact us at (123) 456-7891

In addition to serving as a reminder to the patron checking out the reserve item about the circulation period and providing other valuable information, the label can also serve as a useful tool for staff when they need to enforce reserve policies. For example, if a patron returns a reserve item that circulates for 2 hours to an outdoor book drop that is only checked once a day, then it is likely the patron will incur substantial overdue fines on the item. If the patron later complains about the fine or says they did not know that reserve items could not be returned in the book drop, staff can point out that this information was on the label.

Turnover of the Print Reserve Collection

Staff will have to determine how long they will permit items to remain on print reserve. They may allow instructors to identify a specific date during a semester when they would like an item removed from the collection (e.g., after an item has been used for a class assignment or test). The advantage to allowing instructors to choose a specific date for an item to be removed from print reserve is that an item can be made more widely available to all library users via circulation in the general collection or go out to users at other libraries via consortium lending or ILL. Another advantage is that it helps distribute the workload of removing items from the print reserve collection throughout the semester. Disadvantages to this option include:

- Staff will need to establish a system through which they track these dates.
- If an item is removed from reserve part way through the semester, is returned to the regular circulating collection, and is then checked out by a patron, it may not be readily available should student in the class need to access it at a later time.

Given these challenges, staff could decide that items placed on print reserve at the start of a semester will remain on reserve for the entire semester. The advantage to this option is that items can be made available to students and instructors at any time during the semester. A disadvantage of this system is that at the end of the semester print staff will have to process many items off of reserve instead of doing some gradually throughout the semester.

When a course is taught in back-to-back semesters, staff can choose to give instructors the option to leave the item on reserve for more than one semester. This can be convenient for instructors as it means they may not have to complete a new request form for items each semester it is being used in the course. It can also eliminate the possibility of the item being loaned to another library through consortia lending or ILL, meaning that the work is not available to place on reserve when the course is taught again in subsequent semesters. If a course is taught regularly during a specific semester (e.g., every fall semester), staff could also provide an option to instructors to keep items on reserve for a year or more. However, this option could lead to space on reserve shelving being occupied by books that are not being checked out. Some libraries take this idea a step further and allow instructors to place items on print reserve permanently, meaning that they will not remove the items from reserve until the instructor tells them to do so. While this option can be convenient for instructors in not having to complete request forms each time they are teaching the course, it does mean that access to these works will be limited to reserve circulation periods in perpetuity. Additionally, should the instructor stop teaching the course and forget to notify the library of this fact, then in addition to taking up reserve shelf space, the access to these items would be unnecessarily restricted for library users. Trial and error can help staff determine the best option for establishing pull dates for items.

Print Reserves Copyright Policy

The library will need to establish a copyright policy for their print reserve service. In its simplest form it can state *In support of the teaching and learning mission of the library and the educational institution, library print reserve services will be offered in compliance with U.S. copyright law.* A policy like this highlights the importance of reusing copyrighted works as part of teaching, research, and the creation of new scholarship at the institution and demonstrates that decisions made regarding user rights will be rooted in the law. Libraries wishing to provide additional context for users on copyright may wish to expand this language by citing specific user rights that can be considered when making works available via print reserve, for example, *In support of the teaching and learning mission of the library and the educational institution, library print reserve services will be offered in compliance with user rights U.S. copyright law such as the first sale doctrine (17 U.S.C. § 109) and fair use (17 U.S.C. § 107).* Here, the use of 'such as' indicates there are other user rights libraries can take advantage of when offering print reserves services, such as Reproduction by Libraries and Archives right (17 U.S.C. § 108) and the Reproduction for Blind or Other People with Disabilities right (17 U.S.C. § 121). In the print reserve copyright policy, libraries should be careful not to integrate any wording that may arbitrarily limit their ability to exercise user rights or that is based on common myths and misconceptions about the law, rather than the law itself. For example, a common misconception regarding fair use is that the law limits users to copying no more than 10 percent of a book or one chapter, whichever is less. Section 107 places no such limits on the amount of a work that can be copied and still be considered fair (this misconception and others related to fair use are discussed in depth in Chapter 5).

There will be times when an instructor feels their request to make a work available via print reserve falls within the scope of a user right such as fair use but the library staff supporting this service does not. Because of this, the print reserve copyright policy should contain language that clearly indicates that the library has final say in what works they will make available. For example, *The library reserves the right not to fulfill any print reserve requests if they decide they do not fall within the scope of user rights found in U.S copyright law. A member of the print reserves staff will contact the requestor if any copyright concerns are noted.*

Finally, the print reserve copyright policy should include contact information for members of the library staff who can answer patrons questions regarding the law or the policy. This can be the staff who support this service or a staff member whose job responsibilities include educating members of the campus community about copyright, such as a copyright librarian. The library can also include links to reputable tools and resources, including books and web pages, where they can learn more about the law and user rights.

Placing Items on Print Reserve: Procedures for Instructors

The library will need to develop procedures for instructors to follow when submitting a request to have items placed on print reserve. This should include information regarding:

- The purpose of the service
- The types of items that can be placed on print reserve, including if personal copies will be accepted
- Types of items that cannot be placed on print reserve
- Circulation periods available for print reserve items
- If there is more than one library on campus, which libraries offer course reserve services, and any special policies associated with circulating items from specific libraries
- How the request submission process operates, including a link to or posted copy of the print reserve request form
- How far in advance requests should be submitted
- The amount of time needed by staff to process items being placed on print reserve
- The process for removing items from reserve at the end of the semester
- Contact information for staff or department managing print reserve services

Libraries should provide instructions with information about how works can lawfully be circulated via print reserves. This can include a link to the library's print reserve copyright policy.

The following is an example of what these procedures might look like.

> The library's print reserve service provides instructors and students with short-term access to required and supplementary learning materials in support of the educational mission of the institution.
>
> Items that can be placed on print reserve include copies of books, DVDs, and Blu-rays, and CDs from the library's circulating collections. If you are interested in placing a book, film, or sound recording on print reserve that the library does not

own you should speak with your subject librarian to see if a copy of the item can be purchased for the library's collection. Please allow 2–4 weeks for these items to be ordered, shipped, and processed. Photocopies of works such as articles, selections from books, class notes, practice tests, etc. can also be placed on course reserve. We may also be able to place alternative learning materials on print reserve for your course. For example, models (e.g., a skeleton or anatomical models), a microscope, or technology. Please reach out to us using to contact information found below to learn more about options for placing such items on print reserve.

It is the policy of the library not to place on reserve those materials borrowed from other libraries (e.g., books, DVDs, and CDs borrowed through our consortium).

The library will accept instructor's personal copies of books, films, and CDs to circulate on print reserve. Please be aware that for cataloging purposes tattle-tape, barcodes, and labels will be affixed personal copies and that wear-and-tear caused by frequent use is to be expected. Should a student damage (beyond repair) or lose your personal copy, the library will require the student replace the item.

Print reserve items circulate for 2 hours, 4 hours, 1 day, 3 days, or 7 days. Instructors will be asked to select a circulation period when they submit their print reserve request.

Print reserve requests can be submitted online [embed a link to the form here], or a copy of the request form can be downloaded, printed, and submitted to any campus library at the circulation desk [embed a copy of the document here]. Please complete all required fields on the form and, when applicable, print legibly.

Requests should be submitted at least 1 week prior to the date needed for class, though more processing time may be needed at the beginning of the semester due to the increase in the volume of requests we receive during this time. All requests are processed in the order they are received.

Unless otherwise instructed, items will be removed from print reserve at the end of the semester and be returned to the library collection or, in the case of personal copies, to the rightful owner.

Items will be made available through print reserves in compliance with U.S. copyright law [embed link to print reserve copyright policy here]. If you have questions about copyright or print reserve services, contact us at [insert staff or departmental phone number here] or [insert staff or departmental email here].

Print Reserve Request Forms

The library will need to develop request forms that ask for the information needed to process items onto print reserve. There are several categories of information that should be included on the form:

- Instructor contact information. Instructors should be asked to provide, at minimum, their name, email address, and phone number. If the course is co-taught by another instructor or has TAs the person submitting the request should be asked to provide their names as well.

- Course information. Information collected in this section of the form should include the name of the course, the course code (e.g., psychology courses may be represented in the course catalog as PSY, history classes may be represented as HST, etc.), the course number, and the section number.
- Item information. Instructors should be asked to provide as much information as possible to help staff accurately identify the item they would like to have placed on print reserve. This can include the title of the work; the author, director, or composer; the publisher or distributor; the year the work was published; and the call number for the work, if it is currently held in the library's collection. For articles and book chapters, this can include the name of the publication, the title of the article or chapter, the volume or edition, and the relevant page numbers.
- Intended use. Libraries may wish to ask instructors to briefly describe how the requested work may be used as part of course instruction. This information can be helpful if a copy of a work (e.g., a selection from a book rather than circulating the entire book or a single article from a journal rather than circulating the entire print issue) needs to be made available under user rights found in U.S. copyright law, such as fair use.
- Circulation information. The form should ask instructors to choose from the available circulation periods for print reserve items.
- Location information. If a campus has multiple branch libraries, instructors should identify which library they would like the reserve item circulated from (libraries may also require that print reserve request be submitted at this particular branch).
- The pull date for the item. If the library does not have a set dates when items are removed from print reserve (e.g., the end of the semester), then instructors should be asked when they want the item removed from reserve.

Staff will have to decide whether instructors will need to complete a separate form for each item they would like to place on print reserve or if more than one item can be entered on a single form. Completing a separate form for each requested item may seem time consuming for instructors but could allow staff to more easily track each requested item through processing stages. Some libraries add language to reserve forms asking instructors to certify that their request is made in compliance with U.S. copyright law, such as *Requests must fall within the scope of US copyright law. A librarian will contact me if there are compliance considerations associated with my request.*

Print versus Digital Forms

Staff will need to decide what is the most efficient and practical way to have instructors submit print reserve requests forms. Libraries can create the form as a Word document or portable document format (PDF) and make print copies available in the library. They can also (or alternately) post copies of these forms online for instructors to download and complete. However, this could present some challenges:

- If the form is completed by hand, illegible handwriting may make it hard for staff to read the information that was entered into a field.
- While the digital copies of these forms can be encoded with information that identify which fields users are required to complete, if the instructor prints off the form and completes it by hand these designators may be lost or not be obvious to them.
- If the instructor saves a copy of the form to their computer and uses this version each time they are looking to submit a request, then they may miss seeing revised or updated versions of the form that have been posted to the library's website.
- Requests submitted by instructors on paper can be hard to track and, if lost or misplaced, may result in requests not being processed properly or in a timely manner.

Some of these challenges can be overcome by trying to standardize the form submission process as much as possible. This could include making forms available as Word documents or PDFs but requiring them to be submitted as electronic documents that are sent to a central email account used by staff rather than allowing the submission of them as paper forms. Some of the issues outlined above (e.g., illegible handwriting or incomplete forms) can be overcome by contacting the instructor and asking for clarification or the missing information, but this does mean more work for staff and delays in processing time. If paper forms are submitted in person, then it can be useful for the person accepting them to quickly review them with the instructor to ensure legibility and completeness.

Online Request Submission

Reserve request forms can be set up as an online form using a program such as Google Forms or Formstack. Ticketing systems like TeamDyanmix can also be considered. The advantages to using these online tools include:

- As the information entered into the fields will be typed, handwriting legibility is no longer an issue.
- Form fields can be marked as required fields, requiring the person completing them to enter data before the system allows submission of the form. This can help cut down on the instances of requests that are submitted with incomplete information.

- All submitted requests are stored in a central, online location.
- These forms can be quickly updated if it is identified that a field needs to be changed or added, and once changes are made to the form, all subsequent users will be working from the same form.
- Links can be embedded into the forms directing those completing them to additional information that may be useful to them. For example, a link could be included to an online copy of the reserve copyright policies or to a frequently asked questions page for the services.
- Most form programs allow for email notification as completed forms are submitted. This can help staff identify and track new requests, especially during busy processing times.

Print reserve request forms should include contact information for the person or department managing this service for the library so that instructors who are completing the form have ready access to this information and can use it to get assistance with any questions they may have.

Processing Items onto Reserve: Procedures for Staff

As requests forms are received, staff will need to work through the following steps to process works on to print reserve.

Reviewing Forms for Completeness

All fields on the form should be reviewed to ensure that they have been filled with the information staff will need to process the request. If the form was completed by hand, staff will also need to ensure all the information entered is legible. If any of the information is missing, ambiguous, or illegible, staff will need to follow up with the instructor who submitted the request in order to get the information needed before moving forward with processing.

Checking to See If the Requested Item Is One That Can Circulate on Print Reserve

Staff should check to see if the requested item falls within the scope of the library's print reserve circulation policy. For example, if the item requested is held in the library's reference collection and library policy prohibits these items from being placed on print reserve, then staff will need to determine:

- Whether an exception will be made for this particular item, allowing it to be placed on print reserve

- If, for those institutions that have multiple branch libraries, another copy of the work is available in the circulating collection of one of these libraries that can be transferred over to be placed on reserve
- Whether the library that the work will circulate from might be able to order a second copy of the work that can be placed on reserve
- Whether the instructor who placed the request may be able to supply a personal copy of the work to circulate to students

If an exception cannot be made to the policy, the instructor should be informed if alternate options are available to them, such as directing students to access the item in the reference collection instead of through reserves.

Ensuring the Work Can Lawfully Be Made Available via Print Reserves

Works can lawfully be made available via print reserves when:

1. The work can be circulated under the first sale doctrine (17 U.S.C. § 109).
2. The work is in the public domain.
3. The instructor placing the work on print reserve is the rightsholder.
4. The item is licensed in a way that allows it to be circulated via print reserve.
5. A copy of the item can be circulated under user rights found in U.S. copyright law.
6. Permission or a special license is received to circulate the item through print reserve.

Each of these options will be detailed in Chapter 12, where a copyright workflow for print reserve services can be found. If it is determined that a requested work can be lawfully made available via print reserves, staff should next check to see if a copy of it is available in the library's collection. If the item cannot be lawfully made available via print reserve, staff will need to speak with the instructor to see if another item can be used instead.

Does the Library Own a Copy of the Requested Work?

For this step, staff will have to do more than check to see whether a copy of the requested work is owned by the library, whether the item is available for reserve use, and whether it is in condition to be circulated to students.

Is the Item Available?

Staff will need to check the ILS, online public access catalog (OPAC), or discovery layer to see if the requested work is owned by the library and if it is currently listed as being available on the library's shelves. For those campuses that have multiple libraries, staff will need to check to see if the work is in the collection of the library the instructor wishes the item to circulate from, or is it held at one of the other locations. In these situations, it will need to be decided whether the libraries will transfer items among each other to place on print reserve for the course, or if items will need to be placed on print reserve at the location it is normally housed in. It will be much more convenient for students to be able to access all of the materials placed on print reserve for their course at one location rather than going back and forth between the campus libraries. However, if the requested resource is frequently used by instructors and students at the library it is normally housed at, then staff at that library may be hesitant to send it to the other library. If library policy forbids such transfers, or if the library that has the item is unwilling to agree to the transfer, then the library may need to look into acquiring a copy for their collection or getting a personal copy from the instructor who placed the request

Just because an item is listed as being available in the ILS or OPAC does not mean that it is available for check-out. Items that are listed as being available may not be on the shelf for a multitude of reasons, including:

- The item was recently returned by a patron and is sitting on temporary shelving.
- The item was misshelved.
- A patron removed the item from the stacks and is currently using it in the library.
- If a campus has multiple libraries, it could have been mistakenly shelved at another library.
- The item has been stolen.

If the item is not where it is supposed to be, staff will need to perform a search to see if it can be found. If it cannot be found, staff will have to decide whether they are going to declare the item lost and order a replacement copy. If a replacement copy will not be ordered, staff will need to work through alternate options of obtaining a copy of the work, which are discussed in the section *When the Library Does Not Own a Copy of the Requested Work* found in this chapter. They can also contact the instructor who placed the request to see whether an alternate item can be identified and used as a substitute for the item originally requested.

If the item is currently checked out. If the item is currently checked out, staff will need to determine whether it is in the possession of one of their own patrons or if it has been sent out to a consortium partner or on ILL. If one of the library's own patrons has the item, staff should check to see what the item's due date is. If the due date is only a few days away or a week in the future, a staff member can place a hold on the item so that it is directed to them when it is returned. Here, staff will need to be cognizant of library circulation policies regarding holds placed on items a patron has checked out. Often, if another patron has placed a hold on a checked-out item, this will prevent the patron from securing any renewals. However, if the system is set up to provide patrons with a guaranteed number of renewals, then a staff member may need to recall the item

If an item is checked out to one of the library's own patrons but the due date is far into the future, staff may be able to recall the work if their ILS offers this option. This involves changing the current due date to a new due date a short term out, such as a week or two in the future. In these cases, staff will need to communicate the new due date to the patron. However, just because an item has been recalled, it does not mean that the patron will bring the item back. The library may wish to establish fines for recalled items that are high enough to dissuade patrons from keeping these items past the new due date. When items are recalled to be placed on print reserve, patrons are sometimes responsive to hearing from staff about the reason for the recall, understanding that they will still have access to the item via print reserve and that their classmates will as well.

If a requested item is checked out to a consortium patron or through ILL, it may be harder for staff to get the item back in a timely manner. Staff can try reaching out to the borrowing library to see if they will ask their patron to return the item early, but if they are unwilling to do this, or if the patron decides to keep the item for the full circulation period they were given, staff will have to decide which of the following options might work best for resolving the situation:

- They can let the instructor who placed the request know when they expect to have the item back and see if they still wish to have the item placed on reserve. If the item will not be used as part of class instruction until later in the semester, a delay in getting the item returned may not be an issue.
- They can check to see whether the instructor has a personal copy of the item they could lend to the library to circulate until the library's copy is returned.

In extreme cases, the library could explore options for initiating a rush order of a second copy of the item that could be placed on reserve.

Lost, missing, and damaged items. Staff may find a requested item in the stacks but discover that it is damaged. For example, books may have missing pages, excessive highlighting or pen markings, or a damaged spine, and DVDs or CDs may have scratches on them. Staff will need to determine whether the damage prevents the item from being useful to patrons and, if so, whether they can quickly repair the damage. If not, or if the item is lost or missing, then staff can work through the options outlined in the next section to identify the best way to obtain a copy of the work.

The Library Does Not Own a Copy of the Requested Work

If the library does not own a copy of a requested work, or if their copy is lost, stolen, or damaged beyond repair, the following options can be considered for obtaining a copy of it.

Purchasing a Replacement Copy

If staff find that the requested item is listed as lost or missing or if it is damaged beyond the point that it can be circulated via print reserve, they will need to determine whether the library can order a replacement copy. Often, purchasing decisions will be controlled by the library's collection development policies and procedures and final say regarding the acquisition of items will rest with those librarians charged with collection development. Staff supporting reserve services can work with these librarians to identify requested works that can be purchased for the collection, or, in some libraries, the staff managing reserve services are given their own budget to purchase items for reserve use. In these situations, library administrators should work with staff to decide the amount of funds that will be allocated to this account, how purchase requests will be prioritized, and who among the staff will have final authority in making purchasing decisions. Funds spent on reserve purchases should be reviewed on an ongoing basis to determine whether the amount is appropriate for the use the collection is seeing.

Expiated processing of purchased works. Due to the in-demand nature of reserve services, it will be important to order and process these items as quickly as possible. This can include:

- Acquisitions decisions. Here it will need to be decided whether the decision to purchase requested items will receive expiated review by the appropriate staff.
- Order placement. Once the decision is made to purchase the item, acquisitions staff will need to enter the order into the ILS and place the order for the item with a vendor. Here, it may be decided that, when available, the library will pay for rush shipping for items being used for reserves. Even with rush shipping, it can still take several business days for vendors to

process purchases and get them in the mail. When rush shipping is not available from a vendor, it can take several weeks for items to arrive. Either way, it can be helpful for staff to keep the instructor who requested the item be placed on reserve informed of delays in processing that may result from shipping.

- Cataloging. Once requested orders arrive, staff can choose to move them quickly through the cataloging process as well. Cataloging staff can then notify staff that the items are ready to go so they can pick them up for reserve processing.

For this stage of the process, staff and administration will also need to discuss what the expedited timeframe looks like. For example, it could be established that for reserve items acquisitions decisions, order placement, the cataloging, and the processing of the item onto reserve will all be done within one business day of when each person in this cycle receives the item.

Circulating Instructor's Personal Copies

When the library does not own a copy of a requested item, they may ask the instructor who placed the request if they own a copy they would be willing to donate to or loan to the library to place on reserve.

In these situations, some libraries will require that the instructor donate their copy of the book to the library to incorporate into their circulating collection. The advantage to having such a policy is that the work can be cataloged using normal procedures and easily be attached to a course reserve record. As with other donations, staff will want to review the work first to ensure it is in good enough condition to be accepted for integration to the collection (e.g., making sure there is not excessive wear-and-tear to the work, excessive highlighting or notes, etc.). Some instructors will hesitate at the idea of donating their copy of the work to the library, and in these situations the library can, instead, request they instead temporarily loan the work to the library to circulate to students via print reserve. When an instructor loans a personal copy of a work to the library, it is wise for staff to make them aware that, due to frequent use, it is not uncommon for works circulated through print reserves to be damaged. It could be that their copy may be returned to them with wear-and-tear that can include a broken spine or bent pages on books or scratches on a CD, DVD, or Blu-ray discs. Additionally, if the library will be attaching a barcode, a spine label, or other organizational tag to the work for cataloging purposes, this information should also be shared with the course instructor. As print reserve resources may be lost, could be stolen from the library or from a patron who has it checked out, or could be damaged in a way that renders it useless (e.g., a DVD is broken or a cup of coffee spilled on a book), the library should also inform instructors lending them a personal copy of a work that there is a chance they may not receive their work back at all. If the library has procedures in place to provide a replacement of a personal copy of a work that is lost, stolen, or damaged (e.g., the library purchases a replacement copy or requires the student who had the item checked out to purchase one), this information can be shared with the instructor. Here, staff working at public institutions should note that in some states public funds cannot be used to purchase replacement copies in these situations. Public institutions should check with their campus's purchasing department to see what rules their state has in place that may govern these situations.

Both instructors and library staff will frequently question whether the circulation of instructor's personal copies is a violation of U.S. copyright law or of notices printed on the work stating that they are for the instructor's personal use only. Generally, there are no copyright infringement considerations when circulating these works (a topic discussed in depth is a case study in the section *Circulating Instructor's Personal Copies of Works on Print Reserve* in Chapter 7).

Obtaining Photocopies of Works

If the library is going to circulate photocopies of works via print reserve, staff will need to determine how the photocopies will be obtained. They will also need to determine whether the making and circulating of the photocopies falls within the scope of the options available for lawfully making works available via print reserve, a topic that will be discussed in depth in Chapter 12.

The library owns a copy of the original work. If the library owns a copy of the original work (e.g., a copy of the book or a print copy of the issue the requested journal article is in), from a copyright compliance perspective staff may just wish to circulate the original copy under the first sale doctrine (a topic discussed in Chapter 8). However, if it is decided that selections from the book or the requested article will be photocopied and circulated, then staff will need to locate the item in the collection following the procedures outlined in the preceding sections of this chapter and make the photocopy.

The library needs to acquire a copy. If the library does not currently own a copy of the requested work, they will need to decide how a copy will be acquired. For articles, this could involve obtaining a copy through ILL. For selections from books, this could involve requesting copies of the requested selections through ILL; ordering a copy of the book though consortium lending or ILL and making copies from it; or having the library acquire a copy of the title for their collection that the staff can photocopy. Copyright considerations tied to each of these options will be addressed in Part Two of this book.

ILS Processing

While each ILS system works differently, most ILS systems use the same standard of organization for print reserves: a course record is created, and then item records for the works being placed on reserve are attached to this record. However, staff will want to consult the user manual for their ILS to determine exactly how the print reserve module functions.

Creating Bibliographic and Item Records

For most ILS, items being placed on print reserve will require the creation of two records: a bibliographic record and an item record. Described simply, a bibliographic records contains information about a resource (e.g., a book, DVD, or CD) and includes information such as the title of the work, the creator, the creation or publication year, the International Standard Book Number (ISBN), and the call number. Item records are attached to bibliographic records and contain information about the library's holdings of the bibliographic work. Information found in item records includes:

- The location where the item is kept (e.g., a particular building, collection, or both)
- The type of resource it is (e.g., print or electronic)
- For physical works, the barcode attached to the particular item

For those items that the library owns, these records will have been created when the item was cataloged. Personal copies of works instructors provide to the library to place on print reserve may be treated a bit differently. If the instructor donates their copy of a work to the library to add to their collection, then it should go through the regular cataloging process before being added to a course record. However, if they are only loaning the personal copy to the library, staff will need to decide how it will be cataloged and who will be responsible for doing so. Depending on training and workload, it could be members of the cataloging staff or staff members who support reserve services. Either way, when creating an item record for a personal copy that is on loan to the library, it can be helpful to include a note in the item record stating who owns it. This can provide clarification on who the book should be returned to when its remove from print reserve.

Figure 2.1 provides a basic overview of the workflow staff can use to process print reserve requests from form submission to making the work available for checkout.

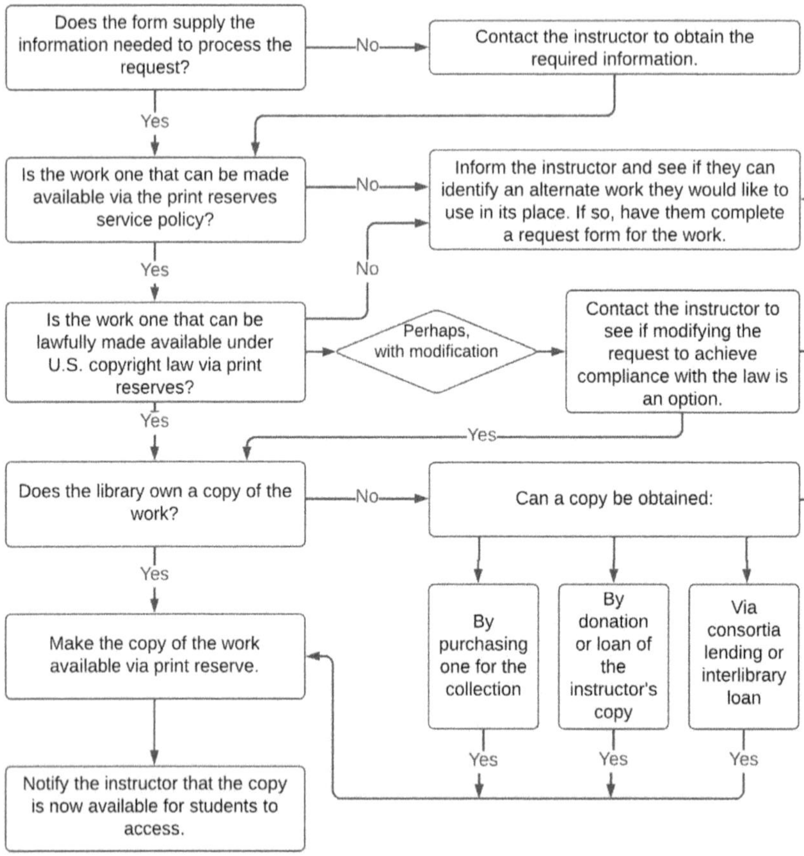

Figure 2.1 The basic workflow of print request processing

Case Study: Organizing Items on the Print Reserve Stacks

There are different ways that items can be organized on the print reserve shelves. For example, some libraries choose to organize works based upon the name of the instructor who placed the item on reserve. Other libraries organize the reserve shelves by the name of the course, grouping together all the items placed on reserve for a specific course together. There are advantages and disadvantages to these two systems. Advantages include:

- If students do not know the titles of the works the instructor has placed on reserve they can, instead, give staff the name of their instructor or their course and staff can pull the item or items for the student to review.
- All items placed on reserve by a particular instructor or for a particular course will be grouped together on the print reserve stacks,

making it easy for staff to pull multiple titles at a time if requested by a student.

Disadvantages to this system include:

- Staff will have to create labels to attach to each print reserve item listing the name of the instructor or the class, and accompanying labels will have to be created and placed on the shelving, marking out the spot where items for that instructor or course are to be placed.
- If an item is requested by more than one instructor or is being used by more than one class, then that items staff may become confused as to which instructor or class space the item should be shelved in.
- If the student does not know the name of their instructor or cannot recall the specific name of their course, staff will have to look the item up in the ILS, catalog, or OPAC to determine which instructor or course it is attached to.

Alternate methods of organizing print reserve collections include organizing items using the course code and number (e.g., PSY 101 or HIST 203). Alternately, some print reserve collections are organized by the department name. For both options, when students ask to check out a specific reserve item, staff will likely be able to quickly locate the portion of the collection it resides in, though them then may have to browse among any books to find the particular title the patron asked for. Some libraries choose to arrange books in call number order on the print reserve stacks. This method also has advantages and disadvantages. One distinct advantage of this system is that a particular work—for example, a film—can be used by multiple instructors or courses and staff will not have to search around to determine which instructor or course the film has been placed under on the stacks. Instead, it will live in one location. A disadvantage to this system is that staff will have to look up the call numbers for works students ask for, though, over time, it is not unusual for staff to have memorized the call numbers for the print reserve items that are most frequently checked-out.

Whatever system of classification the library chooses to use should be the one that allows staff to quickly find items on the shelves so they do not keep students waiting too long to check them out. Staff may wish to try out each classification system over the course of different semesters to see which works best for them.

Processing Items off Print Reserve

It is important for staff to remove items from the print reserve collection when they are no longer being used. This could be at a specific time designated by the course instructor. It could also be in a situation when items were placed on print reserve but are not actually being checked out by patrons. This helps ensure that items that are not circulating are not taking up shelf space in the reserve collection. It also allows items to be returned to their regular location within the collection and their traditional circulation periods.

Dates When Items Are Pulled

As mentioned previously, when submitting the print reserve request, staff can allow instructors to identify a specific date they wish to have items removed from print reserve, or items can be removed at a designated time such as the end of each academic term. If instructors are allowed to designate a specific date for the items to be pulled, staff will need to establish a way of tracking these dates. This could include a print filing system of some sort that is checked on a daily or weekly basis by staff. It could also include notes entered into an electronic calendar that remind staff when it is time to remove a work from print reserve. If items will be removed from reserve at an established time (e.g., the end of each academic term), then extra staff time will likely need to be allotted for to ensure this considerable amount of work goes smoothly.

Communicating with Instructors About the Removal

Before removing items from print reserve, be it during the academic term or at the end of it, it can be helpful to reach out to the instructor who placed the item on print reserve via email to confirm that they still wish to have it removed. This can be especially important if instructors have designated that a work come off reserve during the semester as it could be that a student requested extra time to complete an assignment and needs access to the work beyond the date that the instructor originally identified. Reaching out to instructors at the end of the term to ask them if they still wish to have items removed from reserve may seem like a time-consuming process: however, it may actually prove to be a time-saving measure for staff. For example, if all items placed on reserve for a class are removed at the end of a term and the instructor asks a few days or weeks later for them all to be placed back on reserve for the same course, staff will have to recreate the course records, find the requested items again in the collection, reattach them to the course record, and reshelve the items in the reserve stacks. If staff reaches out to instructors before removing the items from reserve and the instructor informs them then that they wish for the items to remain on reserve for a subsequent semester, then all staff needs to do is to update the course record indicating that it will be active for that future semester. Staff can actually begin reaching out to instructors via email before the end of the term as a way of spreading out the workload and also so that when the end of the term does arrive, they have readily identified which items should be pulled from the reserve collection and which will remain on reserve.

Returning Items

Items that were on print reserve that belonged to the library should be returned to their designated collection or, if on loan from another campus library, sent there. Before doing so, staff may wish to inspect these items to see if there was any significant damage incurred from reserve use that warrants it being repaired or replaced. Personal copies of items that were placed on reserve should be returned to the instructor who owns it. These can be returned through campus mail, can be hand delivered to the instructor office, or staff can ask instructors to stop by and pick up their item from the library. Staff will need to decide whether they will remove barcodes, spine labels, and any other identifying information they attached to the item before returning it to instructors. If the instructor might place the item back on print reserve in the future, it could be helpful for these tags and labels are left on it as this means that staff will not need to recreate them.

Keeping Copies of Reserve Request Forms

Staff will need to decide whether they are going to save copies of reserve request forms and, if so, how long they will keep them. There are several benefits to keeping these records. For example, instructors may contact the library and ask if they can be reminded what they had placed on print reserve for a particular course in a previous semester. In these situations, having access to copies of the request forms can make answering these questions easy. Having copies of the forms can also be useful if staff decide they would like to review them to look for patterns in requests (e.g., which department or instructor may be frequently submitting requests).

If requests are submitted using an online form, then storage space, tracking, and organization will likely present minimal issues. If instructors are permitted to submit copies of the request forms in print or as digital files (e.g., submitting a Word copy of the request form via email), then staff will need to identify a way to store and organize them. This could include making scanned copies of the print forms and saving them all to a shared digital storage area so all those who may need to access them can readily do so. In these situations, staff will want to come up with a naming convention for these files that allows them to identify who submitted the request, what class it was for, and what semester. If requests records will be kept in print, then staff should set aside room in a closet or filing cabinet in which to store them. In all three situations, staff will need to decide how long they wish to keep these records and establish a system for deleting or disposing of them on a regular basis.

Marketing Print Reserve Services

For print reserve services to be successful, instructors and students must be aware of them. Staff will need to carefully consider how print reserve services will be marketed to members of the campus community.

Marketing to Instructors

There are four key areas library staff should emphasize when marketing print reserve services to instructors:

- Promoting print reserve services. Staff will want to ensure that instructors are aware that they offer print reserves, their purpose, and the scope of the service. Here, finding effective ways share the print reserve procedures with instructors can help increase their awareness of the service, including items that can be circulated on reserve, available circulation periods, and how to submit reserve requests.
- Copyright considerations. Information about U.S. copyright law and the ways works can be lawfully shared with students via print reserves should also be marketed to instructors. Providing basic information up front and directing instructors to the print reserves copyright policy can help deepen their understanding of the law and assuage concerns and frustrations they may have about what works can be made available to students.
- Contact information. All marketing done around print reserve services should provide recipients with contact information for the staff overseeing the service that can be used to ask get answers to questions they may have about the service.
- Marketing information for students. Instructors may appreciate receiving marketing information from the library that they can share with students to inform them that they have placed items on print reserve for them to use. This can include text that can be placed in the class syllabus, or information that can be posted to the LMS course page or that can be emailed to students. Information that should be shared with students will be explored in the next section.

Marketing to Students

It is also important to market print reserves to students so they can take advantage of the service. One of the most effective ways of doing so is to have instructors who have placed items on print reserve provide their students with information about:

- The purpose of print reserves
- The titles of the works they placed on print reserve

- The library location where the students can go to check out the reserve items
- The circulation periods

The library can supplement this information with additional marketing about print reserve services, emphasizing the shorter circulation periods, overdue fines, billing procedures, and any other pertinent information that can help students effectively engage with these resources. Any marketing directed to students should also contain contact information for the staff overseeing the service so students can get answers to any questions they may have.

Assessment

Staff should perform assessment on a periodical basis to ensure that print reserve services are functioning optimally and providing a maximum benefit to users. As part of this assessment process, staff should consider several things:

Number of Items Being Placed on Reserve

Staff will want to determine whether the number of items being placed on print reserve are decreasing, increasing, or remaining approximately the same. If the numbers are decreasing, staff should seek to determine why. It could be that instructors are placing items they used to place on print reserve on e-reserve or media reserve. Other factors could be driving their decision not to engage with print reserves though. For example, perhaps instructors find the request submission process too cumbersome or have trouble with making copyright determinations. If the number of items being placed on print reserve has been increasing, staff may wish to speak with instructors to determine what has been motivating them to place items on print reserve so they can identify ways in which to maintain this momentum. If the number of items being placed on print reserve has been remaining approximately the same over years, then assessment can help staff identify if there are ways to promote the service that might increase its use.

Circulation Statistics

The number of check-outs print reserve items are seeing can help indicate the health of the service. If circulation statistics are decreasing:

- It may indicate that students are not aware of the service and how to access items made available through it.

- It could mean that students are aware of the service but some aspect of it does not suit their needs (e.g., the circulation periods are too short).
- It could also mean that students are not finding the items they need to access for classes through the service.

Increasing circulation statistics can indicate that students are aware of and actively engaging with these resources. In these situations, it can be helpful to look at which items are getting the most check-outs to see if there are trends that might help staff identify similar resources that can be placed on reserve to help make the service more functional for others. For example, if it is identified that the textbooks placed on print reserve are the items getting the most check-outs, then this might provide reason for the library to add additional textbooks to the print reserve collection. In the numbers are stagnant, this may show the service is fulfilling a need but needs to be better marketed to students to increase usage. Decreasing circulation numbers could indicate that instructor or student awareness of the services needs to be increased or that the service is no longer being used to the extent it once was that that it could be scaled back by the library accordingly.

Return on Investment

Staff will want to ensure that the levels of resources being invested into print reserve services—including staffing, location and space, technology and equipment, and funding—are reflective of the amount of use it is getting. All of these may need to be increased if reserve usage by instructors and students is increasing. However, if reserve usage by either group or both groups is decreasing, the library may wish to reconsider the resources it devotes to providing print reserve services. Before reducing them, staff should first consider ways in which they may be able to more effectively market the service to renew or increase interest in it.

Putting It All Together

Carefully thinking through the administrative considerations associated with offering print reserve services will provide a solid foundation for launching or expanding the service. Having sound service parameters allows print reserve services to function more smoothly for students looking to use them. It also provides a set of clear rules and expectations for instructors looking to place items on print reserve. A print reserve copyright policy that establishes a balance between the rights granted to the creators of copyrighted works and the user rights found in the law will ensure the library is able to provide a service that meets the needs of users while at the same time mitigating legal risk for the institution (this will be discussed in Chapter 14). Together, all of this should come together to ensure that instructors are able to easily submit reserve requests, that staff are able to process items on to reserve in a timely manner, and that students are able to find the works they need to successfully complete course assignments.

CHAPTER THREE

Electronic and Media Reserves Administration and Management

Electronic reserve (e-reserves) services provide instructors and students with online access to digital copies of textual learning materials, including newspaper and journal articles and selections from books. Some libraries also choose to make digital copies of instructor-generated content such as notes, study guides, and practice tests available via e-reserves. Media reserve services provide instructors and students with online access to digital copies of media such as audiovisual works and sound recordings (e.g., spoken word and music). Both services provide the library with a valuable opportunity to support education by connecting members of the campus community with materials used for teaching, research, and the creation of new scholarship. They can also play a key role in supporting distance education, especially when students live in other states or countries. As these students would be unable to visit the library to access print reserve collections, electronic and media reserve services can help them access course materials that might not otherwise be available to them online.

In addition to providing remote access to course materials for distance learners, electronic and media reserves provide other advantages over print reserves. Items made available via electronic and media reserves can be accessed by students any time of day, whereas print reserves are only accessible to students during its hours of operation. Unless students are working in groups, works placed on print reserve can only be used by one student at a time, whereas items made available via electronic and media reserves can often be accessed by multiple users at once. Print reserve items can usually only be checked out for a few hours, which may not provide the student enough time to complete an assignment or prepare for a test, and if students return the items late, they may be charged overdue fines. As items made available via electronic reserves are not checked out to students in the traditional sense, students are able to access and use the work for as long as needed without fear of incurring overdue fines. Items placed on print reserve may deteriorate quickly from frequent use, but digital copies of items made available via electronic and media reserve services can be used repeatedly without suffering effects from wear-and-tear.

A library's ability to offer electronic and media reserves will be dictated by the availability of resources such as staffing, space, technology, and equipment. The library will also need to be prepared to establish service parameters to guide the administration and use of these services. Both of these topics will be addressed in this chapter, in addition to considerations for processing electronic and media reserve requests, marketing these services, and assessing them for impact. Readers will notice that some information provided in Chapter 2, which explores administrative and management considerations for print reserves, is repeated in this chapter. That is because there are some administrative and management considerations that apply to all three services, and because some readers may not have cause to read Chapter 2 if their library does not offer print reserves. Repeating the information here instead of sending readers to the preceding chapter to review the information seemed to be the most efficient way to address both situations.

Resource Requirements

Before launching or expanding electronic and media reserve services, staff should determine whether they have the staffing, space, technology, and equipment needed to support and maintain them.

Staffing

Staff will need to engage with electronic and media reserve materials in many ways, including:

- Accepting requests to make materials available via these services and answering questions instructors may have about the submission process

- Reviewing submitted requests for completeness and, if needed, following-up with the instructor to obtain supplementary information
- Searching to see if requested items are available in the library's collection
- If requested items are not currently owned by the library, determining how copies might be acquired
- Reviewing requests to see if they can lawfully be made available via electronic and media reserves
- For some requests, creating an electronic copy of the requested work, uploading it to the platform being used to provide the service, and connecting it to the appropriate course
- When appropriate, obtaining permission or a license to make works available via these services
- If needed, also placing copies of requested works on print reserve

Frequently, additional staff support is needed at the beginning of each semester to process the influx of reserve requests submitted by instructors and to help students determine if items they are looking for are available via electronic and media reserve. As many items may come off reserve at the end of each semester, additional staff time should also be allotted then to help support the service.

When launching or expanding reserve services, library administration will need to decide:

- Whether a dedicated position is required to support the services or if these responsibilities will be added to the workload of individuals already employed by the library
- Whether current employees will be reassigned to new positions associated with the services
- Whether new employees need to be hired to help manage the workload

If new employees are hired, administrators will need to determine whether they will be librarians, support staff, student employees, or a combination of the three and how much funding is available to fund these positions.

Staffing may also vary by campus library or location. Smaller libraries on a campus (or regional campus libraries) may not have the staff needed to fully support electronic and media reserve services. In these situations, these services could be administered for that library from a larger campus library. On some campuses that have multiple libraries, one department or group of staff may be responsible for administering electronic and media reserves for the entire campus.

Space, Technology, and Equipment

Additional resources needed to support electronic and media reserve services include:

- Physical space in the library for processing the requests, including workstations with room for computers and digitization equipment.
- Digital space provided by cloud-based or in-house server infrastructure to host the systems and software used to administer electronic and media reserves and to store the associated digital documents and media files.
- A system through which these services can be provided. The library's integrated library systems (ILS) may have a reserve module that can be used for electronic and media reserve services. There are also a variety of commercial systems available to libraries, such as Docutek ERes, Ares, and eReserve Plus. Some libraries choose to use systems developed in-house, whereas others use the institution's learning management system (LMS) (e.g., Blackboard, Canvas, Moodle) to administer these services.
- For media reserves, some type of media hosting platform is required in addition to a system to administer the service. This can be provided in-house or via commercial systems like Kaltura.
- Equipment the library will need to administer electronic and media reserve services, aside from computers used to access the ILS or alternate system includes scanning equipment and software that can be used to make digital copies of requested works.

Case Study: Choosing a System to Administer Reserve Services

Deciding what system to use to administer reserve services can be a daunting task. Often these decisions will be influenced by staffing, features, and the library's finances. For example, if the library has staff who can develop and maintain a system in-house to administer reserve services, then they can likely create a product customized to the institution's specific needs. However, many libraries choose to use an ILS module, commercial system, or the institution's LMS to administer these services because they do not have staff they can dedicate to a project of this magnitude. This also includes time staff would have to spend troubleshooting technical issues, because if a system is developed in-house, library staff will need to resolve issues that arise with it. With ILS modules and commercial systems, vendors will likely provide support to resolve technical issues, or if the LMS is being used, there is likely a department on campus administering the system who can provide support for it.

Features that facilitate access to and administration of reserve services should also be considered. Reserve modules offered by ILS vendors can provide a familiar framework for staff to work in to administer these services but may require that students access works through the library's online catalog, which can be a challenge for a student who does not know how to perform catalog searches. When commercial reserve systems first emerged on the market, students often accessed them through the library's website. However, most commercial systems available today offer options for direct integration with the LMS, allowing students to access reserve materials via their course pages. Commercial systems can also offer additional features, including request submission and tracking, workflow management, email communication with users, copyright management, and use statistic reporting. Using the institution's LMS to administer electronic and media reserve services may be convenient for students and instructors in terms of access, but library staff will likely need to use an alternate system to manage request submission, copyright, and so on, which can create extra work for them in terms of service administration. Ultimately, costs may be a deciding factor, both in terms of a system and staff time. For example, libraries will need to budget for an ILS module or commercial system to administer these services: libraries will likely be able to access the LMS for free, but as these systems were not designed to administer reserve services, they may cost the library in terms of additional staff time needed to navigate the systems or in a lack of features used to manage them.

Libraries looking to offer or expand the reserve services they offer will need to carefully consider staffing, features, and finances and when deciding which system might be the best fit for them, keeping in mind that they can use different systems for different services. For example, a library may use the ILS to administer print reserves, the LMS for media reserves, and a commercial platform for electronic reserves. Whatever platform is selected, staff will need to ensure it meets accessibility requirements outlined in state and federal laws, a topic that is discussed further in Chapter 13.

Service Parameters

Libraries should consider the following question when developing service parameters for electronic and media reserves.

Who Can Place Items on Electronic and Media Reserve?

At most institutions, only instructors and teaching assistants (TAs) have the authority to place items on reserve. However, Hoppenfeld and Arant-Kaspar (2010, 355) argue that students should also be allowed to request that items be placed on reserve for a course, stating that "since the primary users of course reserves are students," they can be well positioned to identify items that might be helpful to classmates. If libraries are not comfortable extending this privilege to students, they can advise students to share with their instructor the list of items they would like to see made available through electronic or media reserves that they can submit to the library on their behalf.

What Types of Items Can Be Made Available via Electronic and Media Reserves?

A variety of items can be made available through these services. For e-reserves, this includes:

- Copies of selections from books
- Copies of newspaper, magazine, and journal articles
- Copies of other textual or graphical works in the library's collections—for example, scans of diaries, journals, and letters held in special collections or scans of pictures and images such as art or maps
- Links to content held in the library's online collections, including electronic books (ebooks), electronic copies of articles, and digital film and music found in library databases
- Links to content made legally available elsewhere online, such as open access works and open educational resources

For media reserves, works that can be made available include:

- Copies of all types of audiovisual works, including motion pictures and documentary films
- Recordings of spoken word (e.g., audiobooks) and all types of music
- Links to digital film and music found in the library databases
- Links to media content made legally and freely available elsewhere online

Some libraries allow instructors to place copies of content they have created for a course on electronic and media reserve. For instance, class notes, study guides, and practice tests as well as audio and video recordings of lectures. However, some libraries decline to make such works available via these services for a variety of reasons, including as a way to manage workload for staff. As part of the policy development process, library administrators will need to decide whether they will allow copies of instructor generated content to be made available through the reserve services they offer.

What Types of Items Cannot Be Made Available via Electronic and Media Reserves?

The nature of the system being used to provide these services may place limitations on the types of works that can be made available through them. For example, if the platform being used to provide reserve services does not support media files, then the library will not be able to offer media reserves. Alternately, the library may have access to a platform that supports media files but does not have access to hardware and software needed to create digital copies of these works to make them available through these platforms. File size may also be a limiting factor for both electronic and media reserves, and staff should be aware of any limitations the system they are using may place on the size of uploads. Aside from these technological considerations and copyright considerations (which will be discussed in Part Two), if the library is able to access, acquire, or create a digital copy of a work, it can generally be made available via electronic and media reserves.

Electronic and Media Reserves Copyright Policy

The library will need to establish a copyright policy for these services. In its simplest form, this policy can state *In support of the teaching and learning mission of the library and the educational institution, library electronic reserve services will be offered in compliance with U.S. copyright law* and *In support of the teaching and learning mission of the library and the educational institution, library media reserve services will be offered in compliance with U.S. copyright law.* Policies like these highlights the importance of reusing copyrighted works as part of teaching, research, and the creation of new scholarship at the institution and demonstrates that decisions made regarding user rights will be rooted in the law. Libraries wishing to provide additional context for users on copyright may wish to expand this language by citing specific user rights that can be considered when making works available via electronic and media reserves—for example, *In support of the teaching and learning mission of the library and the educational institution, library reserve services will be offered in compliance with user rights U.S. copyright law such as fair use (17 U.S.C. § 107).* Here, the use of 'such as' indicates there are other user rights libraries can take advantage of when offering electronic and media reserves services, such as Reproduction by Libraries and Archives right (17 U.S.C. § 108) and the Reproduction for Blind or Other People with Disabilities right (17 U.S.C. § 121). In the electronic and media reserve copyright policies, libraries should be careful not to integrate any wording that may arbitrarily limit their ability to exercise user rights or that is based on common myths and misconceptions about the law, rather than the law itself. For example, a common misconception regarding fair use is that the law limits users to copying no more than 10 percent of a book or one chapter (whichever is less) or 3 minutes from an audiovisual work or 30 seconds from a sound recording. Section 107 places no such limits on the amount of a work that can be copied and still be considered fair (this misconception and others related to fair use are discussed in depth in Chapter 5).

There will be times when an instructor feels their request to make a work available via electronic or media reserve falls within the scope of a user right such as fair use but the library staff supporting this service does not. For this reason, these reserve copyright policies should contain language that clearly indicates that the library has final say in what works they will make available. For example, *The library reserves the right not to fulfill any reserve requests if they decide they do not fall within the scope of user rights found in U.S copyright law. A member of the reserves staff will contact the requestor if any copyright concerns are noted.*

Finally, the electronic and media reserve copyright policies should include contact information for members of the library staff who can answer questions they may have about the law or the policy. This can be the staff who support this service or a staff member whose job responsibilities include educating members of the campus community about copyright, such as a copyright librarian. The library can also include links to reputable tools and resources, including books and web pages, where they can learn more about the law and user rights.

Placing Items on Electronic and Media Reserve: Procedures for Instructors

The library will need to develop procedures for instructors to follow when submitting requests for works to be made available via electronic or media reserves. This document should include information regarding:

- The purpose of the service
- The types of items that can be made available via these services
- Types of items that cannot be made available through them
- How the request submission process operates, including a link to or posted copy of the electronic or media reserve request forms
- How far in advance requests should be submitted
- The amount of time needed by staff to process items being made available through these services
- The library's process for suspending access to items they make available this these systems

This document should also contain the contact information for the people or department responsible for managing reserve services so instructors can ask questions about the submission process. Libraries should provide instructions with information about how works can lawfully be circulated via electronic and media reserves. This can be done by linking to the copyright policies established for these services.

The following is an example of what electronic reserve request submission procedures for instructors might look like.

> The library's electronic reserve service (e-reserves) provides instructors and students with online access to textual learning materials in support of the educational mission of the institution.
>
> Items that can be made available via e-reserves include digital copies of articles and selections from books, and links to the library's online content (e.g., electronic articles). If you are interested in having the library provide access to a work via electronic reserves that is not currently held in our collection, you should speak with a member of the reserves staff to see how a copy might be acquired. Please allow 2–4 weeks for such requests to be processed.
>
> Electronic reserve requests can be submitted online [embed a link to the form here], or a copy of the request form can be downloaded, printed, and submitted to any campus library at the circulation desk [embed a copy of the document here]. Please complete all required fields on the form and, when applicable, print legibly.
>
> Requests should be submitted at least one week prior to the date needed for class, though more processing time may be needed at the beginning of the semester due to the volume of requests we receive during this time. All requests are processed in the order they are received.
>
> Access to copies of works made available via e-reserves may be suspended at the end of the semester, at the end of the period the work is licensed for, or at a time agreed upon by reserve staff and the course instructor.
>
> Items will be made available through e-reserves in compliance with U.S. copyright law [embed link to print reserve copyright policy here]. If you have questions about copyright or e-reserve services, contact us at [insert staff or departmental phone number here] or [insert staff or departmental email here].

The following is an example of what media reserve request submission procedures might look like.

> In support of the educational mission of the institution, the library's media reserve service provides instructors and students with online access to required and supplementary film and sound recordings being used for course instruction.
>
> Items that can be made available via media reserve include digital copies of film and other video recordings, and recordings of music and spoken word (e.g., audiobooks). If you are interested in having the library provide access to a work via media reserves that is not currently held in our collection, you should speak with a member of the reserves staff to see how a copy might be acquired. Please allow 2–4 weeks for such requests to be processed.
>
> Media reserve requests can be submitted online [embed a link to the form here], or a copy of the request form can be downloaded, printed, and submitted to any campus library at the circulation desk [embed a copy of the document here]. Please complete all required fields on the form and, when applicable, print legibly.

Requests should be submitted at least 1 week prior to the date needed for class, though more processing time may be needed at the beginning of the semester due to the volume of requests we receive during this time. All requests are processed in the order they are received.

Access to copies of works made available via media reserves may be suspended at the end of the semester, at the end of the period the work is licensed for, or at a time agreed upon by reserve staff and the course instructor.

Items will be made available through media reserves in compliance with U.S. copyright law [embed link to print reserve copyright policy here]. If you have questions about copyright or media reserve services, contact us at [insert staff or departmental phone number here] or [insert staff or departmental email here].

Electronic and Media Reserve Request Forms

While these are, generally, two separate reserve services, the information needed from instructors placing requests will be similar and include:

- Instructor contact information. Instructors should be asked to provide, at minimum, their name, email address, and phone number. If the course is co-taught by another instructor or has TAs, the person submitting the request should provide their names as well.
- Course information. Information collected in this section of the form should include the name of the course, the course code (e.g., psychology courses may be represented in the course catalog as PSY, history classes may be represented as HST, etc.), the course number, and section number.
- Item information. Instructors should be asked to provide information to help staff accurately identify the item they wish to have made available via electronic or media reserves. This can include the title of the work; the director or composer; the publisher or distributor; the year the work was published; and the call number for the work, if it is currently held in the library's collection. For articles and selections from books, this can also include the name of the publication, the title of the article or chapter, the volume or issue, and the relevant page numbers. For films, instructors will need to identify if they require access to the entire film or, if clips are being requested, the start and stop times for them.
- Intended use. Libraries may wish to ask instructors to briefly describe how the requested work may be used as part of course instruction. This information can be helpful if a copy of a work needs to be made under user rights found in U.S. copyright law, such as fair use.
- The pull date for the item. If the library does not have a set date when access to items made available via electronic and media reserve is suspended, (e.g., the end of the semester), then instructors should be asked if there is a specific date after which they and their students will no longer need access to requested items.

Staff will have to decide whether instructors will need to complete a separate form for each item they would like to place on electronic or media reserve, or if more than one item can be entered in a single form. Completing a separate form for each requested item may seem time consuming for instructors but could allow staff to more easily track each requested item as it is processed.

Some libraries add language to reserve forms asking instructors to certify that their request is made in compliance with U.S. copyright law, such as *Requests must fall within the scope of U.S. copyright law. A librarian will contact me if there are compliance considerations associated with my request.*

Print versus Digital Forms

Staff will need to decide what is the most efficient and practical way to have instructors submit reserve requests forms. Libraries can create the form as a Word document or portable document format (PDF) and make print copies available in the library. They can also (or alternately) post copies of these forms online for instructors to download and complete. However, these two options could present some challenges.

- If the form is completed by hand, illegible handwriting may make it hard for staff to read the information that was entered into a field.
- While the digital copies of these forms can be encoded with information that identify which fields users are required to complete, if the instructor prints off the form and completes it by hand, these designators may be lost or not be obvious to them.
- If the instructor saves a copy of the form to their computer and use this version each time they are looking to submit a request, then they may miss seeing revised or updated versions of the form that have been posted to the library's website.
- Requests submitted by instructors on paper can be hard to track and, if lost or misplaced, may result in requests not being processed properly or in a timely manner.

Some of these challenges can be overcome by trying to standardize the request submission process as much as possible. This could include making forms available as Word documents or PDFs but requiring them to be submitted as electronic documents that are sent to a central email account used by staff rather than allowing the submission of them as paper forms. Some of the issues outlined above (e.g., illegible handwriting or incomplete forms) can be overcome by contacting the instructor and asking for clarification or the missing information, but this does mean more work for staff and delays in processing time.

Online Request Submission

Reserve request forms can be set-up as an online form using a program such as Google Forms or Formstack. Ticketing systems like TeamDyanmix can also be considered. The advantages to using these online tools include:

- As the information entered into the fields will be typed, handwriting legibility is no longer an issue.
- Form fields can be marked as required fields, requiring the person completing them to enter data before the system allows submission of the form. This can help cut down on the instances of requests that are submitted with incomplete information.
- All submitted requests are stored in a central, online location.
- These forms can be quickly updated if it is identified that a field needs to be changed or added and, once changes are made to the form, all subsequent users will be working from the same form.
- Links can be embedded into the forms directing those completing them to additional information that may be useful to them. For example, a link could be included to an online copy of reserve copyright policies or to a frequently asked questions page for the services.
- Most form programs allow for email notification as forms are submitted. This can help staff identify and track new requests, especially during busy processing times.

Reserve request forms should include contact information for the person or department managing these service for the library so that instructors who are completing the form have ready access to this information and can use it to get assistance with any questions they may have.

Processing Items onto Reserve: Procedures for Staff

As requests forms are received, staff will need to work through the following steps to process works on to electronic and media reserves.

Reviewing Forms for Completeness

All fields on the form should be reviewed to ensure that instructors have provided staff with the information they need to process the request. If the form was completed by hand, staff will also need to ensure all of the information entered is legible. If any of the information is missing, ambiguous, or illegible, staff will need to follow-up with the instructor who submitted the request to get the information needed before moving forward with processing.

Checking to See If the Requested Item Can Be Circulated via Electronic or Media Reserves

Staff should next check to see if the requested item falls within the scope of the library's circulation policy for these services. For example, if the instructor wishes to make a copy of a study guide they authored available via e-reserves but the policy does not allow this type of content to be posted, staff will need to decide whether an exception will be made or if the instructor will be directed to share a copy with their students via and alternate method such as email or their LMS course page.

Ensuring the Work Can Lawfully Be Made Available via Electronic and Media Reserves

Works can lawfully be made available via electronic and media reserves when:

1. The work is in the public domain.
2. A link can be provided to a lawful copy of the work.
3. A copy of the work is licensed in a way that allows it to be made available via electronic or media reserve.
4. The instructor placing the request is the rightsholder.
5. A copy of the item can be circulated user rights found in U.S. copyright law.
6. Permission or a license is obtained to make a copy of the work available via electronic or media reserve.

Each of these options will be detailed in Chapter 12, where a copyright workflow for electronic and media reserve services can be found.

If it is determined that a copy of the requested work can be lawfully made available via electronic or media reserve, staff should next check to see if the work is held in the library's collection. If a copy of the work cannot be made available under one of these options, staff may be able to make a physical copy of the original work—for example, a book or Digital Video Disc (DVD)—available via print reserves. Alternately, they can ask the instructor if an alternate item can be used in its place that can be made available via electronic or media reserves.

Does the Library Own a Copy of the Requested Work?

For this step, staff will need to determine whether the library owns a copy of the requested item and, if applicable, if it is in a condition that allows a quality digital copy to be made.

Is the Item Available Electronically?

Staff should first check to see if the library already has electronic access to the requested work. This could include ebooks, online journals, and digital copies of film and music found in the library's databases. When the library has electronic access to a requested work, students and instructors should be directed to it, rather than making an alternate digital copy available via electronic or media reserves. Reasons for doing so include:

- Generally, there are no copyright infringement considerations associated with linking to works.
- Linking promotes user engagement with the library's online resources, raising student and instructor awareness of them and allowing the library to use data about views, downloads, and so on when making collection development decisions about online resources.

When linking to resources, staff will need to be aware of two considerations, license terms and limits on the number of users. Staff will need to review the contract they entered into when licensing or purchasing the electronic resource to determine whether linking is allowed. Most contracts permit the sharing of links via reserve services, but some expressly prohibit this practice. Once staff confirm they are able to share links via electronic and media reserve, next they will want to determine whether they can identify a permanent link, or permalink, to the resource. A permalink is a static hyperlink to a resource found on the Web. As the link does not change over time, students and instructors can rely on consistent access to the work. If the library is using a proxy server to authenticate off-campus user access to its electronic resources, they will need to be sure to attach the proxy prefix to the permalink.

Another factor staff will need to consider when linking to library resources is limits on the number of simultaneous users who are able to access a requested work. Some electronic resources are licensed to libraries in a way that allows only a limited number of users to simultaneously access it at a time. If the work is being used in a smaller class, these limits may not pose significant issues so long as students are made aware of them and are encouraged to end their session as soon as they are done using the work to make it available for others. However, in larger classes low simultaneous user limits may prevent the work from being used effectively by those enrolled in the course. In these situations, libraries can ask the vendor what options are available for increasing the number of simultaneous users or allowing unlimited access to the item. Alternately, some electronic resources, such as ebooks, are available for check-out to only a limited number of users for a time and for a period that could range for several days to several weeks. Such lending models will not work well for reserve use; in these situations, library staff will also want to reach out to vendors to see if the number of users or duration of access granted can be modified.

Is the Item Available in a Physical Format?

If the library does not have access to an electronic copy of the requested work, staff will need to check the ILS, online public access catalog (OPAC), or discovery layer to see if they own a physical copy (e.g., book, DVD, or CD) and if it is currently listed as available for check-out. Even if the item is listed as being available, staff will need to verify the item is actually on hand. Items that are listed as being available may not be on the shelf for multiple reasons, including:

- The item was recently returned by a patron and is sitting on temporary shelving.
- The item was misshelved.
- A patron removed the item from the stacks and is currently using it in the library.
- If a campus has multiple libraries, it could have been mistakenly shelved at another library.
- The item has been stolen.

If the item cannot be found, staff will have to decide whether they are going to declare the item lost and order a replacement copy. If a replacement copy will not be ordered, staff will need to work through alternate options of obtaining a copy of the work, which are discussed in a subsequent section of this chapter. They can also contact the instructor who placed the request to see if an alternate item can be identified and used as a substitute for the item originally requested.

If the item is currently checked out. If the item is currently checked out, staff will need to determine whether it is in the hands of one of their own patrons or if it has been sent out to a consortium partner or on interlibrary loan (ILL). If one of the library's own patrons has the item, staff should check to see what the item is due. If the due date is only a few days away or a week in the future, a staff member can place a hold on the item so that it is directed to them when it is returned. Here, staff will need to be cognizant of library circulation policies regarding holds placed on items that are checked out. Often, if another patron has placed a hold on a checked-out item, this will prevent the patron from securing any renewals. However, if the system is set up to provide patrons with a guaranteed number of renewals, or if an item is checked out to one of the library's own patrons but the due date is far into the future, then a staff member may need to recall the item. This involves changing the current due date to a new date a short-term out, such as a week or two in the future. In these cases, staff will need to make sure communication is sent to the patron who has the item informing them of the new due date. However, just because an item has been recalled it does not mean that the patron will return it. The library may wish to establish fines associated with recalled items that are high enough to dissuade patrons from keeping recalled items past the new due date. When items are recalled in these situations, patrons are sometimes responsive to hearing from staff about the reason for the recall, understanding that they will still have access to the item via electronic or media reserve, and that their classmates will as well. Staff can also offer to check the item back out to the patron it was recalled from after they are done making a copy of the requested portion of the work.

If a requested item is checked out to a consortium partner or through ILL, it may be harder for staff to get the item back in a timely manner. Staff can try reaching out to the borrowing library to see if they will ask their patron to return the item early. However, if the patron is unwilling to do so, they will need to work through alternate options of obtaining a copy of the work, which will be addressed in a subsequent section.

Lost, missing, and damaged items. Staff may find a requested item in the stacks but discover that it is damaged. For example, books may have missing pages or excessive highlighting and pen markings and DVDs or CDs may have scratches on them. Staff will need to determine whether the damage prevents them from making a copy of the work and if they can quickly repair the damage in-house prior to making the copy. If not, or if the item is lost or missing, then staff can work through the options outlined in the next section to identify the best way to obtain a copy of the work.

When the Library Does Not Own a Copy of the Requested Work

If the library does not own a copy of a requested work, they can consider purchasing a copy for their collection, they can see if the instructor who placed the request is interested in donating or lending their own copy of the item (if they have one) to the library to make copies from, or they can consider obtaining a copy of the requested work from another library.

Purchasing Decisions

If an item is being used as part of course instruction, the library may see value in purchasing a copy to add to their collection. If the library already owns a copy but it is checked out and appears unlikely it will be returned in a timely manner, they can consider purchasing another copy of the title to add to their collection. If the library's copy is lost, stolen, or damaged beyond repair, this may prompt staff to purchase a replacement copy. Whatever the reason for the purchase, the library will want to have procedures in place for making these decisions. Often, purchasing decisions will be controlled by the library's collection development policies and procedures, and final approval for purchases will rest with those librarians charged with collection development. Staff supporting reserve services can work with these librarians to identify requested works that can be purchased for the collection; in some libraries, the staff managing reserve services are given their own budget to purchase items for reserve use. In these situations, library administrators should work with staff to decide the amount of funds that will be allocated to this account, how purchase requests will be prioritized, and who among the staff will have final authority in making purchasing decisions. Funds spent on reserve purchases should be reviewed on an ongoing basis to determine whether the amount is appropriate for the use the collection is seeing.

Expiated processing of purchased works. Due to the in-demand nature of reserve services, it will be important to order and process these items as quickly as possible. This can include:

- Acquisitions decisions. Here it will need to be decided whether the decision to purchase requested items will receive expiated review by the appropriate staff.
- Order placement. Once the decision is made to purchase the item, acquisitions staff will need to enter the order into the ILS and place the order for the item with a vendor. Here, it may be decided that, when available, the library will pay for rush shipping for items being used for reserves.
- Cataloging. Once requested orders arrive, staff can choose to move them quickly through the cataloging process as well. Cataloging staff can then notify staff that the items are ready to go so they can pick them up for reserve processing.

For this stage of the process, staff and administration will also need to discuss what the expedited timeframe looks like. For example, it could be established that for reserve items, acquisitions decisions, order placement, and cataloging will be performed within 1 business day of when each person in this cycle receives the item. When items are being ordered for reserve use, it can be helpful for staff to keep the instructor who requested the item be placed on reserve apprised of the situation and when they expect the item to be available.

Donation or Loan from the Instructor

When the library does not own a copy of a requested item, they may ask the instructor who placed the request if they own a copy they would be willing to donate to the library or loan to staff to make copies from. The advantage of having instructors donate the work to the library's collection is that it will be readily available if copies need to be made in the future (e.g., the instructor requests that an alternate selection from a particular book be made available via electronic reserves, or a different clip from a film). As with other donations, staff will want to review the work first to ensure it is in good condition—for example, checking for broken spines, missing pages, excessive highlighting or notes, and so on.

Some instructors will hesitate to donate their copy of the work to the library but may be willing to lend their copy to the library to use to make a digital copy of the requested portion of the work. In situations where the library is making the copy available under user rights found in the law, such as fair use, generally using the instructor's copy to make the scan instead of a copy owned by the library presents no legal challenges so long as the instructor's copy was lawfully made under U.S. copyright law; however, more information about this option can be found in Chapter 8.

Obtaining a Copy from Another Library

Copies of requested works can be obtained from other libraries. For articles, this could include obtaining a copy through ILL. For selections from books, this could include requesting copies of the requested portion through ILL. For books, DVDs, and CDs, staff could request that another library send them their copy of the book, DVD, or CD and then make their own copy of the requested portion from it copies from it. Copyright considerations tied to each of these options will be addressed in Part Two.

Making the Work Available via the Reserve System

How items will be made available for instructors and students to access via electronic and media reserves will depend on the nature of the system being used. Procedures are different for each ILS, commercial platform, LMS, and homegrown system, and addressing all of them here would exceed the scope of this chapter. Instead, this section will address several considerations that will be consistent across the platforms: making copies of works, and the duration of access.

Making Copies

When the request involves making a copy of a work, staff will need to determine who will make the copy and what format it will be made in. The library could require that instructors supply a digital copy of the work they wish to make available via electronic or media reserves. An advantage to doing so is that library staff will not have to spend time hunting down the requested work to make the copies themselves. A disadvantage to this practice is that the quality of the copy the library receives may be questionable. For instance, the digital copy of a film clip an instructor provides may be of low quality, or the instructor may have skipped a page when copying a selection from a book. In these situations, the processing of these items onto reserve may be delayed if staff need to follow up with the instructor to obtain an alternate copy.

Making their own copies of requested works means a larger time investment from the staff supporting reserve services. However, it does allow them to have more control over the quality of the copy. For example, digital copies made from books can be cleaned up by staff to remove a center line, shadows, borders from around the edge of the pages, or other marks. The library may also have technology on hand that allows them to make high-quality copies from films or sound recordings.

Frequently, copies of articles and books will be made in a PDF format. Digital copies made from sound recordings will often be made in an .mp3 or .mp4 file format. Copies made from films will often be made in an .mp4 file format. For media works, these files are often for uploading to the media hosting system rather than sharing downloadable media files with reserve users. Libraries will often have scanning equipment on hand that will allow them to make high-quality digital copies quickly. This may include equipment that is found in other departments—for example, an adjustable high-speed book scanner held in the archives or preservation department. Staff can check with administrators in these departments to see if they might be able to use this equipment, especially around the start of the semester when request submission often peaks. If the number of requests being submitted is significant staff managing reserve services can ask administrators about getting high-speed duplication equipment for their own department. While such scanners are often expensive, the time savings for staff may make it worth the investment.

Duration of Access

Staff will have to determine how long they will permit items to remain available via electronic and media reserves. Decisions about the duration of access will often be made on a case-by-case basis for requested items and will include a combination of short-term access, semester access, and perpetual access options. Two factors will influence these decisions are legal considerations and system parameters.

Legal considerations. If the library is providing instructors and students with links to electronic resources available in their collections, they may make these links available in perpetuity, or for as long as they have access to them. If works are being made available via electronic or media reserves under a permission agreement or a license that places a time limit on how long students and instructors can access the copies, then staff will need to suspend access to these resources via the service platforms on the designated date. When making digital copies of works available via user rights such as fair use or the Technology, Education and Copyright Harmonization (TEACH) Act, staff may consider providing access to them for only a short period of time, such as a few weeks during the semester when it will be used for course instruction. These considerations will be addressed in depth in Part Two, which explores copyright considerations associated with electronic and media reserves.

System parameters. The period of time works may remain accessible to students and instructors through these services may also be influenced by settings available in the system being used to administer them. Some systems allow users to specify a date range when works can be accessed and viewed, which can be especially useful to staff if they are only looking to make certain works available during a certain period of time. If this option is not available in the system the library is using, staff will need to establish a way of tracking these dates, if required. This could include a print filing system of some sort that is checked on a daily or weekly basis by staff. It could also include notes entered into an electronic calendar that remind staff when it is time to remove access to a work from electronic or media reserve platforms.

Some systems may allow staff to suspend access to all works made available via these systems for a particular semester at once, which could be the final date of the semester. If the system the library is using to provide electronic and media reserves does not allow any of these options, then extra staff time will likely need to be allotted at the end of the semester to suspend access to works the library decides to take down.

Figure 3.1 provides a basic overview of the workflow staff can use to process electronic and media reserve requests from form submission to making the work available via the reserve system.

Storing Copies of Digitized Works

Libraries may wish to retain digital copies they made of requested works for use in subsequent semesters. This saves staff from having to re-create the digital copies, which can be a time-consuming process, allowing staff to get requested works posted for student use more quickly in future semesters. Considerations for storing copies are made under user rights such as fair use and the TEACH Act are addressed in Part Two. If the copies were made by obtaining permission or a license from the rightsholder, then copies can be retained for future use under agreed-upon terms.

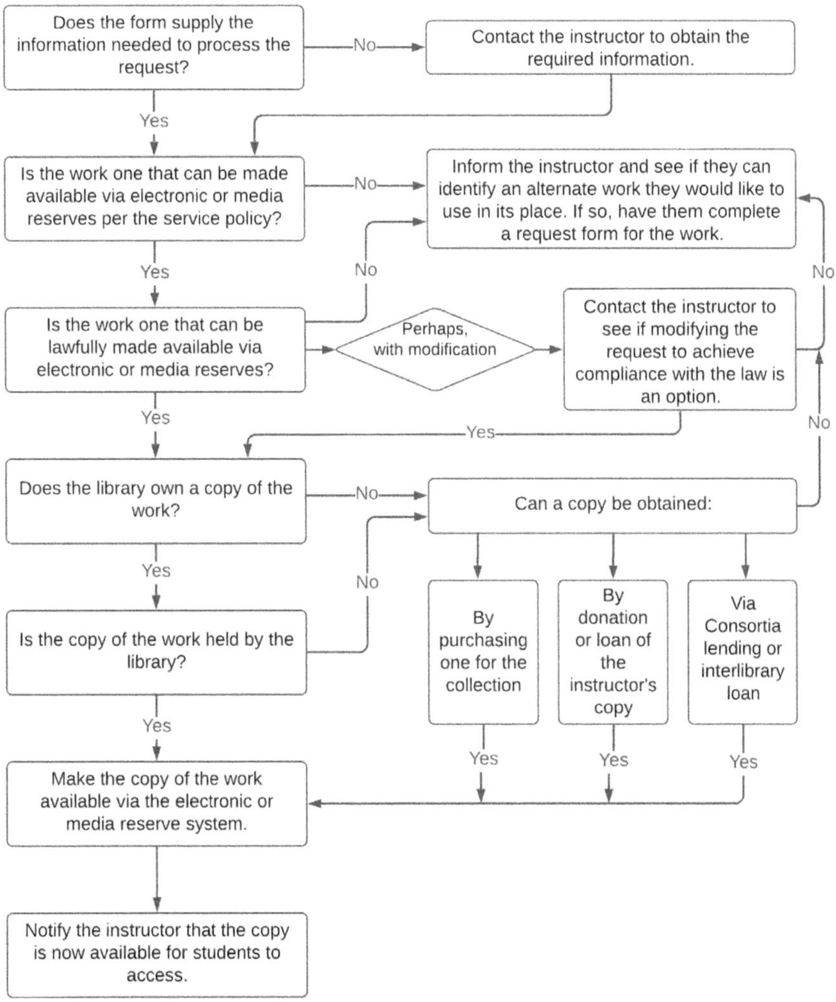

Figure 3.1 The basic workflow of electronic and media reserve request processing

Keeping Copies of Reserve Request Forms

Staff will need to decide whether they are going to save copies of reserve request forms and, if so, how long they will keep them. There are several benefits to keeping these records. For example, instructors may contact the library and ask if they can be reminded what they had placed on reserve for a particular course in a previous semester. In these situations, having access to copies of the request forms can make answering these questions easy. Having copies of the forms can also be useful if staff decide they would like to review them to look for patterns in requests (e.g., which department or instructor may be frequently submitting requests).

If requests are submitted using an online form, then storage space, tracking, and organization will likely present minimal issues. If instructors are permitted to submit copies of the request forms in print or as digital files (e.g., submitting a Word copy of the request form via email), then staff will need to identify a way to store and organize them. This could include making scanned copies of the print forms and saving them all to a shared digital storage area so all those who may need to access them can readily do so. In these situations, staff will want to come up with a naming convention for these files that allows them to identify who submitted the request, what class it was for, and what semester. If requests records will be kept in print, then staff should set aside room in a closet or filing cabinet in which to store them. In all three situations, staff will need to decide how long they wish to keep these records and establish a system for deleting or disposing of them on a regular basis.

Marketing Electronic and Media Reserve Services

For electronic and media reserve services to be successful, instructors and students must be aware of them. For this reason, staff will need to carefully consider how they will be marketed to members of the campus community.

Marketing to Instructors

Staff will want to ensure that instructors are aware of what reserve services they offer, their purpose, and their scope. Here, finding effective ways share electronic and media reserve procedures with instructors can help increase their awareness of them, including items that can be made available through them, and how to submit reserve requests. Information about U.S. copyright law and the ways works can be lawfully shared with students via electronic and media reserves should also be marketed to instructors. Providing basic information up front and directing instructors to the reserve copyright policies can help deepen their understanding of the law and assuage concerns and frustrations they may have about what works can be made available to students. All marketing done for these reserve services should provide recipients with contact information for the staff managing them that can be used to ask get answers to questions instructors may have. Instructors may also appreciate receiving marketing information from the library that they can share with students to inform them how to find and access works made available via electronic and media reserves. This can include text that can be placed in the class syllabus or information that can be posted to the LMS course page or that can be emailed to students.

Marketing to Students

It is also important to market reserve services to those students so they can take advantage of the service. One of the most effective ways is to have instructors who have items posted to electronic and media reserves provide their students with information about:

- The purpose of these services
- The titles of the works made available through them
- Where they can go to access them (e.g., within the LMS course page, or a separate platform)
- If applicable, the password needed to access them

The library can supplement this information with additional marketing about these services via the library's web page or social media accounts. Any marketing directed to students should also contain contact information for the for the staff overseeing the service so students can get answers to any questions they may have about finding and accessing them.

Assessment

Staff should perform assessment on a periodical basis to ensure that electronic and media reserve services are functioning optimally and providing a maximum benefit to users. As part of this assessment process, things to consider should include the number of requests being submitted, the number of uses requested items have, and the return on investment of the library resources being used to support these services.

Number of Requests Being Submitted

Staff will want to determine whether the number of requests for electronic and media reserves are decreasing, increasing, or remaining approximately the same. If the numbers are decreasing, staff should seek to determine why. It could be that instructors understand the options available to them for lawfully connecting students with protected works as part of distance education and have decided to make course materials available themselves in compliance with them rather than relying on the library to do so. Other factors could be driving their decision not to engage with the services though. For example, perhaps instructors find the request submission process too cumbersome or have trouble with making copyright determinations. If the number of items being made available via electronic and media reserves has been increasing, staff may wish to speak with instructors to determine what has been motivating them to increase their engagement with these services so they can identify ways in which to maintain this momentum. If the number of items being made available through these services has been consistent over time, then assessment can help staff identify if there are ways to promote the service that might increase its use.

Usage Statistics

Many electronic and media reserve platforms will allow staff to see the number of engagements (e.g., views, downloads) instructors and students have had with a resource. This can be beneficial in a variety of ways. If a work made available through one of these services sees numerous uses, staff may wish to consider way of expanding access to it. For example, if it is a licensed resource, the library may wish to purchase a perpetual license to it rather than a short-term one, or if an electronic resource limits the number of simultaneous users, they may wish to increase the number that are available. Alternately, if a resource being made available through one of these services sees limited engagement, staff can provide alternate access options that could lead to cost savings for them. For example, if a film the library was licensing access to sees limited use, they may wish to acquire a DVD copy to make available via print reserve instead or renew the license under shorter terms (e.g., one year instead of three years) while continuing to monitor its use. Library staff should consider surveying students and instructors though to try to determine what reasons might exist for the lack of use. For example, an instructor may have decided mid-semester not to use a particular work as part of course instruction, or students may not have known to where to look to engage with items made available via electronic and media reserves.

Return on Investment

Staff will want to ensure that the levels of resources being invested into electronic and media reserve services—including staffing, space, technology, equipment, and funding—are reflective of the amount of use they are getting. Resource allocation may need to be increased if reserve usage by instructors and students is increasing. However, if reserve usage by either group or both groups is decreasing, the library may wish to reconsider the resources it devotes to providing print reserve services. Before reducing them, staff should first consider ways in which they may be able to more effectively market the service to renew or increase interest in them.

Putting It All Together

Carefully thinking through the administrative considerations associated with offering electronic and media reserve services will provide a solid foundation for launching or expanding them. Clearly articulating service parameters provides a set of rules and expectations for instructors looking to make course materials available to students through them. Having procedures for staff to follow when processing reserve requests will allow them to administer the service in an efficient manner. Together, all of this should come together to ensure that instructors are able to easily submit reserve requests, that staff are able to process items on to reserve in a timely manner, and that students are able to find the works they need to successfully complete course assignments, all while mitigating the legal risk of the library and institution as copyrighted works are shared as part of course instruction.

PART II

Copyright and Course Reserves

CHAPTER FOUR

An Introduction to U.S. Copyright Law

To effectively manage course reserves someone in the library, if not multiple people, should have knowledge of the sections of U.S. copyright law applicable to it. This could be a librarian who has been designated as the institution's copyright librarian, it could be a department administrator who is responsible for the management of reserve services, it could be staff members and student employees who handle the day-to-day operations of reserve services, or it could be a combination of some or all of these library employees.

This chapter outlines the basics of U.S. copyright law and provides readers with a foundation of knowledge regarding how copyright is secured, what types of works are eligible for copyright protection, the rights granted to creators, the duration of copyright, and the user rights (exceptions) that can be utilized in providing reserve services. The following chapters will then build upon this knowledge by addressing user rights found in the law, such as fair use and the first sale doctrine, that can be used to make works lawfully available via reserve services. Additional considerations for reserve services that have copyright implications—permissions requests and licensing—will also be discussed in this section, followed by a chapter outlining workflows for making copyright determinations for items instructors wish to place on reserve.

Defining Copyright

Copyright is a form of intellectual property (IP) protection granted to the authors of certain types of works, allowing them to control some uses of their work for a limited time. The World Intellectual Property Organization (n.d.-a) defines intellectual property as "creations of the mind, such as inventions; literary and artistic works; designs; and symbols, names and images used in commerce." The Constitution of the United States of America provides the foundation for the establishment of copyright law, stating in Article 1, Section 8, Clause 8 that Congress shall have power "To promote the Progress of Science and useful Arts, by securing for limited Times to Authors and Inventors the exclusive Right to their respective Writings and Discoveries." As of the writing of this book, U.S. copyright law is governed by the Copyright Act of 1976, as amended, and is codified in Title 17 of the United States Code (U.S.C.).

Securing Copyright

Section 102(a) states that "copyright protection subsists . . . in original works of authorship fixed in any tangible medium of expression." A common misconception regarding copyright law is that a work must be registered with the U.S. Copyright Office (USCO) and include a copyright notice to have copyright protection. However, under the Copyright Act of 1976 a qualifying work only needs to be original, fixed, and fall into one of the categories of works identified in Section 102(a) as being eligible for copyright protection.

Originality

Justice Sandra Day O'Connor, in writing the opinion for the Supreme Court of the United States (SCOTUS) for *Feist Publications, Inc., v. Rural Telephone Service Co.* (499 U.S. 340 [1991]), provides us with a definition of the term "original," stating that "original, as the term is used in copyright, means only that the work was independently created by the author (as opposed to copied from other works), and that it possesses at least some minimal degree of creativity" (Feist v. Rural 1991, 498).

Independent Creation

For independent creation to exist, an author cannot have copied the work of another directly. It is important to recognize that works may be very similar to each other, or even identical to each other, yet still be considered original under the law. For example, in a watercolor class an instructor may place a bowl of fruit on a table and instruct students to paint it. It is likely that the students' final paintings will look like each other's since they were all working from the same model, but each painting will be slightly different as a result of the skill, artistic interpretation, and painting technique used by each student. Each painting will be original to each student, even though all the paintings look alike. Similarly, two or more people could produce identical works that could not be distinguished from each other yet still meet the originality criteria for copyright protection. In *Feist v. Rural* (1991, 499), Justice O'Connor provides an example of such a situation, stating, "[A]ssume that two poets, each ignorant of the other, compose identical poems. Neither work is novel, yet both are original and, hence, copyrightable."

A Minimal Degree of Creativity

The amount of creativity required for copyright protection is truly minimal. In *Feist v. Rural* (1991, 499), Justice O'Connor states that "even a slight amount will suffice [with] the vast majority of works mak[ing] the grade quite easily, as they possess some creative spark." The *Compendium of U.S. Copyright Office Practices* (*Compendium*), a document produced by the USCO to provide "expert guidance to copyright applicants, practitioners, scholars, the courts, and members of the general public regarding institutional practices and related principles of law" (Compendium [Third], Introduction), provides a useful example of the amount of creativity needed to secure protection. It tells us that a listing of all of the restaurants in a city or of the top grossing restaurants in a city would not be eligible for copyright protection as they are made up of facts and do not contain any creativity. However, if a food journalist wanted to compile a list "containing the names of the [their] fifty favorite restaurants . . . [this] may constitute a literary work, which is one of the congressionally established categories of authorship" (Compendium [Third] § 312.1) and, so long as the lists contain some creative input from the author (e.g., the selection of restaurants, and arrangement of the names in their preferred order), then they would be eligible for copyright protection.

Fixation

According to Section 101, "a work is 'fixed' in a tangible medium of expression when its embodiment in a copy or phonorecord, by or under the authority of the author, is sufficiently permanent or stable to permit it to be perceived, reproduced, or otherwise communicated for a period of more than transitory duration." Copies of works are "material objects, other than phonorecords, in which a work is fixed by any method now known or later developed, and from which the work can be perceived, reproduced, or otherwise communicated, either directly or with the aid of a machine or device" (17 U.S.C. § 101). Examples of copies include books; photocopies of articles or digital copies (e.g., portable document format [PDF]) of reports and documents; video home system (VHS) tapes; Digital Video Discs (DVDs) and Blu-ray discs. Phonorecords are "material objects in which sounds, other than those accompanying a motion picture or other audiovisual work, are fixed . . . and from which the sounds can be perceived, reproduced, or otherwise communicated, either directly or with the aid of a machine or device" (17 U.S.C. § 101). Examples of phonorecords include vinyl records, 8-track tapes, audiocassette tapes, CDs (compact discs) and .mp3 files. Crews (2020, 36) identifies several methods of fixation that are inherently impermanent but nonetheless satisfy the fixation requirement: "sandcastles, ice sculptures, and spray-painted graffiti."

Registration and Inclusion of a Copyright Notice

Section 408(a) explicitly states that "registration is not a condition of copyright protection." While not required to secure copyright protection, some rightsholders choose to register their works with the USCO, as doing so conveys certain benefits including:

- Identifying the author of the work
- Identifying the rightsholder of the work (as the author is not always the rightsholder)
- Establishing the creation and/or publication date of the work

A rightsholder must receive registration for their work from the USCO before they can file a copyright infringement lawsuit in court.

Many people incorrectly assume that works that do not have a copyright notice on them do not have copyright protection. Works first published on or before February 28, 1989, were required to have a copyright notice placed on them to have copyright protection. However, this requirement was eliminated as of March 1, 1989, and works published after this date are still fully protected by copyright even if there is no notice on them. Works published on or before February 28, 1989, may not have copyright protection if they were published without a copyright notice. For more information, see the *Duration of Copyright* section of this chapter.

Case Study: Copyright Notices

A copyright notice is a short phrase that is placed on works as a notification to users that the work has copyright protection; to identify the rightsholder; and to identify the date of creation or, in some situations, the date of publication. Section 401(b) outlines the components that should be included in a copyright notice:

> (b) Form of Notice.—If a notice appears on the copies, it shall consist of the following three elements:
>
> (1) the symbol © (the letter C in a circle), or the word "Copyright", or the abbreviation "Copr."; and
> (2) the year of first publication of the work; in the case of compilations or derivative works incorporating previously published material, the year date of first publication of the compilation or derivative work is sufficient. The year date may be omitted where a pictorial, graphic, or sculptural work, with accompanying text matter, if any, is reproduced in or on greeting cards, postcards, stationery, jewelry, dolls, toys, or any useful articles; and
> (3) the name of the owner of copyright in the work, or an abbreviation by which the name can be recognized, or a generally known alternative designation of the owner.

Most notices look something like Copyright © 2022 by Carla Myers, with common variants such as Copr. © 2022 by Carla Myers or © 2022 by Carla Myers. Users may see the symbol ℗ used in place of the © symbol on vinyl records, 8-track tapes, audiocassette tapes, and CDs or in the metadata attached to .mp3 files. Here, the letter "p" stands for phonorecord.

Section 401(c) states that "the notice shall be affixed to the copies in such manner and location as to give reasonable notice of the claim of copyright. The Register of Copyrights shall prescribe by regulation, as examples, specific methods of affixation and positions of the notice on various types of works that will satisfy this requirement, but these specifications shall not be considered exhaustive." The methods of affixation put forward by the Register of Copyrights can be found in Section 202.2 of Title 37, Chapter 2, Subchapter A of *The Code of Federal Regulations.*

Works do not have to be registered with the USCO for the rightsholder to attach a notice to them. While placing a copyright notice on a work is no longer required to secure copyright protection, it does confer certain benefits. These include reminding users that the work is protected by copyright, identifying the author of the work so that those seeking permission for reusing it knows who to contact, and granting the rightsholder additional protection against claims of innocent infringement. Readers can find information on claims of innocent infringement in Chapter 14. Additional information on the structure and use of copyright notices can be found in the USCO's *Circular 3, Copyright Notice*, that can be found online at: https://www.copyright.gov/circs/.

Works Eligible for Copyright Protection

To qualify for copyright protection, works must fall into one of the eight categories identified in Section 102(a) of U.S. copyright law. It is important to understand that these categories are broad and the list of works found in Section 102(a) is by no means exhaustive. Hornick (2003) tells us that "the types of works of authorship qualifying for copyright protection under [Section] 102(a) was intentionally left open-ended by Congress so that new forms of expression not specifically identified in [Section] 102(a) may receive protection under the 1976 Act to the same extent as those works listed in [Section] 102(a)." He goes on to cite a House Report that accompanied the passage of the Copyright Act of 1976 that helps explain Congress's intent in leaving these categories open-ended:

> [A]uthors are continually finding new ways of expressing themselves, but it is impossible to foresee the forms that these new expressive methods will take. The bill does not intend either to freeze the scope of copyrightable subject matter at the present stage of communications technology or to allow unlimited expansion into areas completely outside the present congressional intent. Section 102 implies neither that subject matter is unlimited nor that new forms of expression within that general area of subject matter would necessarily be unprotected. (H.R. Rep. No. 94-1476, 51, 1976)

Congress's foresight in leaving the interpretation of categories found in Section 102(a) open-ended has been especially beneficial to society given the advances in technology made since 1976 and the large body of works that are eligible for copyright protection as a result.

Literary Works (Section 102[a][(1])

Literary works are defined in Section 101 as "works, other than audiovisual works, expressed in words, numbers, or other verbal or numerical symbols or indicia regardless of the nature of the material objects, such as books, periodicals, manuscripts, phonorecords, film, tapes, disks, or cards, in which they are embodied." When referring to literary works most people think of the common examples of books, poetry, newspapers, scholarly periodicals, blogs, and written communications such as letters and emails. This category of works is much more diverse though and includes advertising copy, directories, computer programs, and website text.

Musical Works Section (102[a][2])

Section 802.1 of the *Compendium* states that "musical works (which are also known as musical compositions) are original works of authorship consisting of music and any accompanying words. Music is a succession of pitches or rhythms, or both, usually in some definite pattern." This category of copyrightable works includes new compositions of songs or instrumental pieces as well are rearrangements of older works, such as a new arrangement of a Beethoven symphony or a reworking of the Christmas carol "Silent Night."

Individuals may record the performance of a musical work, in which case they are capturing a sound recording, and this recording will have a copyright that is separate and distinct from the copyright that is held in the musical work. This concept will be discussed further in the *Sound Recordings* section of this chapter.

Dramatic Works Section 102[a][3])

Dramatic works are "composition generally in prose or verse that portrays a story that is intended to be performed for an audience" that frequently "represents the action as it occurs rather than simply narrating or describing the action" (Compendium [Third] § 804.1). For example, the following excerpt is from the play *The Importance of Being Earnest*, by Oscar Wilde (1915, 4–5):

> Algernon. How are you, my dear Ernest? What brings you up to town?
>
> Jack. Oh, pleasure, pleasure! What else should bring one anywhere? Eating as usual, I see, Algy!
>
> Algernon. [Stiffly.] I believe it is customary in good society to take some slight refreshment at five o'clock. Where have you been since last Thursday?
>
> Jack. [Sitting down on the sofa.] In the country.
>
> Algernon. What on earth do you do there?
>
> Jack. [Pulling off his gloves.] When one is in town one amuses oneself. When one is in the country one amuses other people. It is excessively boring.
>
> Algernon. And who are the people you amuse?
>
> Jack. [Airily.] Oh, neighbours, neighbours.

The words in brackets are notes from the playwright instructing the actors on how lines are to be delivered to convey a certain mood to the audience or are instructions (e.g., pulling off gloves) intended to represent action as it should occur as part of the performance.

Pantomimes and Choreographic Works (Section 102[a][4])

The *Compendium* tells us that pantomime involves "imitating, presenting, or acting out situations, characters, or events through the use of physical gestures and bodily movements" whereas chorographical works involve the "composition and arrangement of a related series of dance movements and patterns organized into a coherent whole" (Compendium [Third] Part VIII). As a way of clarifying the difference between the two different types of works, the *Compendium* states that "the physical movements in a pantomime tend to be more restricted than the movements in a choreographic work, while pantomime uses more facial expressions and gestures of the hands and arms than choreography. . . . [and] pantomime usually imitates or caricatures a person, situation, or event" (Compendium [Third] § 806.1). It goes on to state that "while choreography is typically performed with a musical accompaniment, pantomime is commonly performed without music or measured rhythm" (Compendium [Third] § 806.1).

Pictorial, Graphic, and Sculptural Works (Section 102[a][5])

A definition for these types of works can be found in Section 101. It states that "pictorial, graphic, and sculptural works include two-dimensional and three-dimensional works of fine, graphic, and applied art, photographs, prints and art reproductions, maps, globes, charts, diagrams, models, and technical drawings, including architectural plans." The subcategories of pictorial, graphic, and sculptural works are extensive, as illustrated by the examples provided Table 4.1, which come from Section 503.1(B) of the *Compendium*.

Table 4.1 Examples of pictorial, graphic, and sculptural works from Section 503.1(B) of the Compendium of U.S. Copyright Office Practices

Category of Authorship	Examples of Works
Pictorial Works	Paintings, drawings, photographs, prints, art reproductions, maps, technical drawings, diagrams, applied art (i.e., two-dimensional pictorial artwork applied to a useful article), works of artistic craftsmanship (e.g., stained glass, tapestry, wallpaper), online or digital artwork (e.g., computer-aided artwork, digital imaging, pixel art), and similar types of pictorial works.
Graphic Works	Drawings, prints, art reproductions, maps, technical drawings, diagrams, architectural plans, architectural drawings, applied art (i.e., two-dimensional graphic artwork applied to a useful article), works of artistic craftsmanship, online or digital artwork (e.g., computer-aided artwork, digital imaging, pixel art), and similar types of graphic works.
Sculptural Works	Sculptures, globes, models, applied art (i.e., three-dimensional artwork applied to a useful article), works of artistic craftsmanship, and similar types of sculptural works.

Motion Pictures and Other Audiovisual Works (Section 102[a][6])

According to Section 101, audiovisual works "are works that consist of a series of related images which are intrinsically intended to be shown by the use of machines or devices such as projectors, viewers, or electronic equipment, together with accompanying sounds, if any, regardless of the nature of the material objects, such as films or tapes, in which the works are embodied." Examples of audiovisual works include "videogames, slide presentations, online audiovisual works (e.g., smartphone and tablet applications, online courses and tutorials, website content), and similar types of audiovisual works" (Compendium [Third] § 503.1[B]). Motion pictures are a category of audiovisual works that consist "of a series of related images which, when shown in succession, impart an impression of motion, together with accompanying sounds, if any" (17 U.S.C. § 101), such as "films, documentaries, television shows, cartoons, videos, online videos, motion picture soundtracks, and similar types of motion pictures" (Compendium [Third] § 503.1[B]).

Sound Recordings (Section 102[a][7])

Sound recordings "are works that result from the fixation of a series of musical, spoken, or other sounds" but do not include "the sounds accompanying a motion picture or other audiovisual work" (17 U.S.C. § 101) Examples of sounds recordings include recordings of songs and audiobooks.

Hirtle et al. (2009, 18) tell us that the "copyright in a musical work is distinguished from copyright in a sound recording of that work" and that the copyright in a sound recording "is separate from the media on which it is stored . . . or recorded." These are important distinctions. For example, a popular singer-songwriter may be asked to perform a song during the halftime intermission of a major league sporting event. She decides to write a new song for the show, and the musical score and accompanying words of this new song will receive copyright protection as a musical work. When she performs the song during halftime it is video recorded and transmitted digitally on the internet and via cable television, and it is also audio recorded at the same time so that it can be sold online as a downloadable .mp3 file and included on the artist's upcoming "greatest hits live" CD. This recorded performance of the song will receive copyright protection as a sound recording of the musical work and her copyright in the sound recording of the song is the same across all these mediums; it does not differ based on the physical or digital format.

Architectural Works (Section 102[a][8])

Section 101 defines architectural works as "the design of a building as embodied in any tangible medium of expression, including a building, architectural plans, or drawings. The work includes the overall form as well as the arrangement and composition of spaces and elements in the design but does not include individual standard features [e.g., windows and doors].” Here, the term “building” means “humanly habitable structures that are intended to be both permanent and stationary, such as houses and office buildings, and other permanent and stationary structures designed for human occupancy, including churches, museums, gazebos, and garden pavilions” (2 C.F.R. § 202.11[b][2]).

Architectural works were not granted copyright protection until December 1, 1990, when President George H. W. Bush signed the *Architectural Works Copyright Protection Act* (AWCPA) into law, and the copyright protection granted under Section 102(a)(8) extends only to building designs created on or after this date. Works not protected by the AWCPA include:

1. Buildings constructed before December 1, 1990
2. Building drawings or plans that were published before December 1, 1990
3. “The designs of buildings that were unconstructed and embodied in unpublished plans or drawings on December 1, 1990, and remained unconstructed on December 31, 2002” (2 C.F.R § 202.11[d][3][ii] 2003)

Section 926.1 of the *Compendium* tells us that “an architectural work and a technical drawing for an architectural work are separate works.” Drawings of buildings are registered as pictorial works and the copyright protection received is for the drawings themselves: it does not extend to the architectural work the drawings depicts. As a result, architectural drawings that predate the AWCPA will have copyright protection.

Compilation Copyright (Section 103)

Section 103 builds upon the scope of copyrightable works identified in Section 102(a) by outlining the copyright protection in compilations. A compilation is a “work formed by the collection and assembling of preexisting materials or of data that are selected, coordinated, or arranged in such a way that the resulting work as a whole constitutes an original work of authorship” (17 U.S.C. § 101). Examples of compilations identified in Section 508.1 of the *Compendium* are “a directory of services for a particular region, a list of the best short stories of 2014, and a collection of the best sound recordings of 1985.

A compilation can also include collective works, “such as a periodical issue, anthology, or encyclopedia, in which a number of contributions, constituting separate and independent works in themselves, are assembled into a collective whole” (17 U.S.C. § 101). It is important to note that for compilations, the protection granted under the law extends only to the selection and arrangement of the works it contains; it does not necessarily extend to the works themselves. Crews (2020, 41) provides an example of this, stating, "selecting and organizing articles in a journal may entail some originality; an editor selects articles from multiple submissions and organizes them into logical sequence within the journal issue." In this example, the editor can hold a copyright in the compilation of the issue. Whether or not the editor will also hold the copyright in each article included in the issue may actually be a matter of contract law. Section 201(c) states that the "copyright in each separate contribution to a collective work is distinct from copyright in the collective work as a whole, and vests initially in the author of the contribution. In the absence of an express transfer of the copyright or of any rights under it, the owner of copyright in the collective work is presumed to have acquired only the privilege of reproducing and distributing the contribution as part of that particular collective work, any revision of that collective work, and any later collective work in the same series." Under Section 201(c), if there is no transfer of copyright in each article to the editor, then the editor will hold the copyright in the compilation of the issue only and each article author will retain the copyright in their contribution. However, if as a condition of publication the editor requires that the article authors transfer their copyright in their contributions to the editor, then the editor would hold the copyright in the compilation and in the articles.

Works Not Eligible for Copyright Protection

Section 102(b) identifies categories of works that are not eligible for copyright protection. It states that "in no case does copyright protection for an original work of authorship extend to any idea, procedure, process, system, method of operation, concept, principle, or discovery, regardless of the form in which it is described, explained, illustrated, or embodied in such work." Some of these types of works may be eligible for protection under other categories of intellectual property though. For example, procedures, processes, systems, methods of operation, and discoveries may be eligible for patent protection while titles, names, short phrases, and slogans may be protectable under trademark law.

While ideas are not eligible for copyright protection, a person's original expression of an idea in a format that is eligible for copyright protection is. For example, if the idea of writing a novel about a teenage human-vampire romance was copyrightable, then the first person to gain copyright protection for this idea would control production of content in this genre. Instead, this idea is freely available for all to pursue, and each person writing in this genre gains protection for their original expression of this idea. As a result, we have the *Twilight* series from Stephanie Meyer, the *Vampire Academy* series by Richelle Mead, and many, many others. The concept that "copyright law protects only specific expressions of an idea, not an idea itself" is known as the idea–expression dichotomy and is an important principle in U.S. copyright law (Garner 2009, 813). Closely tied to this concept is the merger doctrine. The USCO tells us that "in some cases, there may be only one way or only a limited number of ways to express a particular idea, procedure, process, system, method of operation, concept, principle, or discovery" (Compendium [Third] § 313.3[B]). In those situations where idea and expression merge together, copyright protection cannot be granted for that expression. For example, in the case of *Morrissey v. Procter & Gamble Co.* (379 F.2d 675 [1st Cir. 1967]), the First Circuit Court of Appeals found that simple rules for entering a mail-in sweepstakes (e.g., printing a name and address on a box top or piece of paper and mailing it to a specific address) could not be copyrighted because such rules can only be expressed in a few, simple ways. If one particular person or group was able to copyright the few simple ways that such rules could be expressed, it would effectively give them a monopoly over the idea of conducting a sweepstakes in such a manner. Similarly, stock characters such as star-crossed lovers, a disapproving parent, or a nosy neighbor are not eligible for copyright protection as they are frequently used as a part of storytelling. Basic plots for stories (e.g., friends going on an adventure together, a knight fighting to save a beautiful princess, or people getting stranded on a desert island) are also not eligible for copyright protection. These types of rote characters or plots are known as *scènes à faire*, which is French for "scenes one must do." This term is defined in *Black's Law Dictionary* (Garner 2009, 1462) as "standard or general themes that are common to a wide variety of works and are therefore not copyrightable."

Discoveries and facts are also not eligible for copyright protection as they "do not owe their origin to an act of authorship. The distinction is one between creation and discovery: the first person to find and report a particular fact has not created the fact; they has merely discovered its existence" (Feist v. Rural 1991, 347). For example, the dates, names, and places associated with historical events such as the moon landing by Neil Armstrong and Buzz Aldrin on July 20, 1969, are not information that is arbitrarily made up. Rather, they are facts associated with the event and therefore are not eligible for copyright protection. Writings about facts may be eligible for copyright protection though. For instance, a history textbook may include a lesson on the moon landing, providing a detailed overview of the event. The author's words about the moon landing, as they come together in sentences and paragraphs, can be eligible for copyright protection. Additionally, the selection and arrangement of facts may be eligible for copyright protection, whereas the facts themselves are not protectable. For example, colleges and universities frequently compile and publish statistics about their students, including their age, gender, race, and ethnicity, as well and a total headcount of students, that is often broken down based on status of the student (e.g., undergraduate, graduate, and professional students) and the number of credit hours the student is taking (e.g., full-time and part-time). This data is not eligible for copyright protection, though the ways in which the institution selects and arranges this information in charts, graphs, and tables to visually represent it may be copyrightable.

Other works that are not eligible for copyright protection that are identified in the *Compendium* include works that have not been fixed in a tangible medium of expression and works that do not have a human author, including those "works produced by nature, animals, or plants" or "works produced by a machine or mere mechanical process that operates randomly or automatically without any creative input or intervention from a human author" (Compendium [Third] § 313.2).

RECOMMENDED RESOURCE

Circular 33. The USCO takes an in-depth look at this particular topic in *Circular 33 Works Not Protected by Copyright*, which can be found online at https://www.copyright.gov/circs/.

Works in the Public Domain

Works in the public domain do not have copyright protection. The following types of works are in the public domain:

- Works that contain no copyrightable content
- Works] "prepared by an officer or employee of the United States Government as part of that person's official duties" (17 U.S.C. § 101)
- Works for which the copyright has expired

More information on each of these scenarios can be found in Chapter 5, which explores in depth how to determine the copyright status of a work.

Rights Granted Under the Law

Under Section 106, those who create works that are eligible for copyright protection have certain exclusive rights in them. Here, the term "exclusive" generally means that the rightsholder alone can exercise these rights. However, it is critically important for readers to understand that these rights are not absolute. The rights identified in this section are subject to limitations set forth by Congress in Sections 107 through 122 of the Copyright Act. These user rights (also referred to as exceptions) were established to permit some "uses that would otherwise be infringements" (Crews 2020, 83) and to ensure that the rights granted to the creators of copyrightable works do not impede the promotion of "the Progress of Science and useful Arts" (U.S. Const. art. I, § 8, c8).

Reproduction Rights (Section 106[1])

This right allows the rightsholder, or another acting on the authorization of the rightsholder, to "reproduce the copyrighted work in copies or phonorecords." As mentioned previously, copies of works are defined as "material objects, other than phonorecords, in which a work is fixed by any method now known or later developed, and from which the work can be perceived, reproduced, or otherwise communicated, either directly or with the aid of a machine or device," and phonorecords are "material objects in which sounds, other than those accompanying a motion picture or other audiovisual work, are fixed . . . and from which the sounds can be perceived, reproduced, or otherwise communicated, either directly or with the aid of a machine or device" (17 U.S.C. § 101).

Adaptation Rights (Section 106[2])

Section 106(2) grants the rightsholder the right to prepare derivative works that are "based upon one or more preexisting works, [for example] a translation, musical arrangement, dramatization, fictionalization, motion picture version, sound recording, art reproduction, abridgment, condensation, or any other form in which a work may be recast, transformed, or adapted" (17 U.S.C. § 101). Additionally, "a work consisting of editorial revisions, annotations, elaborations, or other modifications, which, as a whole, represent an original work of authorship, is [also considered to be] a 'derivative work'" (17 U.S.C. § 101).

Public Distribution Rights (Section 106[3])

This right allows rightsholders to control the distribution of "copies or phonorecords of the copyrighted work to the public by sale or other transfer of ownership, or by rental, lease, or lending." Many rightsholders choose to distribute copies by sale, allowing them to profit from the creation of the work, but giving away copies for free also counts as a distribution. It is important for users to understand that ownership of a copy of a work does not mean they own the copyright in a work. Section 202 addresses this, stating "transfer of ownership of any material object, including the copy or phonorecord in which the work is first fixed, does not of itself convey any rights in the copyrighted work embodied in the object."

Public Performance Rights (Sections 106[4])

Section 106(4) states that "in the case of literary, musical, dramatic, and choreographic works, pantomimes, and motion pictures and other audiovisual works," the rightsholder controls the right to "perform the copyrighted work publicly." Under U.S. copyright law, to perform a work means to "recite, render, play, dance, or act it, either directly or by means of any device or process or, in the case of a motion picture or other audiovisual work, to show its images in any sequence or to make the sounds accompanying it audible" (17 U.S.C. § 101). The performance of literary, musical, dramatic and choreographic works, pantomimes, and motion pictures and other audiovisual works becomes public when it is

> (1) [performed] at a place open to the public or at any place where a substantial number of persons outside of a normal circle of a family and its social acquaintances is gathered; or
>
> (2) transmitted or otherwise communicated to a place specified by clause (1) or to the public, by means of any device or process, whether the members of the public capable of receiving the performance or display receive it in the same place or in separate places and at the same time or at different times. (17 U.S.C. § 101)

Examples that illustrate public performances include:

- A person reading aloud from a book of poetry during a poetry night event held at a local coffee shop will be making a public performance of a literary work.
- A marching band playing music during a parade, or a barbershop quartet singing in a talent show will be publicly performing musical works.
- A community theater group performing a play as part of a summer theater series will be publicly performing a dramatic work, which may include the public performance of pantomime by the actors as a way of expressing their character.
- Dance students will be publicly performing choreography for their friends and family sitting in the audience during a dance recital. The students will likely be performing the choreography to songs being played over speakers, which will constitute public performances of the sound recordings of these musical works.
- A popular film being shown in a city park as part of a family night event sponsored by a town would be consider a public performance of a motion picture.

The rightsholders of sound recordings are granted a right in Section 106(6) allowing them "to perform the copyrighted work publicly by means of a digital audio transmission." Section 101 defines a digital transmission as "a transmission in whole or in part in a digital or other nonanalog format." An example of the digital audio transmission of a sound recording would be a song made available streaming over the internet. This can include internet radio stations or online streaming services like Spotify. It can also include music files posted online. For example, the Sleepy Man Banjo Boys are a bluegrass music band made up of three brothers: Jonny, Robbie, and Tommy Mizzone as well as their friend, Josh Thomas. Fans visiting the band's website can listen to some of their most popular songs via a streaming music player. As these songs are made available via the World Wide Web for anyone to listen to, this constitutes a public performance. As the versions found on the band's website are authorized to be there, there is no infringement of the 106(6) right. However, if a fan posted one of the band's songs to their personal website for others to listen to, this would be an infringement of this right.

Public Display Rights (Section 106[5])

Under Section 106(5), the right to make a public display of "literary, musical, dramatic, and choreographic works, pantomimes, and pictorial, graphic, or sculptural works, including the individual images of a motion picture or other audiovisual work," is established. Section 101 states "to 'display' a work means to show a copy of it, either directly or by means of a film, slide, television image, or any other device or process or, in the case of a motion picture or other audiovisual work, to show individual images nonsequentially." The same definition of "public" referred to in the previous section discussing public performances applies here. Examples of public displays of works include:

- Posting a page from a book, musical score, or play online
- Publishing a picture in a newspaper or magazin
- Placing a sculpture in a public garden
- Showing several stills from an animated cartoon show as part of a panel discussion at an art festival as a way of demonstrating how the animation process works

Copyright Ownership

"Copyright . . . vests initially in the author or authors of the work" (17 U.S.C. § 201[a]), and they will be considered the rightsholder. The frequent appearance of the word "author" throughout U.S. copyright law (and in judicial opinions discussing copyright) can be a point of confusion for some as in common vernacular the word author is used in conjunction with literary works (e.g., a book or poem), and other words are used to describe those who create other types of works. For example, a photographer takes a photograph, a sculptor creates a sculpture, a painter paints a picture, a programmer develops software, and a playwright writes a play. However, when reading U.S. copyright law, and in the case of many judicial opinions regarding the law, the word author should be interpreted as "he to whom anything owes its orign [*sic*]" (Burrow-Giles v. Sarony 1884), and generally refers to the creators of all types of works, not just literary works.

Joint Authorship

It is not uncommon for two or more people to decide to work together to create a copyrightable work. For example, several students may team up to develop a PowerPoint presentation as part of a class project, instructors may collaborate on research and the writing of a scholarly article outlining their findings, and members of a band may work together to write a new song. When "a work [is] prepared by two or more authors with the intention that their contributions be merged into inseparable or interdependent parts of a unitary whole" (17 U.S.C. § 101), the resulting work is considered a joint work and the authors are considered to be joint authors. Under this definition, for a copyrightable work to be considered a joint work of authorship two conditions must exist: the authors must each contribute significant copyrightable content to the work, and they must have the intention that their individual contributions will be merged together to form the final, whole work.

Contributing Copyrightable Content

To be considered a joint author of a joint work, a person must contribute to the copyrightable content of the work. For example, a teacher places their students into small groups and assigns each group a famous historical figure to prepare a presentation on. The teacher will not be considered a joint author of the each of the reports as ideas (here, the idea of preparing a presentation on a particular topic) are not eligible for copyright protection and, therefore, they have contributed no copyrightable content to the joint work. Additionally, to be considered a joint author each person must contribute significantly to work. Frequently authors will ask family, friends, and colleagues to review a manuscript they are working on and make recommendations to them regarding the content, the structure and flow of the manuscript, word usage, punctuation, and grammar. The author of the article may make all of the suggested changes proposed by these reviewers, but this will not make their family, friends, and colleagues joint authors of the work. This is because recommended revisions, while important and useful, are usually not considered significant contributions as any changes made will be made at the discretion of the author, who retains control over the final product. In writing his opinion on *Aalmuhammed v. Lee* (202 F.3d 1227 [9th Cir. 1999]), Ninth Circuit Judge Andrew J. Kleinfeld addressed this issue, stating that the "[p]rogress [of Science and useful Arts] would be retarded rather than promoted, if an author could not consult with others and adopt their useful suggestions without sacrificing sole ownership of the work" (Aalmuhammed v. Lee 2000, 1235).

Merging of the Contributions

One of the key aspects of a joint work is that the individual contributions of each author must come together to form "a unitary whole" (17 U.S.C. § 101). For example, an author and an illustrator may decide to work together on a new children's book. The author writes the text (a literary work) and the illustrator develops colorful pictures (pictorial works) depicting the action taking place in the story. Both the author and the illustrator have created works eligible for copyright protection, and these works come together in the final, published children's book, forming a unitary whole.

Ownership of the Copyright in a Joint Work

It is a common misconception that joint authors only hold the copyright in only the portions they have contributed to a work, and that those rights are not shared with their co-authors. This is untrue. Under U.S. copyright law, "the authors of a joint work are co-owners of copyright in the work" (17 U.S.C. 201[a]) and each author owns an undivided share of the rights in the whole work.

As co-owners of the copyright in a work, each joint author may, without the consent of the other joint authors exercise any of the rights granted to rightsholders under the law. For example, any joint author may make and distribute a copy of the work. Each joint author may also authorize others to exercise any of the rights granted in Section 106 on a nonexclusive basis. However, if joint authors authorize any commercial use of the work, they must make an accounting of any profits they receive to the other joint authors. Joint authors may not grant an exclusive license to any or all of the rights in the work to another without the prior authorization of the other joint authors. More information about exclusive and nonexclusive licenses can be found in the *Transfer of Rights* section of this chapter.

Works Made for Hire

The person who creates the work may not be the author for the purposes of copyright law. Section 101 identifies two situations in which a work may be considered a work made for hire.

Works Created by Employees

When a work is "prepared by an employee within the scope of his or her employment" (17 U.S.C. § 101), "the employer or other person for whom the work was prepared is considered the author for purposes of this title," and they will own "all of the rights comprised in the copyright" unless the parties "have expressly agreed otherwise in a written instrument signed by them" that states otherwise (17 U.S.C. § 201[b]). For example, a graphic designer employed by a large company to design advertisements for their products to be used in newspapers, magazines, and on social media will not own the copyright in these works even though they are clearly the author of the work. As they are preparing the work "within the scope of his or her employment" (17 U.S.C. § 101), the copyright will be held by the advertising agency.

Ordered or Commissioned Works

If the creation of a copyrightable work is "specially ordered or commissioned" (17 U.S.C. § 101), then it may also be considered a work made for hire even if the person creating it does not work directly for the person or organization that ordered or commissioned it. In these situations, the work being created must fall into one of nine categories identified in Section 101: "a contribution to a collective work, as a part of a motion picture or other audiovisual work, as a translation, as a supplementary work, as a compilation, as an instructional text, as a test, as answer material for a test, or as an atlas."

Here, the party that ordered or commissioned the work will only be considered the rightsholder "if the parties expressly agree in a written instrument signed by them that the work shall be considered a work made for hire" (17 U.S.C. § 101). For example, a company hires a freelance videographer to make training videos for them to use to help employees better understand workplace safety. In this situation, the company will only hold the copyright in the training videos if they and the videographer "expressly agree in a written instrument signed by them that the work shall be considered a work made for hire."

RECOMMENDED RESOURCE

Circular 30: Works Made for Hire. Published by the USCO, it explores work-for-hire situations in depth and can be found online at: https://www.copyright.gov/circs/.

Transfer of Rights

Under Section 201(d)(1), "the ownership of a copyright may be transferred in whole or in part by any means of conveyance or by operation of law, and may be bequeathed by will or pass as personal property by the applicable laws of intestate succession," which is the "acquisition of rights or property by inheritance" by the heirs of a person who has died without a will (Garner 2009, 1569).

A rightsholder may transfer one, some, or all the rights they have in a work to another individual or organization. Transfers may be made for a specific period of time, from hours to years, or for the duration of time the work has protection. Transfers may be made applicable for a specific territory, such as a specific country or a group of countries, or they may be granted for worldwide use. The transfer may be made on a nonexclusive basis or exclusively.

Nonexclusive Licenses

A nonexclusive license is "a license of intellectual property rights that gives the licensee a right to use, make, or sell the licensed item on a shared basis with the licensor and possible other licensees" (Garner 2009, 1004). With nonexclusive licenses, the rightsholder may authorize multiple individuals or organizations (e.g., a publisher, an academic institution, or a library) to exercise one or more of the rights they possess in a work. As indicated by the definition, the rightsholder can grant these rights in a way that multiple individuals or organizations may be taking advantage of them. An example of a nonexclusive license is the public performance licenses libraries and educational institutions obtain for certain public screenings of a film. In these situations, the rightsholder often grants the organization the short-term right to publicly perform the film on a particular day and at a specific location. The rightsholder can grant this same public performance right many times over to other institutions and can even grant multiple institutions the rights to hold their screenings on the same day. With nonexclusive licenses, the rightsholder is not giving up the copyright they hold in a work. Rather, they are sharing those rights with others under certain terms that are often outlined in a license. Nonexclusive licenses may be made verbally, though it is always best to set forth the terms of the license in writing so they are clear both for the licensor and for the licensee.

Transfer of Rights

Section 201(d)(2) states that one, some, or all of the exclusive rights granted to a rightsholder under Section 106 may be transferred to another. Often this process will be talked about in terms of exclusive licenses; however, Hirtle et al. (2009, 131) state that the "exclusive licenses are a bit of a misnomer [as] . . . the granting of an exclusive license is the equivalent of transferring copyright ownership of that right [or rights]" to another. Unlike a nonexclusive license where the copyright holder retains their rights in the work, once an exclusive transfer of one or more of their rights in a work is made in compliance with the law, the new rightsholder is entitled "to the extent of that right, to all of the protection and remedies accorded to the copyright owner by this title" (17 U.S.C. § 201[d][2]). This means that the original rightsholder may have to seek permission from the new rightsholder (the person or organization they transferred the right or rights to) to reuse the work they authored. Otherwise, they may be placing themselves at risk of claims of copyright infringement, so rightsholders should carefully consider if a nonexclusive license might work before making an exclusive transfer.

Under Section 204(a), an exclusive transfer of any or all rights in a work "is not valid unless an instrument of conveyance, or a note or memorandum of the transfer, is in writing and signed by the owner of the rights conveyed or such owner's duly authorized agent." The transfer of exclusive rights can be done via a contract drafted, reviewed, and approved by legal counsel. It can also be performed more informally, including via a hand-written transfer that is signed and dated, or via an email that includes an electronic signature from the rightsholder. It is important for users to recognize that the date on which a document transferring the copyright to another is signed may be different from the date in which the transfer becomes effective. For example, a person may sign a transfer document on March 1 of a given year that states that the transfer of rights will become effective on July 1 of that same year. For works that have been registered with the USCO, it is a best practice to record the transfer of the exclusive rights in a work with them, though this is not required by law. Doing so has distinct advantages though, which include helping users of the work identify the correct person to whom requests to reuse the work can be directed.

The Termination of Transfers

Except in those situations where a work is considered a work made for hire, under Section 203 an exclusive transfer of rights or nonexclusive license that was executed on or after January 1, 1978, may be terminated under certain conditions. In these situations, upon the effective date of the termination, "all rights that were covered by the terminated [license] revert to the author, authors, and other persons owning termination interests under clauses"—for example, a rightsholder's heirs (17 U.S.C. § 203[5][b]). When a termination takes place, it is important for the rightsholder to realize that it affects only those rights covered by the original transfer agreement. For example, an author may have made an exclusive transfer of the different rights they held in a novel they wrote to different people or organizations (e.g., they granted the rights to reproduce and distribute the novel in print or electronic formats to a publisher and the right to make a movie version of the novel to a film studio). If the author successfully pursues a termination of the rights they transferred to the publisher, this would not impact the transfer of rights they granted to the movie studio: they would have to pursue that termination separately. The circumstances under which a termination can take place are detailed in Section 203.

Duration of Copyright

The term of copyright protection granted to a work depends on when the work was created and published. Generally, the term of works created after January 1, 1978, are as follows:

- Works created by a single author are protected for the life of the author and 70 years after their death.
- For works of joint authorship, the term of protections lasts for 70 years after the passing of the last surviving author.
- For anonymous works, works created under a pseudonym, and works made for hire, the term of protection lasts for 95 years from the year of the works first publication, or 120 years from the year of its creation, whichever expires first.

For works created prior to January 1, 1978, the term of protection it received will depend on its publication status (published or unpublished) and the rightsholder's compliance with formalities found in the law during this time. A more thorough overview of these terms and requirements can be found in Chapter 5. Under Section 305, the term of copyright in a work "run[s] to the end of the calendar year in which they would otherwise expire."

The International Treatment of Copyright

It used to be that copyright was not recognized across borders. For example, the first Copyright Act was passed in the United States in 1790, but it was not until 1891, when the International Copyright Act (also called the Chace Act) was passed by Congress, that copyright protection was extended to certain foreign copyright holders. In recognizing the value and importance of providing copyright protection to the authors internationally, numerous international treaties, agreements, and conventions dealing with copyright law have been established between countries. *The Convention for the Protection of Literary and Artistic Works* signed in Berne, Switzerland, in 1886, is one such treaty. Frequently referred to as the *Berne Convention*, this treaty:

- Established a system of equal treatment, requiring participating countries (who are members of the *Berne Union*) to agree to set minimum standards of copyright protection in their law to ensure that the copyright of foreign authors is granted, at minimum, the same amount of protection as those authors of their country. These standards include a minimum term of copyright protection, which is currently the life of the author and 50 years after the authors death.

- Eliminated requirements, more frequently referred to as formalities, for securing rights. This includes a prohibition on formal registration requirements or the placement of a copyright notice on a work.

The United States joined the Berne Convention in 1989. As of the writing of this book (2022), 176 countries are members or signatories of the *Berne Convention*, which is managed by the World Intellectual Property Organization (WIPO). In-depth information regarding the treaty and a list of member countries can be found on their website: http://www.wipo.int/treaties/en/ip/berne/.

The United States is party to many other international treaties that address the international protection of copyright. The USCO provides information about these on their website: https://www.copyright.gov/international-issues/. As these treaties, conventions, and agreements are subject to revision and new treaties, conventions, and agreements may be proposed by WIPO and other international agencies, those who frequently engage with copyright law should periodically check this website to keep themselves up to date on the law and the ways in which such agreements may their work.

Putting It All Together

Key points readers should take away from this chapter include:

- Copyright protection is instantly granted to original, creative works upon fixation.
- Many types of works are eligible for copyright protection.
- Not all types of work are copyrightable though.
- Works without copyright protection are in the public domain and may be freely reused.
- Certain rights are granted to those who create works that are eligible for copyright protection.
- The person who creates a copyrightable work is usually considered the author, but copyright can also be held by joint authors or, in some situations, the employer of the person who created the work can be the author.
- These rights can be licensed to others on a nonexclusive basis or transferred to others exclusively.
- The copyright in works last for a long, though limited, time.

- International treaties and agreements ensure that copyrightable works created by foreign authors are protected in the United States, and that works created by U.S. authors receive copyright protection in foreign countries.

To effectively administer reserve services, library staff should have an understanding of these concepts as well as the user rights found in Sections 107, 108, 109, 110, and 121 that establish limitations that the exclusive rights granted under Section 106 are subject to. In the following chapters, readers will find information on the user rights (also referred to as exceptions) that can be taken advantage of when providing reserve services to the campus community. Combined, this information will help staff make thoughtful and informed decisions when looking to make copyrighted works lawfully available via reserve services.

Case Study: A Boy, His Dragon, and Copyright: A Review of the Basics of U.S. Copyright Law, Courtesy of Christopher Paolini

The novel *Eragon* was written by Christpoher Paolini. Set in the fictional land of Alagaësia, the book follows the adventures of a teenage boy named Eragon. While in the mountains located near his village, a mysterious blue stone suddenly appears before Eragon. He takes the stone home with him, but the stone is not really a stone: it is actually a dragon's egg, and a beautiful blue dragon hatches from it. Eragon names the dragon Saphira, and the two instantly bond. The evil King Galbatorix, who rules Alagaësia, has been hunting for the egg as he wants the dragon for himself. He has sent mercenaries into Alagaësia to find the egg, and the story unfolds as Eragon and Brom, a storyteller from his village with a mysterious background, try to evade the mercenaries while seeking out a group of rebels called the Varden, whom they believe can help them bring about the downfall of Galbatorix.

Securing Copyright

As *Eragon* was Paolini's original, creative work and was fixed in a tangible medium of expression it qualified for copyright protection as a literary work. Paolini also created the cover art (a dragon's eye) for the original version of the book, and as this was also an original, creative, fixed work, it too qualified for copyright protection, though as a graphic work.

Idea vs. Expression

Paolini said that "[o]ne of the things that inspired me [to write *Eragon*] was an image—inspired by the book Jeremy Thatcher, Dragon Hatcher, by Bruce Coville—of a dragon egg appearing before a young man deep within a dark pinewood forest" (Paolini n.d.). Here we see the application of the idea/expression dichotomy. The idea of a dragon egg appearing before a young man deep within a forest is free for anyone to use, and both Bruce Coville and Christopher Paolini received copyright protection for their individual expressions of these ideas.

Authorship

As Paolini wrote the novel, he is considered the author of it, and the copyright in the work vested with him.

Exercising Rights Granted Under the Law

Paolini took advantage of many of the rights granted to him under U.S. copyright law or, in some situations, authorized others to do so on his behalf.

- Reproduction and Distribution: *Eragon* was originally self-published (reproduced in copies and distributed) by his parents in 2001; however, the novel was brought to the attention of the publishing house Alfred A. Knopf, which republished and distributed the book on Paolini's behalf starting in 2003.
- The Making of Derivatives: Given the popularity of the novel, derivative versions have been made of it, including an audiorecording of the novel, translations, and a videogame.
- Public Performances of the Movie: Another derivative of the book, a movie, was produced by the Twentieth Century-Fox Film Corporation. The screenplay for the movie qualified for copyright protection as a dramatic work, and the movie itself received copyright protection as an audiovisual work. This movie was publicly performed in theaters throughout the world.
- Public Displays: Stills from the movie were included in movie reviews published in magazines, newspapers, and online, constituting public displays of images from the movie. If you are looking to purchase a copy of Paolini's book or the movie, you'll find the cover art for the book and DVD/Blu-ray being publicly displayed by online by retailers such as amazon.com and barnesandnoble.com.

Duration of Copyright Protection

The copyright protection in *Eragon* lasts for Paolini's life and 70 years after his passing. Once this term of protection expires, the work will pass into the public domain and be freely available for all to reuse.

"Authors" Among Us

Christopher Paolini was 17 when he published his first novel. People can look with amazement at what he accomplished, but often do so not realizing that they are "authors" themselves. Authors, as defined by U.S. copyright law, are everywhere. Almost everyone living in the United

States, from toddlers drawing with crayons, to aspiring teen authors, to senior citizens snapping selfies, creates copyrightable works on a daily basis. Authors should be aware of the rights granted to them under U.S. copyright law. Unfortunately, few of them are. This chapter challenges readers to learn the fundamentals of U.S. copyright law so they can make informed decisions when dealing with copyright questions and issues related to reserve services. This knowledge can hopefully also empower readers to act as "sources of copyright information for their user communities," preparing them to confidently "inform or properly refer users with questions pertaining to copyright" (Committee on Professional Ethics, 2013–14, 9. Readers should also remember that they are "authors" as well, and use this knowledge to make thoughtful decisions about how they wish to manage their own copyrights. "Promot[ing] the Progress of Science and useful Arts" (U.S. Const. art. I, § 8, c8) may be the foundational principle of U.S. copyright law, but the phrase could also be used when describing the mission of libraries. Staff can truly "advocate [for] balance between the interests of information users and rights holders" (6) by being informed about their own rights and the rights of other creators, and by encouraging library users to do the same.

CHAPTER FIVE

Determining the Copyright Status of a Work

When an instructor asks the library to make a work available via reserve services in a way that would exercise rights granted to rightsholders under Section 106 of U.S. copyright law, it can be helpful to begin the copyright review process by trying to identify its status as a copyrightable work. For example, if it can be determined the work is in the public domain, then as it has no copyright protection it can be freely reused, including making copies available via print, electronic, or media reserves. Alternatively, if it is determined the work is protected by copyright, then the library can consider exercising rights found in U.S. copyright law, such as the first sale doctrine (17 U.S.C. § 109) or fair use (17 U.S.C. § 107), for making copies available via reserve services.

The Public Domain

Public domain works are works that do not have copyright protection. Works enter the public domain when they have no copyrightable content, when the "work prepared by an officer or employee of the United States Government as part of that person's official duties" (17 U.S.C. § 101), or when the copyright in the work expires.

The Work Contains No Copyrightable Content

Works that consist solely of material that is not eligible for copyright protection are in the public domain. Examples include fact-based works such as multiplication tables and a table converting inches to centimeters or ounces to liters. Another example includes the alphabetical listing of names in the white pages of a phone book as "in preparing its white pages, [the telephone provider] simply takes the data provided by its subscribers and lists it alphabetically by surname. The end product is a garden-variety white pages directory, devoid of even the slightest trace of creativity" (Feist v. Rural 1991, 362).

Works of the U.S. Government

Section 105(a) tells us that "[c]opyright protection . . . is not available for any work of the United States Government." Section 101 states that a "Work of the United States Government" is any "work prepared by an officer or employee of the United States Government as part of that person's official duties." For example, satellite photos taken by National Aeronautics and Space Administration (NASA), NASA-created content found on their website, and video and reports published by NASA are in the public domain. NASA's *Media Usage Guidelines* (Daines 2022) state that "NASA material is not protected by copyright unless noted [and], if not copyrighted, NASA material may be reproduced and distributed without further permission from NASA."

Exceptions for Certain Works of the U.S. Government

Section 105(b) states that "subject to subsection [105](c), the covered author of a covered work owns the copyright to that covered work." Section 105(c)(1) tells us that "the term 'covered author' means a civilian member of the faculty of a covered institution." These covered institutions are identified in Section 105(c)(2) and include:

- The National Defense University
- The United States Military Academy
- The Army War College
- The United States Army Command and General Staff College
- The United States Naval Academy
- The Naval War College
- The Naval Post Graduate School
- The Marine Corps University
- The United States Air Force Academy

- The Air University
- The Defense Language Institute
- The United States Coast Guard Academy

According to Section 105(c)(3), "the term 'covered work' means a literary work produced by a covered author in the course of employment at a covered institution for publication by a scholarly press or journal." In qualifying situations, covered authors would be able to transfer their copyright in the work in whole or in part to another, such as the publisher of a scholarly press or journal.

Works created as part of U.S. government grant-funded projects are also not necessarily public domain works as they are often not being created by employees of the U.S. federal government. However, more frequently the U.S. government is requiring recipients of its grants to make the results of research it funds, including published works and data, freely available to the public within one year of publication. Users must recognize that these works are often not in the public domain. Rather, they are licensed in such a way that allows their reuse so long as users provide attribution to the copyright holder of the work. Failure to abide by the terms of the license may place the user at risk of claims of copyright infringement by the rightsholder.

Case Study: Copyright in State Government Works

Section 105(a), (b), and (c) only applies to works created by employees of the U.S. federal government. The copyright status of works produced by state governments vary by format and by state. The *government edicts doctrine*, an exception to copyright created judicially by the SCOTUS in 1834 as part of their decision on the case of *Wheaton v. Peters* (33 U.S. 591 [1834]), prohibits copyright from protecting for works considered to be government edicts, such as judicial decisions and statutes. The copyright status of informational works created by states (e.g., posters, flyers, photographs, maps, and pamphlets) is not so clear cut. Some states have passed laws placing such works in the public domain, while other states consider such works to be fully protected under U.S. copyright law. In an effort to provide information to the public about the copyright status of state publications, Kyle Courtney, copyright adviser and program manager at Harvard's Library Office for Scholarly Communications and Katie Zimmerman, Director of Copyright Strategy at the Massachusetts Institution of Technology (then copyright fellow at Harvard's Library Office for Scholarly Communications) worked with members of the Free State Government Information Network to develop the *State Copyright Resource Center*, which can be found online at http://

copyright.lib.harvard.edu/states/. This resource provides the public with information on the copyright status of works produced by state governments and can be a valuable resource when engaging with materials published by states.

The Copyright in the Work Expires

A work will pass into the public domain once its term of copyright expires. As of the writing of this book (2022), works first published in the United States or works registered with the U.S. Copyright Office (USCO) in unpublished form prior to January 1, 1927, are in the public domain. Barring any legislative action by Congress, this date will move progressively forward year by year. This means that on January 1, 2023, unpublished works registered with the U.S. Copyright Office (USCO) or works first published in the United States prior to January 1, 1928, will also pass in to the public domain, and so forth. Extensions of the term of copyright have been passed by Congress in the past. For example, when the Copyright Act of 1976 was passed, the term of protection granted to many works was for the life of the author and then 50 years after their death. However, the Sonny Bono Copyright Term Extension Act, passed in 1998, added 20 years to the existing terms of copyright, extending the term mentioned previously to 70 years after the death of the author. As of the writing of this book, there is no pending legislation intended to extend the current terms of copyright; however, legislation could be passed that applies retroactively, bringing works that were once in the public domain back under copyright protection. Readers should pay attention to the actions of Congress and take note if any legislation regarding the extension of copyright is put forward and passed and, if so, whether it is applied retroactively.

Works first published in the U.S. or works registered with the USCO in unpublished form between January 1, 1927, and December 31, 1977, may or may not be in the public domain. Much will depend if the rightsholder complied with the formalities found in the law during this time. Determining the public domain status of these works can be a complex process. Prior to this date, works had to comply with the formalities found in the law in order to receive copyright protection; failure to do so meant the work passed into the public domain. A brief synopsis of the terms of protection and formalities is found below. Readers should consult Peter Hirtle's *Copyright Term and the Public Domain in the United States* charts for additional information. A copy of them is included in Appendix A of this book. They can also be found online at https://guides.library.cornell.edu/copyright/publicdomain.

Determining the Status of Works Registered or First Published from 1927 Through 1963

Works created during this time period secured copyright protection when they were first published in the United States or, for unpublished works, were registered with the USCO. Published works had to include a properly formatted and placed copyright notice. If the rightsholder failed to place a copyright notice on a published work, or if the notice was not properly formatted or placed in the location identified by the law, the work automatically passed into the public domain. Works that were published with a properly formatted and placed copyright notice received a term of copyright protection of 28 years, and rightsholders could renew this term for an additional 28 years during the last year of the first term. Subsequent updates to the U.S. Copyright Act extended this term to a total of 95 years after the date of publication. If the rightsholder failed to renew the copyright in their work during the last year of the initial term, it passed into the public domain.

Determining the Status of Works Registered or First Published from 1964 Through 1977

Works first published in the United States with a properly formatted and properly placed copyright notice and unpublished works that were registered with the USCO during this time receive a term of copyright protection that lasts for 95 years after the date of publication. This is due to automatic renewal being granted to these particular works. For works that were published during this time period, if the rightsholder failed to place a copyright notice on a published work, or if the notice was not properly formatted or placed in the location identified by the law, the work automatically passed into the public domain.

Determining the Status of Works Registered or First Published Between 1978 and March 1, 1989

Works published in the United States during this time period were also required to have a properly formatted and placed copyright notice on them. However, if the copyright notice was omitted the rightsholder had the opportunity to remedy the situation and prevent the work from passing into the public domain. Section 405 addresses these situations. It states:

> With respect to copies and phonorecords publicly distributed by authority of the copyright owner [from the implementation date of the 19766 Copyright Act (January 1, 1978)] before the effective date of the Berne Convention

Implementation Act of 1988 [March 1, 1989], the omission of the copyright notice described in sections 401 through 403 from copies or phonorecords publicly distributed by authority of the copyright owner does not invalidate the copyright in a work if—

(1) the notice has been omitted from no more than a relatively small number of copies or phonorecords distributed to the public; or

(2) registration for the work has been made before or is made within five years after the publication without notice, and a reasonable effort is made to add notice to all copies or phonorecords that are distributed to the public in the United States after the omission has been discovered; or

(3) the notice has been omitted in violation of an express requirement in writing that, as a condition of the copyright owner's authorization of the public distribution of copies or phonorecords, they bear the prescribed notice.

If the rightsholder did not take steps to correct the omission of the notice on these published works, they passed into the public domain.

Determining the Status of Unpublished Works Created Between 1927 and 1978

Under the Copyright Act of 1978, literary works; musical works; dramatic works; pantomimes and choreographic works; pictorial, graphical, and sculptural works; and motion pictures and other audiovisual works created during this time period that were never published or registered with the USCO receive a term of copyright protection that lasts for the life of the author plus 70 years after their death. Works of joint authorship receive a term of protection that lasts for 70 years after the passing of the last surviving author. Works that were published anonymously, under a pseudonym, or that were works made for hire receive a term of protection that lasts 120 years from the year of its creation.

Determining the Status of Unpublished Works Created Between 1927 and 1978, but Published Between 1978 and March 1, 1989

Literary works; musical works; dramatic works; pantomimes and choreographic works; pictorial, graphical, and sculptural works; and motion pictures and other audiovisual works that were created between 1927 and 1977 that were never published and never registered with the USCO but were then published between January 1, 1978, and March 1, 1989, receive the following copyright protection:

- Works created by a single author: 70 years after the passing of the author or protection through December 31, 2047, whichever term is greater

- Works created by joint authors: 70 years after the passing of the last surviving author or protection through December 31, 2047, whichever term is greater
- For anonymous works, pseudonymous works, and works made for hire: 95 years from the year of its first publication, or a term of 120 years from the year of its creation, whichever expires first, or protection through December 31, 2047, whichever term is greater

Determining the Copyright Status of Sound Recordings

The copyright term for sound recordings that were published in the United States prior to February 15, 1972, used to be controlled by state law. With the passage of the Music Modernization Act (MMA) in 2018, new federal terms were established for these works:

- Sound recordings published in the United States prior to 1923 passed into the public domain on January 1, 2022.
- Sound recordings published in the United States between 1923 and 1946 receive a term of copyright protection of 100 years from publication.
- Sound recordings published in the United States between 1947 and 1956 receive a term of copyright protection of 110 years from publication.
- Sound recordings published in the United States between 1957 and February 14, 1972, will pass into the public domain on February 15, 2067.

Sound recordings that were published after February 15, 1978, receive the same terms of protection as identified for all other types of copyrightable works created after January 1, 1978.

Determining the Copyright Status of Works First Published Abroad

Works first published abroad between 1927 and 1977 are treated differently, though most that complied with formalities in place at the time receive a term of protection similar to those of works first published or registered here in the United States prior to during these time periods. Sounds recordings that were published outside the United States prior to February 15, 1972, receive the same terms of protection that sound recordings published in the United States under the MMA, though sound recordings published after this time receive slightly different terms of protection.

Determining the Copyright Status of Architectural Works

As discussed in Chapter 4, architectural works were not granted copyright protection until December 1, 1990. Because of this, copyright protection extends only to building designs created on or after this date. Architectural works without copyright protection include:

- Buildings constructed before December 1, 1990
- Building drawings or plans that were published before December 1, 1990
- "The designs of buildings that were unconstructed and embodied in unpublished plans or drawings on December 1, 1990, and remained unconstructed on December 31, 2002" (2 C.F.R § 202.11[d][3][ii] 2003)

Architectural plans and drawings may be eligible for copyright protection as literary works or pictorial, graphical, and sculptural works, in which case they would receive terms of protection as afforded by the Copyright Act.

Putting It All Together

When it comes to determining the copyright status of works instructors request to place on print, electronic, or media reserve, some decisions will be fairly straight forward and others will be complicated. Staff can safely assume that works on or created after March 2, 1989, are protected by copyright. For these works, they can consider the options identified in this book for making these works lawfully available via the reserve services they offer.

For works created prior to March 1, 1989, staff can perform an analysis to determine whether the work is in the public domain, but these determinations are not always as straight forward as one might hope. For example, an instructor teaching an American literature class may request that *The Wonderful Wizard of Oz*, written by L. Frank Baum, be made available via reserve services for their students. This book was published in the United States in 1900 and the original published text and illustrations found in it are in the public domain in the United States (see Figure 5.1).

If the library owned an original copy of this book, its public domain status means they could scan it in its entirety and make it available for students to access, download, and share via electronic reserves. However, most libraries will likely have newer editions of this title in their collection, as a variety of new editions have been published in the past decides and these editions may have new, copyrightable components added to them that are eligible for copyright protection. This could include an introduction written by a notable scholar who specializes in American literature, new illustrations, and new cover art. Staff could still scan and post in its entirety the original text of *The*

Figure 5.1 The copyright page from the first edition of The Wonderful Wizard of Oz. This image is in the public domain due to its term of copyright protection expiring.

Wonderful Wizard of Oz found in these edition to an electronic reserve platform, but they would need to consider alternate reuse options (e.g., fair use, obtaining permission, or obtaining a license) for the parts of the new edition that are copyrightable. Barring situations where staff can be confident that a requested work is in the public domain, they may wish to proceed under the assumption that a work is fully protected by copyright and then consider exercising user rights found in U.S. copyright law, such as those discussed in the following chapters, for making the work available via reserve services.

RECOMMENDED RESOURCES

Is it in the Public Domain? A Handbook for Evaluating the Copyright Status of a Work Created in the United States Between January 1, 1923 and December 31, 1977 was created on behalf of the Samuelson Law, Technology and Public Policy Clinic at the University of California, Berkeley, School of Law by Menesha A. Mannapperuma, Brianna L. Schofield, Andrea K. Yankovsky, Lila Bailey, and Jennifer M. Urban. It is a valuable resource for performing in-depth determinations of the copyright status of a work and can be found online at https://www.law.berkeley.edu/files/FINAL_PublicDomain_Handbook_FINAL(1).pdf. Users will need to modify the dates found in the handbook slightly based the advancing public domain date in the United States.

The USCO's Circular 22, *How to Investigate the Copyright Status of a Work*, also provides quality information that can be used to learn more about this topic. It includes information about performing searches of USCO's renewal records or utilizing their staff to perform these searches (for which a fee is charged). This circular can be found online at https://www.copyright.gov/circs/. Project Gutenberg is an online library with more than 60,000 books that are made freely available as they are in the public domain in the United States. If staff suspect a title that has been requested for reserve is in the public domain, they can check the Project Gutenberg library to see if it is listed there: https://www.gutenberg.org/catalog/. If it is, staff can save time by providing the instructor and students with a link to the full text work, instead of having to make new scans themselves. Staff can also use the public domain search feature of Google Books to identify works that are in the public domain and share them via electronic reserve services: https://books.google.com/.

CHAPTER SIX

Section 107: Fair Use

In Sections 107 through 122, Congress establishes limitations that exclusive rights granted under Section 106 are subject to. These user rights (which are also referred to as exceptions or exemptions) allow "the public to make limited uses of copyrighted works—uses that might otherwise constitute infringement—especially for advancing knowledge or serving other important social objectives" (Crews 2020, 95). Some of these user rights can be taken advantage of when providing reserve services. The fair use right found in Section 107 may be the best known of these user rights, and one of the most flexible. This statue reads:

> Notwithstanding the provisions of sections 106 and 106A, the fair use of a copyrighted work, including such use by reproduction in copies or phonorecords or by any other means specified by that section, for purposes such as criticism, comment, news reporting, teaching (including multiple copies for classroom use), scholarship, or research, is not an infringement of copyright. In determining whether the use made of a work in any particular case is a fair use the factors to be considered shall include—
>
> (1) the purpose and character of the use, including whether such use is of a commercial nature or is for nonprofit educational purposes;
> (2) the nature of the copyrighted work;
> (3) the amount and substantiality of the portion used in relation to the copyrighted work as a whole; and
> (4) the effect of the use upon the potential market for or value of the copyrighted work.

> The fact that a work is unpublished shall not itself bar a finding of fair use if such finding is made upon consideration of all the above factors.
> (17 U.S.C. § 107)

While some user rights found in U.S. copyright law provide an exception only to certain exclusive rights granted to a rightsholder (e.g., the exception to the right of distribution found in the first sale doctrine), fair use can be considered when looking to exercise any of the exclusive rights found in Section 106, including the right of reproduction, distribution, the creation of derivative works, and public performances or displays. This is one of the reasons fair use is an extremely useful right for libraries seeking to make services and resources available for their patrons.

Making a fair use determination involves working through the four factors found in the statute to determine if the use might be considered fair or infringing. In the sections below, considerations tied to each of the four factors of fair use will be explored within the context of reserve services.

The First Factor of Fair Use

This factor requires users to consider "the purpose and character of [their] use, including whether such use is of a commercial nature or is for nonprofit educational purposes" (17 U.S.C. § 107[1]).

Purpose and Character of Reserve Uses

Reserve services provide instructors and students with access to required and supplementary learning materials in support of the educational mission of the library and the academic institution. This purpose aligns closely with the purpose of copyright, that is, "to promote the Progress of Science and useful Arts" (U.S. Const. art. I, § 8, c8). Educational resources made available through reserve services also closely align with the language of Section 107 that states that fair uses can include works being used "for purposes such as criticism, comment, news reporting, teaching (including multiple copies for classroom use), scholarship, or research" (17 U.S.C. § 107).

Commercial Versus Nonprofit Use

Section 107(1) specifically identifies "nonprofit educational purposes" as an important consideration when evaluating the first factor of fair use. Indeed, in the case of *Diversey v. Schmidly* (738 F.3d 1196 [10th Cir. 2013]) the court stated that the distribution of works by libraries with "a non-commercial, educational purpose [is] at the heart of the protection for fair use"

(1203). As most libraries offering reserve services will be part of nonprofit educational institutions, the first factor will often weigh strongly in their favor. However, it is important to note that "the mere fact that a use is educational and not-for-profit does not insulate it from a finding of infringement, any more than the commercial character of a use bars a finding of fairness" (Campbell v. Acuff-Rose Music 1994, 584). Numerous commercial uses have been found to be fair uses by the courts. In fact, SCOTUS tells us that "many uses Section 107 lists as paradigmatic examples of fair use, including criticism, comment, and news reporting, are generally conducted for-profit in this country, a fact of which Congress was obviously aware when it enacted Section 107" (Harper & Row v. Nation Enterprises 1985, 470). If a library looking to offer reserve services is affiliated with a for-profit academic institution they can still consider fair use, they will just need to do so understanding that their commercial nature could offset somewhat the more favorable view that nonprofit libraries and educational institutions might enjoy under the first factor.

Case Study: Transformative Uses and Course Reserves

Transformative uses of copyrighted works are often viewed very favorably under the first factor of fair use. Pierre Leval, Senior United States Circuit Judge of the United States Court of Appeals for the Second Circuit, has provided a well-respected definition of transformative use. He says they are uses that are "productive and must employ the [copied portion of a work] in a different manner or for a different purpose from the original" (Leval 1990, 1111). For example, "a quotation of copyrighted material that merely repackages or republishes the original is unlikely to pass the [transformative] test . . . [as] it would merely 'supersede the objects' of the original [quoting Folsom v. Marsh (F.Cas. 342, 345 (C.C.D. Mass. 1841)]" (1111). However, if "the secondary use adds value to the original—if the [copied] matter is used as raw material, transformed in the creation of new information, new aesthetics, new insights and understandings—this is the very type of activity that the fair use doctrine intends to protect for the enrichment of society" (1111). Judge Leval cites examples of transformative uses, including those uses "criticizing the quoted work, exposing the character of the original author, proving a fact, or summarizing an idea argued in the original in order to defend or rebut it" (1111). It is not uncommon for works made available through reserve services to be employed by students and instructors in all of these ways as part of teaching, research, and in their creation of new scholarship. As such, it would seem that transformative uses can be considered under the first factor when looking to make copies of works available through reserve services. However, this is a point of contention between libraries and the courts, who have argued that such uses may not be transformative. In *Campbell v. Acuff-Rose Music* (510 U.S. 569 ([1994]), Justice Souter, writing the majority opinion of the SCOTUS, states that "the obvious statutory exception to this focus on transformative uses is the straight reproduction of multiple copies for classroom distribution" (579). In the case of *Cambridge Univ. Press v. Becker* (863 F. Supp. 2d 1190 [N.D. Ga. 2012]), better known as the Georgia State electronic reserves (e-reserves) case, a lawsuit was filed against Georgia State University (GSU) over their e-reserve practices. In this case, both the district court and the U.S, Circuit Court of Appeals for the Eleventh District stated that reserve uses were not transformative, with the court of appeals arguing that

> GSU's electronic reserve system are verbatim copies of portions of the original books which have merely been converted into a digital format. Although a professor may arrange these excerpts into a particular order or combination for use in a college course, this does not imbue the excerpts themselves with any more than a de minimis amount of new meaning . . . nor do Defendants use the excerpts for anything other than the same intrinsic purpose—or at least one of the purposes—served by Plaintiffs' works: reading material for students in university courses. (Cambridge Univ. Press v. Patton 2014, 1263)

It is worth noting, however, that the attorneys for GSU did not argue that the school's uses were transformative, focusing instead on their educational, nonprofit character. The courts' relatively hasty analysis of transformative use in this case may thus reflect the parties' failure to raise or vigorously defend the point. Transformativeness in teaching has been recognized by the courts in other cases. For example, in *Sundeman v. Seajay Society* (142 F.3d 194 [4th Cir. 1998]), the U.S. Court of Appeals for the Fourth Circuit ruled that a scholar's quotation from an unpublished manuscript outlining their critical analysis of the work as part of a lecture was transformative use. Butler (2015) outlines many other instances where transformativness may exist in educational uses, including:

- Using media about current events as problems or illustrations
- Teaching history with primary materials
- Using expressive works to teach theories and methods of critical thought and analysis
- Teaching with archival materials
- Teaching skills and methods with exemplars of good and bad practice
- Teaching technological tools and content manipulation skills using raw material from existing works
- Teaching lectures with third-party media

- Teaching themes, genres, or stylistic movements in music, film, or literature by assigning outside reading of exemplary works
- Assembling galleries, playlists, and other large collections of representative works to facilitate student exposure to genres, movements, styles, and other shared characteristics of expressive works

Readers should remember that while educational uses and transformative uses are often highly favored under the first factor of fair use, the other three factors must be taken into consideration as well. And, fortunately, the courts have said that "while a transformative use is generally more likely to qualify as fair use, 'transformative use' is not absolutely necessary for a finding of fair use" (Authors Guild v. HathiTrust 2014, 102).

The Georgia State e-reserves case will be explored in depth in a case study at the end of this chapter.

The Second Factor of Fair Use

The second factor of fair use asks users to consider "the nature of the copyrighted work" (17 U.S.C. § 107[2]) they are seeking to reuse. The SCOTUS tells us that "the law generally recognizes a greater need to disseminate factual works" (Harper & Row v. Nation 1985, 563) and, therefore, the sharing of works of nonfiction, biographies, textbooks, scholarly monographs, research articles, and documentary films may be viewed as favorable under the second factor. More creative works such as "works of fiction or fantasy" (563) can be considered when seeking to reuse works under fair use, but the courts do call "for recognition that some works are closer to the core of intended copyright protection than others, with the consequence that fair use is more difficult to establish when [they] are copied" (Campbell v. Acuff-Rose Music 1994, 586). Library staff will likely be asked by instructors to make both factual and creative works available via reserve services as both are used as part of course instruction. When more creative works are used, the second factor may be weighed as "neutral, or even weighed against fair use" (Cambridge Univ. Press v. Patton 2014, 81). However, this does not preclude the library staff from determining the use would be fair as no one factor is dispositive. Indeed, courts generally give very little weight to the second factor in the overall analysis.

Publication Status of the Work

Another consideration tied to the second factor is the publication status of the work being used. Generally, the use of published works is more likely to be viewed as fair. However, Section 107 tells us that "the fact that a work is unpublished shall not itself bar a finding of fair use if such finding is made upon consideration of all [four] factors." The courts have stated that an author does have a "right to control the first *public* appearance of his expression" (emphasis added) and that this right "encompasses not only the choice whether to publish at all, but also the choices of when, where, and in what form first to publish a work" (Harper & Row v. Nation 1985, 471). As a result, the unpublished nature of a work could weigh against findings of fair use if they preempt the first publication of the author. However, as access to copies of works made available via reserve services under the auspices of fair use are frequently only made available to a limited group of users (e.g., library patrons for copies circulated via print reserves and students enrolled in a specific course for electronic and media reserves), the impact of sharing unpublished works would not be as significant as if they were being made publicly available via the internet.

The Third Factor of Fair Use

The third factor of fair use requires users to think "not only about the quantity of the materials used, but about their quality and importance, too" (Campbell v. Acuff-Rose 1994, 587).

The Amount Used

Contrary to popular belief, "there are no absolute rules as to how much of a copyrighted work may be copied and still be considered a fair use. In some instances, copying a work wholesale has been held to be fair use . . . while in other cases taking only a tiny portion of the original work has been held unfair" (Maxtone-Graham v. Burtchaell 1986, 1263). Instructors may ask to make copies of entire works, such as a journal article or film, available to students via reserve services, or they may request for smaller sections of a work, such as a section from a book or a clip from a film, be made available for student use. How much of a work they need to make available to students will often be closely tied to the first factor of fair use, their purpose. When the amount used is appropriate to a purpose that the court has found to be legitimate (especially if the purpose is transformative), the court will tend to find that the third factor is at least neutral or perhaps even favorable to the use.

Courts also examine the amount used through the lens of the fourth factor, market effect. Here, courts will ask whether the amount made available is sufficient to "serve as an effectively competing substitute for the original, and might therefore diminish the original rights holder's sales and profits" (Authors Guild v. Google 2015, 29). In evaluating the amount used through this lens, a court may take into consideration the formats and licensing options typically used by a copyright holder. In cases where a work is only available for purchase as a complete text, the court may find that a modest excerpt does not provide a competing substitute. For example, in the GSU case, the court held that the excerpts at issue there were typically too small to substitute for a purchase of the complete work from which they were taken. However, in cases where the publisher had a robust licensing market in place, the court considered whether the excerpt was large enough to threaten their licensing revenues and weighed the factor against GSU.

The Fallacy of Limits on the Amount Used

Over time, myths and misconception regarding the third factor of fair use have been perpetuated in librarianship and academia. These include numerical limits on the amount of a work that can be reproduced and still be considered fair use. Many of these misconceptions stem from 'guidelines' put forward by various interest groups seeking to instruct users on how fair use determinations should be made. Crews (2001, 609) tells us that "negotiations in the mid-1970s gave rise to the first set of guidelines," the *Agreement on Guidelines for Classroom Copying in Not-For-Profit Educational Institutions with Respect to Books and Periodicals on the Issue of Photocopying for Classroom Handouts* [*Guidelines for Classroom Copying*], and soon after "came guidelines on making copies of musical works for education and later emerged guidelines on sending copies of journal articles for interlibrary loans and recording television broadcasts off-air for classroom use."

The *Guidelines for Classroom Copying* may the best known of all of these 'guideline' documents and, perhaps, the one that most often causes confusion when fair use is being utilized for reserve services. Among other things, the *Guidelines for Classroom Copying* limits the amount of a work that can be copied under fair use to specific, small amounts that are used in a spontaneous manner. A review of Section 107 shows that the law itself places no such limits, requirements, or prohibitions on fair use. Crews (2001, 664) emphasizes that "all of the guidelines fail any valid claim that they might have binding, legal authority. Congress never enacted them. No court ever has read them into law in a legal decision. From a source-based analysis, one can unequivocally conclude that the guidelines are not themselves binding on the public as a rule of law." The courts have also disputed the legal validity of the *Guidelines for Classroom Copying*. In the district court ruling from the district court in the GSU e-reserves case, Judge Orinda D. Evans stated that "the Court does not accept Plaintiffs' argument that the outcome on the third fair use factor should turn on what is in the Classroom Guidelines" (Cambridge Univ. Press v. Becker 2012, 1229) as "the Guidelines establish numerical caps on how many words a teacher may copy . . . which would preclude a use from falling within the safe harbor [of fair use] solely on the basis of the number of words copied, is not compatible with the language and intent of § 107" (59). The U.S. Circuit Court of Appeals for the Eleventh District's 2014 ruling on this case emphasized that the *Guidelines for Classroom Copying* "do not carry force of law" (Cambridge Univ. Press v. Patton 2014, 1273) and that "we must keep in mind that they . . . were drafted by partisan groups" (1246), not lawmakers, and that "to treat [them] as indicative of what is allowable [under Section 107] would be to create the type of 'hard evidentiary presumption' that the Supreme Court has cautioned against (quoting Campbell, 510 U.S. at 584, 114 S. Ct. at 1174 [quoting Sony, 464 U.S. at 455, n. 40, 104 S.Ct. at 795, n. 40])" (1273). Because of this, when working through the third factor of fair use, library staff should consider the "amount and substantiality of the portion used in relation to the copyrighted work as a whole" as the fair use statute directs, rather than using arbitrary guidelines.

The Fourth Factor of Fair Use

Those making fair use determinations are charged with determining if their reuse of a work "brings to the marketplace a competing substitute for the original" and, in the process, deprives "the rightsholder of significant revenues because of the likelihood that potential purchasers may opt to acquire the copy [being made available to them] in preference to the original" (Authors Guild v. Google, Inc. 2015, 205). An individual making a fourth factor analysis should also consider if "unrestricted and widespread conduct of the sort" they are engaging in "'would result in a substantially adverse impact on the potential market' for the original" (Campbell v. Acuff-Rose Music, Inc., [1994], 590, citing Nimmer § 13.05[A][4], p. 13102.61). For reserve services, the ability to license a work for use should be considered. In the GSU e-reserves case, the Circuit Court of Appeals for the Eleventh District stated that "if a copyright holder has not made a license available to use a particular work in a particular manner, the inference is that the author or publisher did not think that there would be enough such use to bother making a license available. In such a case, there is little damage to the publisher's market when someone makes use of the work in that way without obtaining a license, and hence the fourth factor should generally weigh in favor of fair use. This is true of Plaintiffs' works for which no license for a digital excerpt was available" (Cambridge University Press v. Patton 2014, 1277).

When licenses are available to use in a particular manner (e.g., reserve uses), this should be considered as part of the analysis performed for the fourth factor. In the GSU e-reserves case, the appellate court found that "the District Court properly took license availability into account in determining whether the fourth factor weighted for or against fair use" (1279). License availability may be especially important when an instructor asks that an entire work be made available to students via reserve services (e.g., an entire film, rather than film clips). However, "the ability to license does not demand a finding against fair use" (1276).

Out-of-Print Works

Instructors may ask that works that are out of print be made available for students to access via reserve services as they may not be readily available for students to acquire on their own. A Senate Report that accompanied the passage of the Copyright Act of 1976 states that "a key, *though not necessarily determinative*, factor in fair use is whether or not the work is available to the potential user. If the work is 'out of print' and unavailable for purchase through normal channels, the user may have more justification for reproducing it than in the ordinary case" (emphasis added) (S. Rep. No. 94-473, 64, 1975). Here, a work being out of print will not automatically make a use fair. Rather, its out-of-print status can weigh favorably when evaluating the fourth factor.

Using Fair Use for Reserve Services

When it comes to utilizing user rights found in U.S. copyright law to make works available via reserve services, library staff will find fair use to be the most flexible and, perhaps, the most useful. Fair use determinations must be made on a case-by-case basis. This means that each request submitted for reserves that involves making and distributing a copying of a work must be reviewed to determine if will falls within the scope of this user right. When making a fair use determination, library staff must consider each of the four factors outlined in the statute. However, these factors should not "be treated in isolation, one from another" (Campbell v. Acuff-Rose 1994, 578). Instead, each factor must "be explored, and the results weighed together, in light of the purposes of copyright" (578). Determinations of fair use should be made in good faith, with library staff being comfortable acknowledging when a particular use may not be considered fair. There are resources and tools that library staff can use to make thoughtful applications of fair use: two of the most well known and well respected ones are discussed next.

Code of Best Practices

The *Code of Best Practices in Fair Use for Academic and Research Libraries* (*Code*), developed by the Association of Research Libraries (ARL), the Center for Social Media (School of Communication) at American University, and the Program on Information Justice and Intellectual Property at the Washington College of Law at American University, is a resource that "enhances the ability of librarians to rely on fair use by documenting the considered views of the library community about best practices in fair use, drawn from the actual practices and experience of the library community itself" (ARL et al. 2012, 3). Like the various documents discussed earlier in this chapter, the *Code* does not carry the force of law. However, the *Code* differs substantially from the various 'guideline' documents in that:

- The 'guidelines' "often misinterpret fair use, infusing it with variables and conditions that are not part of the law" (Crews 2020, 132) such as the tests of 'brevity' and spontaneity.' The *Code* does not.
- The 'guidelines' "create rigidity in the application of fair use [e.g., using only 10% of a work], sacrificing the flexibility that allows fair use to have meaning for new needs, technologies, and materials" (132). Whereas the *Code* seeks to empower members of the library community in making thoughtful applications of the statute based upon the profession's mission and values.

Drafted after interviews and discussions with members of the library community, the *Code* identifies eight situations that represent a "current consensus about acceptable practices for the fair use of copyrighted materials" and how the right of fair use "should apply in certain recurrent situations" (ARL et al. 2012, 3). One of these situations includes "supporting teaching and learning with access to library materials via digital technologies" (13). The consensus among the profession is that "it is fair use [for libraries] to make appropriately tailored course-related content available to enrolled students via digital networks" (14). These digital networks can include electronic and media reserve platforms. It is critical for readers to understand that this does not mean that the making of any copyrighted work available via reserve services is a fair use. Rather, library professionals involved in the development of the *Code* argue that a strong argument for fair use can be made when the four factors are applied to these situations alongside limitations and enhancements the represent professional practices and values.

Limitations

Within the *Code*, limitations are identified "that should be observed to assure that the case for fair use is strong" (11) when libraries are providing access to materials that support teaching and learning via digital networks. For example, the *Code* states that libraries should only make materials available via digital networks when "there is a clear articulable nexus between the instructor's pedagogical purpose and the kind and amount of content involved" (14). Additionally, closer scrutiny should be applied to requests for "content created and marketed primarily for use in courses" such as "a textbook, workbook, or anthology designed for the course" (14). This is because the "use of more than a brief excerpt from such works on digital networks is unlikely to be transformative and therefore unlikely to be a fair use" (14). Libraries should also seek to provide "full attribution" for works they make available via such services "in a form satisfactory to scholars in the field." Not only does this provide acknowledgement to the original creator, but if a student is interested in engaging more fully with the work (e.g., reading the entire book a selection is taken from or watching an entire film after viewing a clip), then they will have the information they need to locate a copy.

Another limitation identified in the *Code* addresses who should have access to materials made available in these situations: "only eligible students and other qualified persons (e.g., professors' graduate assistants)" (14). Fortunately, most learning management systems (LMS) and commercial electronic and media reserve platforms allow library staff to easily limit access to works made available through these services to these groups in this way. Additionally, the availability of materials made available via these services "should be coextensive with the duration of the course or other time-limited use (e.g., a research project)" (14). Staff supporting reserve services can have a discussion with the instructor placing reserve requests to identify the duration of time works should be made available during an academic term to best support their pedagogical needs, and many LMS and commercial electronic and media reserve platforms have features that allow documents and films to be visible to students only for certain periods of time. Finally, "libraries should provide instructors with useful information about the nature and the scope of fair use, in order to help them make informed" decisions when placing requests (14). This can be done by having a well-crafted copyright policy for reserve services, a topic discussed in Part One. Libraries should also seek to provide students with "information about their rights and responsibilities regarding their own use of course materials" (14). This could be made available via a statement instructors place in their syllabus or as a note or announcement made available in the course's LMS page or via the commercial electronic or media reserve system.

Enhancements

The *Code* also includes enhancements, which are actions that, if taken, could further strengthen the case made for fair use. When providing access to materials that support teaching and learning via digital technologies,

> the case for fair use is enhanced when libraries prompt instructors, who are most likely to understand the educational purpose and transformative nature of the use, to indicate briefly in writing why particular material is requested, and why the amount requested is appropriate to that pedagogical purpose. An instructor's justification can be expressed via

> standardized forms [such as reserve request forms] that provide a balanced menu of common or recurring fair use rationales. In order to assure the continuing relevance of those materials to course content, libraries should require instructors of recurrently offered courses to review posted materials and make updates as appropriate. (ARL et al., 2012, 15)

Using the Code

While the section of the *Code* discussed here focuses on making works available to students and instructors via digital networks, which can include electronic and media reserve platforms, it can, with slight modifications, also provide guidance to library staff on making determinations of fair use when making photocopies from a work, such as a selection from a book, to circulate via print reserve services. For example, when placing print reserve requests libraries can "provide instructors with useful information about the nature and the scope of fair use, in order to help them make informed" decisions about the law (14). Information for students "about their rights and responsibilities regarding their own use of course materials" could be made available where print reserve materials are borrowed or via the library webpage (14). Some academic libraries choose to only may reserve items available for students to check out, rather than to anyone who may be visiting, such as community patrons. This practice could be seen as limiting access to materials to "eligible students and other qualified persons" (14). As discussed in Part One, staff supporting reserve services can consider if their workflow allows them to make works made available under fair use via reserve services available for "the duration of the course or other time-limited use" (14). Library staff can also consider only making materials available via print reserves under fair use when "there is a clear articulable nexus between the instructor's pedagogical purpose and the kind and amount of content involved," and give extra consideration to requests that require the copying and distribution of "content created and marketed primarily for use in courses" such as "a textbook, workbook, or anthology designed for the course" (14). Libraries can provide "full attribution, in a form satisfactory to scholars in the field" (14) for works they make available via print reserve under fair use by providing a full citation to the original work on the copy itself or on the folder or case containing the copied work.

Again, it is important to understand that adhering to the limitations and enhancements found in the *Code* does not mean that any work made available by libraries via digital networks is automatically considered to be a fair use. Library staff supporting reserve services still need to make a fair use determination on a case-by-case basis for requested works by working through the four factors found in the statute. However, the *Code* can help library staff identify common values and community practices in the field and use this information to make thoughtful applications of the law and demonstrate good faith in balancing the needs of instructors and students utilizing these services in balance with rights granted to creators.

Checklists

Checklists have also been developed to aid users in making thoughtful fair use determinations. Generally, these documents list the four factors and, under each factor, examples of actions that can be seen to weigh for and against fair use are provided. Perhaps the best known of these checklists is the *Fair Use Checklist* developed by Dr. Kenneth D. Crews, formerly of Columbia University, and Dwayne K. Buttler of the University of Louisville. This original version can be found on the Columbia University's Copyright Advisory Services website at https://copyright.columbia.edu/index.html. In 2020, Crews published a revised version of the checklist, which is reproduced here in Appendix B.

While theses checklists can help users thoughtfully work through a fair use determination, it is important to understand that it should not been seen as an exercise in checking bokes and seeing which side—those uses favoring fair use or those opposing fair use—has the most. Determinations of fair use must be made by deciding "whether the cumulative weight of the four factors favors or opposes fair use" (Crews 2020, 287). Checklists are most effective in helping users make fair use determinations when those complete them use a "reasonable perspective" (287) and their knowledge and understanding of the situation at hand (here, reserve access).

Putting It All Together

Fair use is a flexible user right that many people take advantage of daily without even being aware of it. For example, quoting a favorite author in a Tweet or integrating a third-party photograph into a meme they share via Facebook or Instagram. When providing reserve services, library staff can conscientiously consider fair use whenever an instructor asks them to make a copy of a work (print or digital) and make it available to students. Fair use determinations must be made on a case-by-case basis and involve working through the four factors found in the statute, weighing them against the facts of the situation and with each other. The flexibility found in the four factors is what allows this user right to be applicable to so many different situations. Library staff supporting reserve services can use quality resources and tools to help them make thoughtful applications of the law, including the *Code of Best Practices in Fair Use for Academic and Research Libraries* and fair use checklists. These resources provide "sources of guidance that [take them through] the reasoning process that goes into making . . . good and robust decisions about what is and isn't acceptable [fair use] practice . . . They aren't designed to proscribe, [and] they aren't designed to provide rules of thumb" (Jaszi et al., 2017, 8) like many of the 'guideline' documents that have been published about fair use do. If, after working through the four factors, it is determined that a particular use may not be fair, all is not lost. There are other options, including other user rights found in the law, that can be considered for making works available via reserve services as well as options for obtaining permission or a license for the use.

Case Study: The Georgia State E-Reserves Lawsuit

In 2008, three plaintiffs, Cambridge University Press, Oxford University Press, and Sage Publications, with financial backing from the Copyright Clearance Center and the Association of American Publishers filed suit against Carl V. Patton, the president of GSU (Patton retired in 2008 and Mark P. Becker replaced him in office and the lawsuit), and other university officials in the federal District Court for the Northern District of Georgia claiming they "had infringed copyrights held by Plaintiffs, publishing houses, by allowing unlicensed portions of Plaintiffs' copyrighted books to be posted electronically and made available electronically to students" via an electronic reserves system (Cambridge Univ. Press v. Becker 2012, 1201). The three publishers sought, among other things, an injunction forcing GSU to stop making excerpts available and an award of the attorneys' fees and court costs accrued in bringing suit against GSU, as is allowed under Section 505 of U.S. copyright law.

The case was litigated over 12 years, reaching a conclusion in late 2020 when Judge Orinda Evans filed a final order and declared GSU to be the prevailing party. Of the original 99 claims of infringement put forward by the publishers, Judge Evans ruled that only 10 of these were valid.

In her order, Judge Evans stated that the ""Defendants [GSU] are ORDERED AND DIRECTED to maintain copyright policies which are not inconsistent with the rulings of the United States Court of Appeals for the Eleventh Circuit in this case" and "to inform all Georgia State professors and other instructors in writing of these rulings" (Evans 2020, 13).

In her final order, Judge Evans decided not to make the plaintiffs pay GSU attorneys' fees and court costs despite finding GSU to be the prevailing party.

Readers are encouraged to review each of the opinions and orders issued in this case. All seven, along with links to articles and resources summarizing the case, can be found on this LibGuide developed by Laura Burtle, Associate Dean for the Georgia State University Library: https://libguides.law.gsu.edu/gsucopyrightcase. Key takeaways regarding fair use determinations for making items available for students and instructors via electronic reserves are identified below.

Factor One: The Purpose and Character of the Use

While "verbatim copying 'may be transformative so long as the copy serves a different function than the original work' (Citing Perfect 10, Inc. v. Amazon.com, Inc., 508 F.3d 1146, 1165 [9th Cir. 2007])" (Cambridge University Press v. Patton 2014, 1262), here, GSU's copying was found not to be transformative as "works posted on GSU's electronic reserve system are verbatim copies of portions of the original books which have merely been converted into a digital format" (1262) and though "a professor may arrange these excerpts into a particular order or combination for use in a college course, this does not imbue the excerpts themselves with any more than a de minimis amount of new meaning" (1262). However, as "Congress devoted extensive effort to ensure that fair use would allow for educational copying under the proper circumstances" and as "allowing latitude for educational fair use promotes the goals of copyright ["to promote the Progress of Science and useful Arts" (U.S. Const. art. I, § 8, c8)] the Circuit Court agreed with the District Court that the use of the book selections "for teaching purposes by a nonprofit, educational institution such as [GSU] favors a finding of fair use under the first factor, despite the non-transformative nature of the use" (1267). As such, libraries serving non-profit educational institutions can feel fairly comfortable arguing that when they make copies of works available via reserve services under the auspices of fair use the first factor will weigh in their favor so long as the material truly is being used for teaching purposes (as opposed to being used for students' entertainment).

Factor Two: The Nature of the Copyrighted Work

In her 2012 ruling, Judge Evans noted that "none of the books at issue are fictional. All of them are intended to inform and educate," though some "are not merely descriptive; they contain material of an evaluative nature, giving the authors' perspectives and opinions" (Cambridge Univ. Press v. Becker 2012, 1223) and, therefore, found that "factor two favors [GSU] in this case" (1358). The Circuit Court disagreed with this somewhat, stating in its opinion that

> the District Court did err in holding that the second fair use factor—the nature of the copyrighted work—favors fair use in every case. *Though this factor is of comparatively little weight in this case* particularly because the works at issue are neither fictional nor unpublished, where the excerpts in question contained evaluative, analytical, or subjectively descriptive material that surpasses the bare facts, or derives from the author's own experiences or opinions, the District Court should have held that the second factor was neutral or even

weighed against fair use where such material dominated (emphasis added). (Cambridge Univ. Press v. Patton 2014, 1283)

The Circuit Court's statement that those works that include more creative components may move an analysis of the second factor to a more neutral position or may even weigh as unfair should be kept in mind by library staff making fair use determination, but they should also recognize that that the courts do not give this factor much weight in their analysis, perhaps in recognition that a variety of works many legitimately be used for teaching.

Factor Three: The Amount and Substantiality of the Portion Used

Here, perhaps the most important lesson for libraries is that both courts set aside the *Guidelines for Classroom Copying*, stating that they are "not compatible with the language and intent of § 107" (Cambridge Univ. Press v. Becker 2012, 1229) and that they "do not carry force of law" (Cambridge Univ. Press v. Patton 2014, 1273). Instead of relying on the arbitrary limits of brevity, spontaneity, and cumulative effect set forth by the *Guidelines for Classroom Copying*, when working through the third factor of fair use for reserve requests library staff should consider "the amount and substantiality of the portion used in relation to the copyrighted work as a whole" (17 U.S.C. § 107). It will also be helpful for them to keep in mind that the third factor "is intertwined with the first factor" (Cambridge Univ. Press v. Patton 2014, 1271), and when analyzing the two together users should determine if the amount taken is "excessive in relation to [the] pedagogical purpose." The fourth factor of fair use, the effect on the market may also impact an analysis of the third factor if the amount taken is "excessive in light of the educational purpose of the use" and, as a result, poses a "threat of market substitution" (1275).

Factor Four: The Effect upon the Potential Market

In the GSU case, the Circuit Court "agree[d] with the District Court that the small excerpts [GSU] used do not substitute for the full books from which they were drawn" and, therefore, they "did not affect [the publishers'] actual or potential sales of books" (94, citing Cambridge Univ. Press v. Becker 2012, 1236). However, the availability of a license for the excerpt being used received special consideration. As mentioned earlier, the Circuit Court stated that "if a copyright holder has not made a license available to use a particular work in a particular manner, . . . there is little damage to the publisher's market when someone makes use of the work in that way without obtaining a license, and hence the fourth factor should generally weigh in favor of fair use" (1277). And while "the ability to license does not demand a finding against fair use" (1276), the Circuit Court noted that "where the evidence showed that there was a ready market for digital excerpts of a work . . . [at] the time of the purported infringements, the District Court found that there was small—due to the amount of money involved—but actual damage to the value of Plaintiffs' copyright" (1278) and, because of this, "the District Court also properly took into account that widespread use of similar unlicensed excerpts could cause substantial harm to the potential market . . . [and] held that the fourth factor weighed against a finding of fair use (1278). Given this, when considering fair use for making works available via reserve services, library staff will likely wish to determine if a license can be obtained for the excerpt in question and factor its availability (or lack thereof) into their fourth factor analysis.

While this case focused on GSU making excerpts of books available via its electronic reserve service, it is not unreasonable to argue that information about making fair use determinations found in this case can be applied to other reserve services, including print and media reserve. What the GSU case should not do is make libraries hesitant to offer or discontinue offering reserve services out of fear that they may be sued by the parties involved in this case. In addition to the importance of remembering the mission of libraries, as discussed in Chapter 14, it is important for library staff to recognize that many of "the big principles that the publishers were trying to gain" in filing this lawsuit against GSU "are all lost" (Smith, October 20, 2018). Smith correctly predicted that there were "no sweeping injunction[s]" issued in the case, "nor any broad assertion that e-reserves always require a license" (October 20, 2018) Instead, the case "continue[d] to chew over issues that seem less and less relevant" and, over time, "devolve into insignificance" especially as "library practices have evolved [since 2008], and publishing models [such as] open access and the movement toward OERs [open educational resources] have had a profound impact on the way course materials are provided to students." So, while the GSU e-reserves case can provide some guidance on reserve practices, libraries should not let fear of claims of infringement prevent them from exercising their fair use rights when providing these services.

CHAPTER SEVEN

Section 108: Reproduction by Libraries and Archives

Section 108 offers user rights to libraries and archives that can be considered when seeking to make copies of works available via print, electronic, and media reserves. Like other user rights, the rights granted to the creators of copyrightable works in Section 106 are subject to those granted in Section 108, allowing libraries and archives to make "uses that might otherwise constitute infringement—especially for advancing knowledge or serving other important social objectives" (Crews 2020, 95). While qualifying libraries and archives can take advantage of Section 108, in keeping this chapter aligned with the scope and spirit of this book the statute will frame the discussion of the stature using only the term 'libraries.'

Qualifying Libraries

The reproduction and distribution rights found in Section 108 allow qualifying libraries to, among other things:

- Make copies of unpublished works "for purposes of preservation and security or for deposit for research use in another library" (17 U.S.C. § 108[b])
- Make copies of published works "for the purpose of replacement of a copy or phonorecord that is damaged, deteriorating, lost, or stolen, or if the existing format in which the work is stored has become obsolete" (17 U.S.C. § 108[c])

- Make, distribute, display, or perform copies of published works "for purposes of preservation, scholarship, or research" (17 U.S.C. § 108[h][1]) during the last 20 years of its term of protection

To take advantage of the rights found in Section 108, libraries must meet the following requirements:

1. Reproductions and distributions of works must be made in a way that provide no "direct or indirect commercial advantage" (17 U.S.C. § 108[a][1]) to the library or archive. As students and instructors are not charged for accessing copies of works made available through reserve services, academic libraries should easily be able to meet this requirement of the law. A library having nonprofit status or that is part of a nonprofit origination can also be viewed favorably here.
2. The library must be "open to the public" (17 U.S.C. § 108[a][2][i]) or make its collections "available not only to researchers affiliated with the library . . . or with the institution of which it is a part, but also to other persons doing research in a specialized field" (17 U.S.C. § 108[a][2][ii]). So long as an academic library makes its collections available to the public (and most do), they will qualify under this requirement. While not often encountered, some libraries (e.g., private or corporate libraries) do not make their collections open to the public, but they can still meet this requirement if they make their collections open "to other persons doing research in a specialized field" (17 U.S.C. § 108[a][2][ii]).
3. Copies made under Section 108 must include "a notice of copyright that appears on the copy or phonorecord . . . or [include] a legend stating that the work may be protected by copyright if no such notice can be found on the copy or phonorecord" (17 U.S.C. § 108[a][3]). For example, when making copies from a book under Section 108, the library should include the page where its copyright notice is found. For those works that do not have a copyright notice, Crews (2020, 170) tells us that the following statement is used by many libraries to meet the requirements of Section 108(a)(3): "Notice: This material is subject to the copyright law of the United States."

Options for making copies of works under Section 108 vary depending on the publication status of the work. Section 101 states that publication involves "the distribution of copies or phonorecords of a work to the public by sale or other transfer of ownership, or by rental, lease, or lending," that "the offering to distribute copies or phonorecords to a group of persons for purposes of further distribution, public performance, or public display, constitutes publication," and that "a public performance or display of a work does not of itself constitute publication." For example, a book is published when copies of the work are distributed online or in book-stores. A newspaper is distributed when copies are sold at newsstands or delivered to subscribers' doorsteps. A song is distributed when print copies or phonorecords are sold (e.g., on sheet music or in .mp3 format). Software is distributed when copies are distributed by purchase or license, whether in CD-ROM format or online (provided that the copies are actually downloaded and not merely accessed online). (Compendium [Third] § 612.2)

An unpublished work is "a work for which publication, as defined in the Copyright Law, has not occurred" (Compendium [Third] Part VIII). For instance, private letters, diaries, manuscripts, and photographs that were donated to a library or archive and that have not otherwise been made available in a way that would constitute publication under the law are considered unpublished.

Making Copies of Unpublished Works

Section 108(b) allows libraries to make copies of unpublished works in two situations:

1. Libraries can make and distribute "copies or phonorecords of an unpublished work duplicated solely for purposes of preservation and security" (17 U.S.C. § 108[b]) so long as "the copy or phonorecord reproduced is currently in the collections of the library" (17 U.S.C. § 108[b][1]).
2. Libraries may obtain a copy of an unpublished work held in the collection of another qualified library (one that meets the requirement found in Section 108[a][2]) for "deposit for research use" in their collection. For example, a library may have received a donation of unpublished manuscripts from a notable author. An instructor teaching a literature class may be interested in having their students review the manuscripts and asks if their library can obtain copies. Section 108(b) allows staff to ask the library that holds the manuscripts to make copies for them to add to their collection.

Both of these options have applications for reserve services.

Print Reserve Applications of Section 108(b)

Section 108(b) could be utilized if an instructor asks the library to circulate via print reserves an unpublished work held in their collection that is fragile or deteriorating. In this situation, a physical copy of the work could be made available to students for check-out instead of lending the original. Alternately, if the library is asked to make a unique or rare unpublished item they hold in their collection available to students via print reserve, a physical copy could be made under this exception to ensure the security of the original.

Electronic and Media Reserve Applications of 108(b)

Section 108(b)(2) allows digital copies of unpublished works to be made for preservation and security purposes so long as the digital copy "is not otherwise distributed in that format and is not made available to the public in that format outside the premises of the library." Depending on the library's interpretation of the term premises, these copies could be made available via electronic and media reserves.

What is a premises? The law does not provide a definition of the term premises, so library staff and administrators will want to work with their legal counsel to determine how they will interpret this word. Some libraries make a strict interpretation of it, allowing digital copies of work made under Section 108(b) to only be accessed inside the building where the original work is held. Other institutions, viewing all campus libraries as being interconnected, allow digital copies made under Section 108(b) to be accessed from inside any of their libraries. Under these two interpretations of the word premises, works digitized under Section 108(b) could be made available via electronic and media reserve services, though the library would need to inform users that they had to visit a campus library to access them.

Some libraries believe that their patrons enter a virtual library premises when they use credentials issued by the academic institution to access services and resources the library offers online, including digital collections. Under this interpretation of the word premises, libraries make works digitized under Section 108(b) available online but require users to log in to view them in order to verify that they are currently affiliated with the academic institution. Libraries interpreting the word this way could argue that works digitized under Section 108(b) could be made available via electronic and media reserve services so long as instructors and students were required to log into the system to access them.

Making Copies of Published Works

Section 108(c) allows libraries to make copies of published works, in whole or in part, for the purpose of replacement of a copy or phonorecord that is damaged, deteriorating, lost, or stolen" or if the existing format in which the work is stored has become obsolete"

Section 108(c)(2) tells us that "for purposes of this subsection, a format shall be considered obsolete if the machine or device necessary to render perceptible a work stored in that format is no longer manufactured or is no longer reasonably available in the commercial marketplace."

Section 108(c)(2) requires that, in both situations, the library put forth a reasonable effort to determine "that an unused replacement cannot be obtained at a fair price" before they make a copy. In performing a search for a replacement copy it could be argued that a reasonable effort would involve checking the market outlets and vendors the library normally peruse when looking to acquire a new item for their collection. Staff could also check with online sellers like Amazon, Barnes and Noble, and eBay to see if they have an unused copy of the work in question available for sale. The law does also not tell us what might constitute a fair price, but it may be considered reasonable to argue that, generally, it might not be much more than the original list price of the work.

Print Reserve Applications of 108(c)

As mentioned in Chapter 2, it is not uncommon for works circulated via print reserves to receive excessive wear-and-tear from use. For instance, books being circulated via print reserves may have pages removed or be lost or stolen by users. Under Section 108(c) libraries may make full replacement copies of these works if they are lost or stolen, or make copies of the missing pages to bind into their original copy of a book. Here replacements could be obtained in one of two ways. For example, if pages are missing from a book the library could order replacement pages via interlibrary loan, or they could request a physical copy of the book from consortia partners or via interlibrary loan and make the replacement copies of the pages themselves.

The option to make copies of works in obsolete formats may be especially useful for libraries when instructors ask that older media works be made available via print reserves. For example, many libraries have extensive collections of VHS (video home system) tapes. In July 2016, it was reported that "Japan's Funai Electric, a company that claims to be the last manufacturer of videocassette recorders (VCRs), will manufacture its last VHS player this month" (Hodak). A search of many major electronics websites will show that VCRs are becoming harder to find for sale commercially, making it difficult for libraries to replace players they own when they break. Some may argue that VCRs can be purchased secondhand, but a Senate report published in 1998 tells us that under the "reasonably available in the commercial marketplace" found in Section 108(c)(2), "if the needed machine or device can only be purchased in secondhand stores, it should not be considered "reasonably available'" (S.R. Rep. No. 105-190, 62, 1998). Together, this information can help support a reasonable argument that VHS are tapes obsolete under the definition provided in Section 108(c)(2). However, technology to play DVDs (Digital Video Discs) is still readily available on the market. Therefore, libraries may wish to make DVD copies of VHS tapes to circulate via print reserve. Under Section 108(c), staff should first perform a reasonable search to see if an unused DVD copy of a requested film is available for purchase at a reasonable price. If it is, the library will want to consider acquiring it for patrons to use. However, if no unused copy of the work can be found for sale at a reasonable price, then the library can make a DVD copy of the work to circulate to via print reserve.

Electronic and Media Reserve Applications of 108(c)

When looking to make copies of works for electronic or media reserves, staff may find the item on the shelf but discover it has been damaged. For instance, a DVD may be scratched, causing skips or sticks in the performance of the film when staff are trying to make a copy of the requested portion of the work to make available via media reserve. So long as an unused replacement copy of the disc cannot be purchased at a reasonable price, Section 108(c) would also allow staff to make a physical replacement copy of the DVD from a nondamaged copy so they can then copy the requested portion without error to make available via media reserves. Such copies do need to be made in compliance with the Digital Millennium Copyright Act, a topic that is discussed in Chapter 10.

Digital copies of obsolete works can also be made under Section 108(c). However, like Section 108(b)(2), these copies must "not made available to the public in that format outside the premises of the library . . . in lawful possession of such copy" (17 U.S.C. § 108[c][2]). The library's ability to make these digital copies available via electronic and media reserve will depend on their interpretation of the word premises, a topic discussed in the preceding section on making copies of unpublished works under Section 108(b).

Circulating Copies of Published Works in the Last 20 Years of Their Term of Copyright

Section 108(h) states that "during the last 20 years of any term of copyright of a published work, a library . . ., including a nonprofit educational institution that functions as such, may reproduce, distribute, display, or perform in facsimile or digital form a copy or phonorecord of such work, or portions thereof, for purposes of preservation, scholarship, or research." This right could provide an opportunity for libraries to connect patrons with access to qualifying works via reserve services. However, the law sets forth three terms under which libraries cannot utilize Section 108(h). They are: "(A) the work is subject to normal commercial exploitation; (B) a copy or phonorecord of the work can be obtained at a reasonable price; or (C) the copyright owner or its agent provides notice pursuant to regulations promulgated by the Register of Copyrights that either of the conditions set forth in subparagraphs (A) and (B) applies" (7 U.S.C. §108[h]).

Staff could perform a search of vendors and other online websites to see if a work they are looking to make available under Section 108(h) is subject to the terms outlined in Sections 108(h)(2)(A) and 108(h)(2)(B). The requirement found in Section 108(h)(2)(C) may appear to be more troublesome; however, a report put forward by the Registrar of Copyrights in 2017 states that "as of the date of this report, no rightsholder has ever filed such a notice with the Copyright Office (Weston et al. 2017, 44). Nevertheless, libraries can contact the U.S. Copyright Office by email or at Library of Congress, U.S. Copyright Office—NLA, 101 Independence Avenue SE., Washington, DC 20559-6000—to see if such a notice has been filed for the work in question.

Print Reserve Applications of 108(h)

For print reserves, the rights granted under Section 108(h) may prove valuable if the library is interested in making a copy of qualifying works via print reserve.

Electronic and Media Reserve Applications of 108(h)

Section 108(h) allows for the creation and distribution of digital copies of qualifying works that could made available via electronic and media reserves or even the library's catalog so that other users can discover them.

RECOMMENDED RESOURCE

Sonny Bono Memorial Collection. The Internet Archive (IA), a nonprofit archive dedicated to "building a digital library of Internet sites and other cultural artifacts in digital form" (Internet Archive 2017), has been taking advantage of Section 108(h) to make eligible copies of works publicly available online for users. When libraries are considering taking advantage of Section 108(h) to make copies of works available via reserve services, they may wish to first check this collection to see if the work is available there. If it is, providing users with a link to this copy will save staff time in in making a copy themselves. The collection can be found online at: https://archive.org/details/last20?tab=collection.

Limitation and Special Considerations for Sections 108(b), 108(c), and 108(h)

There are a few considerations associated with these three sections of the law that staff should be familiar with when looking to utilize them.

Qualified Works

The reproduction and distribution of some types of works, (e.g., musical works; pictorial, graphic, or sculptural works; a motion picture or other audiovisual works) are not allowed under some sections of Section 108.

Fortunately, "no such limitation shall apply with respect to rights granted by subsections (b), (c), and (h)" (17 U.S.C. § 108[i]), which are the three subsections that may be applicable to reserve use.

Number of Copies

The number of copies that can be made under Sections 108(b) and 108(c) are limited to three. This includes both print and digital copies. Section 108(h) places no such specific limits on the number of copies a library can make, though Section 108(g) states that "the rights of reproduction and distribution under this section extend to the isolated and unrelated reproduction or distribution of a single copy or phonorecord of the same material on separate occasions." Staff can make multiple copies of a work over time so long as employees are not aware of or have no "substantial reason to believe that [they are] engaging in the related or concerted reproduction or distribution of multiple copies or phonorecords of the same material, whether made on one occasion or over a period of time, and whether intended for aggregate use by one or more individuals or for separate use by the individual members of a group" (17 U.S.C. § 108[g][1]).

Contractual Limitations Still Apply

Section 108(f)(4) states that nothing in Section 108 "in any way affects . . . any contractual obligations assumed at any time by the library . . . when it obtained a copy or phonorecord of a work in its collections." This means that libraries will not be able to take advantage of the rights granted in Section 108 if they have entered into some type of enforceable agreement that prohibits them from doing so. Libraries should carefully read all contracts and licenses put forward by vendors as they are licensing or acquiring works for their collection and, should language be found that would curb rights they would otherwise have under U.S. copyright law, negotiate to have them removed from the agreement.

The Fair Use Savings Clause

Section 108 will not address all of the library's needs when it comes to making copies of works for services it provides, including reserves. Fortunately, libraries are not bound to utilizing Section 108 only. Libraries can consider fair use for making and distributing copies of works via reserve services, even when the use is similar to one permitted by 108, a fact made clear in Section 108(f)(4), which states that nothing in Section 108 "in any way affects the right of fair use as provided by section 107."

Putting It All Together

Section 108 is somewhat more limited in scope that other user rights, such as fair use. However, it can still play a critical role in making copies of protected works lawfully available to students via reserve services. In order to ensure their compliance with the requirements outlined in the various section of Section 108, the staff supporting reserve services will want to work with administrators and legal counsel to determine how they wish to interpret text found in the statute (for instance, the term premises), and then develop workflows or checklists to guide them working through applications of Section 108 as part of the reserves processing workflow.

Case Study: Making Copies of Works Obtained Through Interlibrary Loan Available via Reserve Services

Interlibrary loan (ILL) services play a critical role in supporting the information needs of patrons. Frequently, ILL requests are submitted by patrons for copies of works their library does not own. In these situations, staff identify another library that owns the item and request that they lend their physical copy of the work (e.g., a book, CD, or DVD) to them to circulate to their patron, or ask that they make a physical (e.g., a photocopy) or digital copy such as a PDF (portable document format) of the work that can be given to their patron. ILL services are somewhat outside the scope of this book: however, as it is not unusual for instructors to ask if materials obtained through ILL can be placed on reserve, it can be prudent for readers to have an understanding of the sections of U.S. copyright law relevant to them.

Section 108 and ILL

Section 108 allows qualified libraries to make physical and digital copies of works for other libraries' patrons to fulfill ILL requests. Here, library staff must offer the service in compliance with the rules outlined in subsections (d), (e), (g), and (i).

Under Sections 108(d) and 108(e), a library or archive can make a copy of a work to send to users "of another library." Section 108(d), allows libraries to make and distribute "no more than one article or other contribution to a copyrighted collection or periodical issue, or to a copy or phonorecord of a small part of any other copyrighted work" to users at other libraries. Section108(e) allows libraries to make a copy of an entire work in their collection, or "a substantial part of it," for users at other libraries so long as they have determined "on the basis of a reasonable investigation, that a copy or phonorecord of the copyrighted work cannot be obtained at a fair price."

Both of these sections require that:

(1) "[T]he copy or phonorecord becomes the property of the user" (17 U.S.C. § 108[d][1]; 17 U.S.C. § 108[e][1]).
(2) "[T]he library . . . has had no notice that the copy or phonorecord would be used for any purpose other than private study, scholarship, or research" (17 U.S.C. § 108[d][1]; 17 U.S.C. § 108[e][1]).
(3) "[T]he library . . . displays prominently, at the place where orders are accepted, and includes on its order form, a warning of copyright in accordance with requirements that the Register of Copyrights shall prescribe by regulation" (17 U.S.C. § 108[d][2]; 17 U.S.C. § 108[e][2]), the text of which can be found in 37 C.F.R. § 201.14.

Limitations on the Types of Works That Can Be Copied

Section 108(i) limits the types of works that can be made available under Section 108(d) and 108(e). It tells us that "the rights of reproduction and distribution under [these sections] do not apply to a musical work, a pictorial, graphic or sculptural work, or a motion picture or other audiovisual work other than an audiovisual work dealing with news." However, it does allow for the copying of "pictorial or graphic works published as illustrations, diagrams, or similar adjuncts to works of which copies are reproduced or distributed in accordance with subsections (d) and (e)."

ILL Request Monitoring

When placing ILL requests on behalf of their patrons under Section 108, library staff must monitor their request practices to ensure that they do not "as their purpose or effect . . . substitute for a subscription to or purchase of such work" 17 U.S.C. § 108[g][2]). When it comes to determining whether ILL requests may be substituting for a subscription, some libraries choose to operate under the *Rule of Five*, "which permit[s] each requesting library up to five copies of articles from the most recent five years of each journal title to which it does not subscribe" (Library of Congress 1978, 128). The *Rule of Five* was put forward by the *Commission on New Technological Uses of Copyrighted Works* (CONTU), which was established by Congress in 1975 to discuss how the Copyright Act of 1976 should be revised to address the impact of "the new technologies of photocopying and computers on the authorship, distribution, and use of copyrighted works" (Library of Congress 1978, 1). Discussions included the making and distributing of copies of works via ILL, and the *Rule of Five* was included in the appendixes of the commission's *Final Report*. Despite its inclusion in this document, the *Rule of Five* holds no force of law. Section 108(g)(2) is law, and it requires only that libraries make sure their ILL borrowing does not exceed "such aggregate quantities as to substitute for a subscription to or purchase of such work." When it comes to reserve services, if instructors are consistently requesting articles from a particular journal title and then asking that those copies be shared with students, this could indicate a need for the library to obtain a subscription to the title. However, isolated and unrelated requests for copies from a particular journal title made over time would likely not meet this threshold, even if the instructor is interested in sharing copies with students.

Downstream Uses

Some libraries hesitate to make copies of works provided to instructors under Sections 108(d) or 108(e) available via reserve services as they believe that such copies can only be used for *private* "study, scholarship, or research" (17 U.S.C. § 108[d][1]; 17 U.S.C. § 108[e][1]). Here, the language of the statute is interpreted to mean that the copy is intended to be used only by the person who requested it for their own study, scholarly, and research purposes and not shared with others. Other libraries take a broader interpretation of the statutory language that allows the copy to be used for private study, *or* scholarship, *or* research purposes. As the purpose of reserve services is to make works available for teaching, research, and the creation of new scholarship, reserve uses would fall within the scope of this requirement. Library staff and administrators will need to determine how they wish to interpret this language found in Section 108(d)(1) and 108(e)(1). Should libraries choose the narrower interpretation, this only means they cannot make the particular copy the instructor received via ILL under Sections 108(d) and 108(e) available via reserves. In these situations, staff could request a copy of the work from another library under fair use, as it can also be considered for ILL requests. Fair use provides two unique advantages for ILL borrowing. It does not place restrictions on the types of works a library may copy and distribute, and it can apply even if the library has notice that the copy will be used for something other than private study, scholarship, or research Alternatively, the library could request a loan of the physical item and make the copy themselves under fair use.

Other 108 Considerations

The contractual provision limitation that is also found in Section 108(i) may come into play for copies of works an instructor is looking to make available to students via reserve services. For example, as an alternative to ILL lending, some libraries might choose to purchase a copy of an article directly from the journal publisher or through the Copyright Clearance Center's *Get it Now* service. Such purchases often come with their own terms and conditions, and while the library may be acting within the scope of the license to provide the instructor with the copy for their own personal use, the license may prohibit the making of additional copies of the work or sharing copies with others. In these situations, neither the library nor the instructor could provide copies of the work to students.

Libraries will want to carefully review such terms before acquiring copies of works these ways and decide whether they and the patron receiving the copy are willing and prepared to abide by them.

ILL Requests for Physical Works

As mentioned at the beginning of this case study, for some ILL requests staff may ask another library to loan them their physical copy of a work (e.g., a book, CD, or DVD) to circulate to their patron. Under the first sale doctrine found in Section 109 of U.S. copyright law, a library may loan their lawfully made copy of a work to another library without fear of claims of copyright infringement (a topic that is discussed in depth in Chapter 8). However, many libraries do not allow instructors to place physical copies of works obtained via ILL or consortia lending on print reserve. Instead, libraries often acquire their own copy of the work or see whether the instructor can lend to them or donate their personal copy of the work to circulate to students.

Using Section 108 for Course Reserves

Section 108 offers options for libraries to connect their patrons with resource via ILL lending, but with some restrictions, and library staff will need to work with administrators and their institution's legal counsel to determine what answer they will give to instructors who ask if they can make copies of works they received under Section 108 available to students via reserve services. When offering ILL services, it is important for staff to remember there are a variety of user rights found in the law that can be used to obtain works from other libraries, including fair use and Section 109. To ensure maximum flexibility in providing ILL services, the library's ILL copyright policy may simply state that requests will be fulfilled in compliance with U.S. copyright law. This will allow the staff to choose from the different user's rights available to them when placing requests on behalf of their patrons, with implications for potential downstream uses in mind.

CHAPTER EIGHT

Section 109: The First Sale Doctrine

Section 109, which is often referred to as the first sale doctrine, is a limitation on the exclusive right of distribution granted to rightsholders under Section 106(3) and permits copies of copyrighted works to be transferred to others in a variety of ways.

Section 109(a) reads, in part, "[N]otwithstanding the provisions of section 106(3), the owner of a particular copy or phonorecord lawfully made under this title, or any person authorized by such owner, is entitled, without the authority of the copyright owner, to sell or otherwise dispose of the possession of that copy or phonorecord." Under Section 109, rightsholders are able to control only the first distribution of their copyrightable works. When lawfully made copies have been acquired by someone (e.g., an instructor) or by an entity (e.g., a library), they are free to make subsequent distributions of the work, such as lending it to others or reselling it. Most physical copies of works circulated by libraries, including books and Digital Video Discs (DVDs), will be made legally available to patrons under Section 109. This section of the law also allows patrons to donate copies of works they own to the library, and it allows libraries to sell copies of discarded works to patrons through book sales, all without having to obtain permission from or paying a fee to the rightsholder. As the copyright owner's rights to control the distribution of works is limited by Section 109 to the first sale of the work only, this section of the law is also sometimes referred to and the *exhaustion of rights* granted under Section 106(3).

Section 109(2)(b)(1)(A) addresses the right of first sale for sound recordings of musical works (e.g., songs recorded on a compact disc [CD]). It states that "in the case of a sound recording in the musical works embodied therein, neither the owner of a particular phonorecord nor any person in possession of a particular copy . . . may, for the purposes of direct or indirect commercial advantage, dispose of, or authorize the disposal of, the possession of that phonorecord or computer program . . . by rental, lease, or lending." Technically this would mean that libraries are unable to circulate such works to patrons. However, the statute goes on to state that this language does not "apply to the rental, lease, or lending of a phonorecord for nonprofit purposes by a nonprofit library or nonprofit educational institution" (17 U.S.C. § 109(2)[b][1][A]).

Under the first sale doctrine, physical works such as books, DVDs, Blu-rays, and CDs that have been lawfully made can be circulated by the library via print reserve with no infringement considerations. This includes circulating multiple copies of works. A common misconception regarding print reserve services is that only a single copy of a work can be circulated to students or that only one copy can be made available via print reserve for every 15 students enrolled in a course. Both of these arbitrary limits hold no force of law, especially when it comes to application of the first sale doctrine. In the same way that public libraries serving large communities may have hundreds of print copies of a popular reading title or a newly released DVD in its collection to meet patron demand for it, so too can academic libraries circulate an unlimited number of lawfully made print copies of works to students via print reserves.

Case Study: Circulating Copies of Computer Programs

Section 109(2)(b)(1)(A) addresses the right of first sale for computer programs, saying:

> Notwithstanding the provisions of subsection (a), unless authorized by the owners of copyright . . . in a computer program (including any tape, disk, or other medium embodying such program) . . . any person in possession of a particular copy of a computer program . . . may [not], for the purposes of direct or indirect commercial advantage, dispose of, or authorize the disposal of, the possession of that . . . computer program by rental, lease, or lending, or by any other act or practice in the nature of rental, lease, or lending (17 U.S.C. § 109[2][b][1][A]).

It is rare for libraries to lend copies of computer programs to patrons anymore as most software is now downloaded directly from the internet and is frequently licensed to individual users. However, if a library is asked to circulate a copy of software via print reserves, they can do so under Section 109(b)(2)(1)(A), as it goes on to state that "nothing in [Section 109(b)(2)(1)(A)] shall apply to the lending of a computer program for nonprofit purposes by a nonprofit library." There are, however, requirements outlined here that libraries must follow. Section 109(b)(2)(1)(A) states that "each copy of a computer program which is lent by such library [must have] affixed to the packaging containing the program a warning of copyright in accordance with requirements that the Register of Copyrights shall prescribe by regulation." These requirements can be found in Section 201.24 of Chapter 37 of the *Code of Federal Regulations*. As of the writing of this book (2022), the required notice reads as follows:

> **Notice: Warning of Copyright Restrictions**
>
> The copyright law of the United States (title 17, United States Code) governs the reproduction, distribution, adaptation, public performance, and public display of copyrighted material.
>
> Under certain conditions specified in law, nonprofit libraries are authorized to lend, lease, or rent copies of computer programs to patrons on a nonprofit basis and for nonprofit purposes. Any person who makes an unauthorized copy or adaptation of the computer program, or redistributes the loan copy, or publicly performs or displays the computer program, except as permitted by title 17 of the United States Code, may be liable for copyright infringement.
>
> This institution reserves the right to refuse to fulfill a loan request if, in its judgement, fulfillment of the request would lead to violation of the copyright law. (37 C.F.R. § 201.24[b])

Section 201.24(c) of Chapter 37 of the *Code of Federal Regulations* outlines how this notice should be affixed to computer programs, requiring that it "shall be affixed to the packaging . . . by means of a label cemented, gummed, or otherwise durably attached to the copies or to a box, reel, cartridge, cassette, or other container used as a permanent receptacle for the copy of the computer program. The notice shall be printed in such manner as to be clearly legible, comprehensible, and readily apparent to a casual user of the computer program."

Libraries can take advantage of the first sale doctrine for circulating copies of computer programs to patrons so long as they follow the requirements outlined in the statute and so long as, when they acquired the copy of the computer program, they did not enter into a license that prohibits them from taking advantage of this right.

What Constitutes a Lawfully Made Copy of a Work?

The SCOUTS decision in the case of *Kirtsaeng v. John Wiley & Sons, Inc.* (Wiley) (568 U.S. 519 [2013]) helps us understand what constitutes a lawfully made work under the first sale doctrine. In this case, Supap Kirtsaeng, a student from Thailand studying in the United States, had "asked his friends and family in Thailand to buy copies of foreign edition English-language textbooks at Thai bookshops, where they sold at low prices, and mail them to him in the United States" (Kirtsaeng v. Wiley 2013, 527). He would then sell the copies, reimburse his friends and family for both the costs of the books and shipping expenses they incurred mailing them to him, and keep the profits for himself. Wiley, a textbook publisher, brought suit against Kirtsaeng for copyright infringement, claiming that, among other things, Kirtsaeng's importation and resale of copies of its textbooks infringed on their Section 106(3) right of distribution. This was because the textbooks Kirtsaeng was selling had been manufactured abroad and were only intended for sale overseas in specific countries, as indicated by notices printed by Wiley in the front of the books, such as the following notice on page vi in the 2008 Wiley International Student edition of J. Walker, *Fundamentals of Physics:*

> Copyright © 2008 John Wiley & Sons (Asia) Pte Ltd[.] All rights reserved. This book is authorized for sale in Europe, Asia, Africa, and the Middle East only and may be not exported [*sic*] out of these territories. Exportation from or importation of this book to another region without the Publisher's authorization is illegal and is a violation of the Publisher's rights. The Publisher may take legal action to enforce its rights. . . . Printed in Asia. (Kirtsaeng v. Wiley 2013, 526)

Both the district court and the United States Court of Appeals for the Second Circuit ruled in favor of Wiley, arguing that the words "lawfully made under this title" referred to works manufactured in the United States, not those manufactured abroad. The SCOTUS disagreed, stating that "both historical and contemporary statutory context indicate that Congress did not have geography in mind when writing the present version of § 109(a)" (Kirtsaeng v. Wiley 2013, 533). Justice Breyer, who wrote the majority opinion of the SCOTUS decision, explained that "the first two words of the phrase, 'lawfully made,' suggest an effort to distinguish those copies that were made lawfully from those that were not and the last three words, 'under this title,' set forth the standard of "lawful[ness]" (530) that means the work was made "'in accordance with' or 'in compliance with' the [U.S.] Copyright Act" (520). Therefore, a copyrightable work that is manufactured with authority of the rightsholder or their representative in a way that would grant them protection under U.S. copyright law will be considered lawfully made and subject to the first sale doctrine. This does include "copies of a copyrighted work lawfully made abroad" (525).

The Kirtsaeng case had far-reaching implications for libraries as it reinforces their right to circulate physical copies of works to patrons, including those manufactured abroad. If the SCOTUS would have upheld the decisions of the lower courts, then libraries would have found themselves in the position of having to obtain permission from rightsholders (and perhaps also paying a license fee) to circulate foreign-made works in their collections. Fortunately, the majority of the SCOTUS recognized that "reliance upon the 'first sale' doctrine is deeply embedded in the practices of [institutions], such as booksellers, libraries, museums, and retailers, who have long relied upon its protection" (Kirtsaeng v. Wiley 2013, 544). However, in response to the SCOTUS ruling in this case, rightsholders may pursue alternate means of restricting the first sale rights of users, such licensing works to libraries and individuals rather than selling them, a topic discussed in the *Section 109 and Licensed Resources* section of this chapter.

Case Study: Circulating Instructor's Personal Copies of Works on Print Reserve

Book publishers and film distributors may offer an instructor a gratis copy of a monograph, textbook, or documentary film to review, and instructors sometimes ask if they can donate these copies to the library to circulate to students. Under the first sale doctrine, instructors are free to donate their copy of lawfully made copies of works to the library, and the library may then loan it to others under the same statute.

Rather than donating a personal copy of a work to the library, instructors will sometimes ask that if they can lend the copy to the library for the duration of time they wish to make it available to students via print reserve. Section 109 states, "Notwithstanding the provisions of section 106(3), the owner of a particular copy or phonorecord lawfully made under this title, *or any person authorized by such owner*, is entitled, without the authority of the copyright owner, to sell or otherwise dispose of the possession of that copy or phonorecord" (emphasis added). In these situations, the library is being authorized by the owner of the copy to loan it on their behalf, so the circulation of the work is lawful.

Sometimes gratis copies of works that have been given to instructors have a notice printed on or inside it stating the work is for the instructor's personal use only and cannot be loaned, given, or sold to another. Smith (2014) tells us that "our courts have looked very unfavorably on licenses that attempt to curtail first sale, in cases as old as *Bobbs-Merril v. Straus* (1908) and as recent as *Kirtsaeng v. Wiley* (2012)." In the case of *Bobbs-Merrill Co. v. Straus* (210 U.S. 339 [1908]), book publisher Bobbs-Merrill had printed a notice inside copies of the book *The Castaway* that stated "the price of this book at retail is $1 net. No dealer is licensed to sell it at a less price, and a sale at a less price will be treated as an infringement of the copyright" (Bobbs-Merrill v. Straus 1908, 341). Isidor and Nathan Straus, who were partners at R. H. Macy & Company, purchased copies of the book wholesale and sold them for 89 cents. Bobbs-Merrill brought suit against the Straus' for copyright infringement, claiming that the "power to control further sales is given by statute to the owner of such a copyright in conferring the sole right to 'vend' a copyrighted book" (343). The SCOTUS disagreed, stating that "in our view the copyright statutes, while protecting the owner of the copyright in his right to multiply and sell his production, do not create the right to impose, by notice, such as is disclosed in this case, a limitation at which the book shall be sold at retail by future purchasers, with whom there is no privity of contract" (350). Essentially, this meant that because there was no enforceable contract or license between Bobbs-Merrill and the Straus's, the terms the publisher printed in the book were unenforceable.

In a similar case, *Universal Music Group (UMG) Recordings, Inc., v. Augusto* (558 F. Supp. 2d 1055 [2008]), the United States Court of Appeals for the Ninth Circuit upheld a ruling by the district court that the following notices UMG had printed on promotional music CDs were not enforceable:

> This CD is the property of the record company [UMG] and is licensed to the intended recipient for personal use only. Acceptance of this CD shall constitute an agreement to comply with the terms of the license. Resale or transfer of possession is not allowed and may be punishable under federal and state laws" or, in some cases "Promotional Use Only—Not for Sale. (UMG v. Augusto 2008, 328)

UMG had mailed promotional CDs "to individuals such as music critics and radio disc jockeys" (UMG v. Augusto 2008, 326). There had been "no prior agreement or request by the recipients to receive the CDs," and "UMG [did] not seek or receive payment for [them]" (327). UMG argued that "the statements on the discs and the circumstances of their distribution granted only a license to each recipient, not a transfer of ownership (or 'sale') of the copy" (327) and that UMG remained the owners of the discs. Troy Augusto obtained copies of these CDs from used record stores and sold many of them on eBay. UMG claimed that since the individuals who originally received the CDs from them were not owners, they did not enjoy a first sale right to sell them to Augusto, nor did the first sale doctrine cover his selling of the CDs to others. The court of appeals disagreed, stating that "because the record here is devoid of any indication that the recipients agreed to a license, there is no evidence to support a conclusion that licenses were established under the terms of the promotional statement" (336) and that as "UMG dispatched the CDs in a manner that permitted their receipt and retention by the recipients without the recipients accepting the terms of the promotional statements . . . UMG's distribution of the promotional CDs under the circumstances effected a sale (transfer of title) of the CDs to the recipients. Further sale of those copies was therefore permissible without UMG's authorization" (338).

Because of this, the mere printing of such notices on or inside of gratis copies of books, DVDs, or CDs sent to instructors by publishers and distributors will likely not be viewed as legally enforceable and prevent them from donating or loaning the copy to the library to circulate via print reserves. However, the courts do warn us that in situations where an individual or entity enters into a contract or license through which they sign away their first sale rights, then such terms may be enforceable, a concept that is explored in the next section of this chapter.

Limitations and Special Consideration for the First Sale Doctrine

While the first sale doctrine is a powerful right granted to users, there are some factors that limit its application that staff should be aware of.

Distribution Only

Sections 109(a) and 109(b) allow libraries to circulate copies of works to patrons; however, their scope is limited to distribution only. These two sections do not allow users to take advantage of others rights granted to rightsholders in Section 106, for example the right to make reproductions of a work in part or in total. Libraries may wish to photocopy and make available part of a work (e.g., a selection from a book or an article from an issue of a journal) to circulate via reserve services. When a library makes such copies, it must be under user rights found in U.S. copyright law, such as fair use, or done with the permission of the rightsholder.

Ownership

The first sale doctrine applies to an "owner of a particular copy or phonorecord . . . or any person authorized by such owner" (17 U.S.C. § 109[a]). It does not convey rights to "sell or otherwise dispose of the possession of that copy" to those who are not owners, such as a licensee. Remington argues that after the *Kirtsaeng v. Wiley* SCOTUS decision, the licensing model of acquisitions would likely increase "at the expense of the 'sale model' . . . so that copyright holders can more easily argue that first sale rights do not apply because the recipient of the copyrighted work is merely a 'licensee' of the work, not an 'owner'" (Jaszi et al. 2016, 37). He goes on to warn that "user interests now need to focus on whether an agreement is a license or sale, whether there are significant restrictions on a purchaser's ability to transfer a copyrighted work, and other use restrictions" (37). This concept is addressed in *UMG v. Augusto*. There, the United States District Court for the Central District of California stated that "particularly with regard to computer software, we have recognized that copyright owners may create licensing arrangements so that users acquire only a license to use the particular copy of software and do not acquire title that permits further transfer or sale of that copy without the permission of the copyright owner" (UMG v. Augusto 2008, 332).

Staff are more likely to run into such licensing and contractual restrictions when dealing with electronic works rather than physical copies of books, DVDs, Blu-rays, and CDs. Nevertheless, they should still be aware of purchases of physical copies of works that are being construed as a licensed acquisition rather than a sale.

Even in those situations where libraries are acquiring ownership of works, libraries can sign away their first sale rights as part of a contract or license agreement. This fact is also emphasized by the courts. For example, in the case of *Bobbs-Merrill Co. v. Straus* (210 U.S. 339 [1908]) Justice Day states that the question before them "is purely a question of statutory construction [as] there is no claim in this case of contract limitation, nor license agreement controlling the subsequent sales of the book" (Bobbs-Merrill v. Straus 1908, 350). This confirms that a valid contract or license agreement that bars the resale or redistribution of the work that a rightsholder and purchaser enter into could can trump rights they might otherwise have under the law. In contracts or licenses where such language exists, libraries should attempt to negotiate to have it removed.

Case Study: Digital First Sale

Even in those situations where an individual clearly owns a digital copy of a work, there are currently limits on how they may be able to resell it under the first sale doctrine. In the case of *Capitol Records LLC et al. v. ReDigi Inc. et al.* (934 F. Supp. 2d 640 [2013]), ReDigi is a company that created an online platform that allowed people to resell digital music files they has purchased from iTunes. Users downloaded ReDigi's Music Manager software to their computer, which identified music files the user had purchased from iTunes. As part of the reselling process, the Music Manager transferred the digital music file to ReDigi's servers and ensured that the music file was removed from the seller's device. ReDigi was found guilty of copyright infringement because copies of the music files were made as part of the transfer process from the seller's electronic device to ReDigi's servers, and then from these servers to the device of the person purchasing the file. ReDigi argued that the sale of the music files was allowed under the first sale doctrine as the sellers lawfully owned the files. However, the United States Court of Appeals for the Second Circuit upheld the ruling of the district court that found infringement of the plaintiff's rights of reproduction under Section 106(1), stating that "the fixing of the digital file in ReDigi's server, as well as in the new purchaser's device, creates a new phonorecord" and that "the creation of such new phonorecords involves unauthorized reproduction, which is not protected, or even addressed, by § 109(a)" (Capital v. ReDigi 2018, 16–17). Judge Leval, who wrote the court's opinion in the case, states that "it is undisputed that one who owns a digital file from iTunes of music that is fixed in a material object qualifies as 'the owner of a particular . . . phonorecord lawfully made,' [under] 17 U.S.C. § 109(a), and is thus entitled under § 109(a) 'to sell or otherwise dispose of the possession of *that* . . . phonorecord,' id. (emphasis added), without violating § 106(3)" (13). He explains that "first purchasers . . . [could] place 50 or 100 (or more) songs on an inexpensive device such as a thumb drive and sell it" (21) and this would be within the scope of their first sale rights as the original copies of the files are being sold. However, any resale of a digital work that would involve the making "of at least one unauthorized reproduction" of the file, as ReDigi's system did, would not be lawful as "unauthorized reproduction is not protected by § 109(a)" (22). ReDigi asked the SCOTUS to hear their appeal of the case. However, they denied their petition for certiorari in 2019, which means the ruling of the Second Circuit Court stands. Given library's reliance on the first sale doctrine to circulate works to patrons, it will be important for them to continue to monitor the issues related to the concept of digital first sale rights, especially if Congress would decide to pursue legislation making it clear that such a right exists.

Section 109 and End User License Agreements

As part of the acquisition process, those purchasing digital works such as music, film, and ebooks are often required to agree to an end user license agreement (EULA) that place restrictions on how they can be used. For example, an instructor may ask to place on print reserve music they purchased online and burned to a CD, thinking that they own the songs and can, under the first sale doctrine, lawfully request the library to circulate the CD to students. However, many online vendors have terms and conditions in a EULA that individuals are required to agree to when creating an account with the service or at the time of purchase that would not allow this. For example, the Amazon's *Music Terms of Use* states, among other things, the following:

> We grant you a non-exclusive, non-transferable right to use Purchased Music, Music Service Content, and any additional Music Content we provide you access to through the Services only for your personal, non-commercial purposes, subject to the Agreement. Except as set forth in the preceding sentence, you may not redistribute, transmit, assign, sell,

> broadcast, rent, share, lend, repurpose, modify, adapt, edit, license or otherwise transfer, or use Purchased Music or Music Service Content. (Amazon.com 2021)

An instructor burning digital music they purchased from Amazon to a CD to circulate via print reserves would violate terms of this EULA. In these situations, staff could see if they could acquire CD copies of the music that they could circulate to students under the first sale doctrine. Alternately, the instructor could have students purchase copies of the songs themselves via an online music vendor for use in the course.

Putting It All Together

Taking advantage of the first sale doctrine for circulating works via print reserve involves making a good faith effort to ensure that copies of works such as books, DVDs, and CDs placed on print reserve are lawfully made. This does not need to involve tracing the manufacturing origins of each work to ensure it was made under the authorization of the rightsholder. Staff can be fairly confident that most works they obtain from directly from reputable vendors will be will be copies the rightsholder or their representative authorized to be made and sold and so will be considered lawfully made under the first sale doctrine. Situations where staff may be most likely to encounter pirated works would be when purchasing from third-party reseller online. This should not be taken to mean that all third-party resellers are disreputable and that libraries should not purchase from them. There are bad actors in this market though, so libraries should give such works a more careful review before adding them to their collection. Pirated copies are often identifiable due to their poor quality. If staff have serious reason to believe that a copy of a work they received from any vendor may be a pirated copy, they should contact the vendor to ask about its origins and options for returning it for a refund.

Case Study: Showing Reserve DVDs in the Classroom

Instructors may place DVDs or Blu-rays on print reserve so that students can borrow them and watch them outside of class time. However, sometimes instructors wish to check out a copy of a film they have placed on print reserve to show part or all of it as part of face-to-face classroom instruction. These situations are often covered under U.S. copyright law, which states:

> [The] performance or display of a work by instructors or pupils in the course of face-to-face teaching activities of a nonprofit

> educational institution, in a classroom or similar place devoted to instruction, [are not infringements of copyright] unless, in the case of a motion picture or other audiovisual work, the performance, or the display of individual images, is given by means of a copy that was not lawfully made under this title, and that the person responsible for the performance knew or had reason to believe was not lawfully made. (17 U.S.C. § 110[1])

So long as the copy of the film the library is circulating via print reserves was lawfully made under U.S. copyright law, the instructor may show it to students as long as they meet the other qualifications outlined in this statute.

Some film vendors sell copies of films with something they call educational rights that they say allow classroom performances of the film. Libraries are not obliged to purchase these rights from the film vendor, as the right to perform a copy of a film in a face-to-face classroom setting is already grated to them under Section 110(1); rather, they are free to purchase physical copies of films being sold online by vendors like Amazon or Barnes and Noble or at brick-and-mortar businesses such as a department store if they are finding them priced much cheaper there so long as, as part of the purchase transaction, the do not encounter any license language that contractually binds the user to personal uses of the film only or asks that they sign away any rights they may have under U.S. copyright law (e.g., their Section 110[1] rights). Under the first sale doctrine, libraries could actually purchase a physical copy of a film from a private seller on eBay so long as they are able to verify the copy they received is an original copy of the work that was lawfully made under U.S. copyright law.

Many copies of films that are sold by commercial retailors have warnings that state the use of the film is for home use only and that it may not be performed publicly. Such statements and warnings placed on items generally will not override rights granted to users under U.S. copyright law, as discussed in the *Ownership* section in this chapter.

Sometimes the only way a library can obtain a physical copy of a film is to go through a vendor who has a variety of pricing models that include one price for individuals looking to acquire a copy of the film and another higher priced copy that they sell to libraries and educational institutions with a vendor's version of classroom rights. In these situations, staff can try explaining to the vendor that they do not need to acquire classroom rights from them since these are already available to users under Section 110(1). Some vendors will still insist that the library purchase the higher priced version, and in these cases, the library may wish to see if, as part of the purchase they can or will obtain additional rights that are not actually available to them under U.S. copyright law, such as the right to make a public performance of the film as part of a campus film festival or the right to stream a copy of the film to patrons. Alternately, libraries should carefully read any contracts or licenses a vendor is requiring them to sign as part of the purchase of a work to make sure that they are not prohibiting uses that would normally be allowable under the law (e.g., a license that prohibited classroom screenings). Smith tells us that the rights users have under U.S. copyright law "are in place unless they have been changed but an agreement between two individual parties" and, in those situations "it is the agreement they provides the rules and restrictions for those parties" (2015).

CHAPTER NINE

Section 110(2): The Technology, Education, and Copyright Harmonization Act

Section 110 of U.S copyright law provides limitations on the exclusive rights of performances and displays granted to the creators of copyrightable works in Section 106. When users meet the requirements outlined in the various sections of this statute, their performances and displays are not "infringements of copyright" (17 U.S.C. § 110).

Section 110(2), which is often referred to as the TEACH (Technology, Education and Copyright Harmonization) Act, was signed into law by President George W. Bush on November 2, 2002, in response to changes in distance education brought about by advances in technology in the preceding years. It allows qualifying institution to transmit copyrighted works to students as part of distance education. Section 101 of U.S. copyright law tells us that a transmission of a work will involve a performance or display of it "by any device or process whereby images or sounds are received beyond the place from which they are sent." Given this transmission component, the TEACH Act can be considered by libraries as option for making works lawfully available via electronic reserve (e-reserves) and media reserve services. However, first, library staff must be prepared to work with campus administrators, information technology (IT) staff, and instructors to ensure they are meeting all of the requirements set forth by the statute.

Institutional Requirements

Only "a governmental body or an accredited nonprofit educational institution" (17 U.S.C. § 110[2][A]) may use the TEACH Act. Section 110(11)(A) provides additional information about accreditation requirements, including those for institutes of higher education. It states that "with respect to an institution providing post-secondary education, [accreditation] shall be as determined by a regional or national accrediting agency recognized by the Council on Higher Education Accreditation or the United States Department of Education." Many academic libraries that offer reserve services are part of accredited nonprofit educational institutions, so they will readily meet this requirement of the statute. However, libraries associated with for-profit educational institutions will not be able to utilize the TEACH Act, even if their institution meets the accreditation requirements in Section 110(11)(A). Likewise, institutions that to not meet the accreditation requirements set forth by this law will not be able to use the TEACH Act, even if they are nonprofit educational institutions. This does not mean that institutors that find themselves in either of these two situations will not be able to offer reserve services, though, as there are other use rights, such as fair use and the first sale doctrine, that can be considered when seeking to connect students with works via reserves.

Section 110(2)(D)(i) requires that institutions using the TEACH Act institute "policies regarding copyright." Many institutions of higher education will have some type of intellectual property policy in place that addresses copyright considerations for members of the campus community. Others might have an independent policy that addresses the reuse of copyrighted works on campus. If library staff are having trouble finding a policy that addresses copyright for their educational institution, they should reach out to their campus legal counsel to see if they can confirm if such a policy exists and, if so, what language is included in it. Hopefully the copyright policy for the institution is straightforward and legally sound (a topic discussed more in depth in Chapter 14). Some institutions may have copyright policies in place that include myths and misconceptions about the law, such as those discussed in the section "The Fallacy of Limits on the Amount Used" in Chapter 5). If library staff find their institutions have such policies in place, they may wish to speak with administrators about revising them to actually reflect the scope and intent of copyright law. If no copyright policy exists, the library will want to work with campus administrators to establish one for the institution before they can use the TEACH Act.

Under the TEACH Act, institutions must provide "informational materials to faculty, students, and relevant staff members that accurately describe, and promote compliance with, the laws of the United States relating to copyright" (17 U.S.C. § 110[D][i]). This information can be communicated to members of the campus community in a variety of ways—for example, having quality copyright polices that inform users about their rights and their responsibilities when engaging with third-party works and having informational resources available they can consult to learn more about the law. Librarians may be ideally placed to support the institution in meeting this requirement as they can use their training in evaluating information to identify quality resources about the law to make available to the campus community. This could include having books (print and electronic [ebooks]) on the law in their collection and a page or guide on the library's website that provides information, tools, and resources on copyright. If the library has the resources to do so (e.g., having a copyright librarian on staff), it could provide workshops on copyright for instructors, students, and staff.

Section 110(D)(i) also requires that the institution provide "notice to students that materials used in connection with the course may be subject to copyright protection." The statute does not specifically dictate how it must be provided to students, only that it be provided. Therefore, institutions can consider a variety of methods for notifying students, including placing a notice on the learning management system (LMS) page for courses, asking instructors to place the notice on their syllabus, or placing the notice directly on any third-part copyrighted materials made available under the TEACH Act. The statute also does not dictate how the notice should be worded. As a best practice, keeping the notice short and using plain language can be helpful to those who receive the notice. For example, it could read *The copyrighted materials made available to you via this course may be protected by copyright. They are provided to support research and learning in this course. We ask that you refrain retaining copies beyond the course session or sharing copies with others.*

Technological Requirements

Section 110(2) sets forth several technological requirements for making copyrighted works available via the TEACH Act. When the transmission of works is made for distance education under the TEACH Act, "to the extent technologically feasible," it should be made "solely for" and "limited to" (17 U.S.C. § 110[2][C]) those students who are "officially enrolled in the course for which the transmission is made" (17 U.S.C. § 110[2][C][i]). Fortunately most LMS (e.g., Canvas, Blackboard, Moodle) or commercial reserve platforms (e.g., eReserves Plus) libraries might use to provide electronic or media reserve services easily allow them to meet this requirement. Under Section 110(C)(ii), access can also be provided to "officers or employees of governmental bodies as a part of their official duties or employment." Here, especially for government bodies such as state schools, this could include those on campus who may be supporting the courses where these materials are being used—for example, teaching assistants (TAs) or staff providing technological support for the LMS or reserve platform. Institutions must apply technological measures to these digital transmissions that "reasonably prevent" (17 U.S.C. § 110[2][D][1]) the students who access them from retaining "the work in accessible form. . . for longer than the class session" (17 U.S.C. § 110[2][D][1][aa]). Here there is some debate as to what is meant by the term "class session." Some institutions interpret this to mean the duration of the class itself (e.g., a 60- or 90-minute class session). Other institutions work with instructors to identify the period of time that they will be using the work as part of course instruction, which could be days or weeks, and limit students access to the work to that period. Other institutions believe that the class sessions cover the entire academic term, as students may need to access the work repeatedly for class assignments or to prepare for quizzes, tests, or the final examination. Libraries utilizing the TEACH Act for reserve services will want to have a discussion with their institution's legal counsel to decide how they wish to interpret this phrase. Fortunately, most LMS and reserve platforms allow access to works such as documents and videos to be visible to students for a set period of time ranging from minutes, to hours, to days, and these can be used to meet this requirement of the law.

Another technological requirement set forth by the TEACH Act is that institutions apply "technological measures that reasonably prevent" (17 U.S.C. § 110[2][D][1]) the "unauthorized further dissemination" of works made available "in accessible form. . . to others" (17 U.S.C. § 110[2][D][1][bb]). In terms of media reserve services, libraries often stream videos and music they are making available in an effort to meet this requirement. Here, readers who are technologically savvy will realize that there are ways for students to get around such protective measures the library may put in place to make a copy of the work that they can keep beyond the class session or share with others. They law recognizes that this can happen, and instead of putting an absolute mandate on institutions to prevent such actions, which may be impossible to accomplish, instead it requires that reasonable measures be taken and that controls are established "to the extent technologically feasible" for the intuition (17 U.S.C. § 110[2][C]). Fortunately, as discussed here, the technology and commercial platforms used to provide access to learning materials for students under the TEACH Act facilitate compliance with the law.

Finally, the institution cannot "engage in conduct that could reasonably be expected to interfere with technological measures used by copyright owners to prevent such retention or unauthorized further dissemination" (17 U.S.C. § 110[2][D][ii][II]) of copyrighted works.

Instructor Requirements

Instructors must be prepared to meet the requirements set forth for them in the TEACH Act as well. Fortunately, many of them align with common pedagogical practices. For example, the performance or display of the copyrighted work must be "made by, at the direction of, or under the actual supervision of an instructor as an integral part of a class session offered as a regular part of the systematic mediated instructional activities of . . . an accredited nonprofit educational institution" (17 U.S.C. § 110[2][A]). Here, the law is emphasizing that performances and displays made under the TEACH Act should be made at the request of the instructor as part of courses they are teaching. Generally, this is a key component of how reserves services work; the instructor asks the library to make available to students works they are using as part of course instruction. As such, this requirement closely aligns with reserve request practices. The law also requires that "the performance or display [of the copyrighted work] is directly related and of material assistance to the teaching content of the transmission" (17 U.S.C. § 110[2][B]). Requests the library receive from instructors to make works available via reserve services can be for materials students are required to engage with as part of the course and supplementary learning materials. Either way, it is likely that they are related to the teaching content of the course. However, for those libraries using the TEACH Act to make works available via reserve services, if they struggle to make a connection between the work requested and how it might be of "material assistance to the teaching content of the transmission" (17 U.S.C. § 110[2][B]), they can follow up with the instructor who placed the request for additional information.

Content That Can Be Made Available Under the TEACH Act

If members of an institution of higher education are able to work together to meet all of the requirements outlined above, then the following works can be made available to students via reserve services such as e-reserves and media reserves in support of distance education.

Performances of Works

The performance of a work involves "recit[ing], render[ing], play[ing], dance[ing], or act[ing] it, either directly or by means of any device or process or, in the case of a motion picture or other audiovisual work, . . . show[ing] its images in any sequence or to make the sounds accompanying it audible" (17 U.S.C. § 101). Under the TEACH Act, libraries can make performances of "reasonable and limited portions" (17 U.S.C. § 110[2]) of certain types of works available via media reserve services, including motion pictures, such as feature films, documentary films, television shows, and video games; and of sound recordings, which could include recordings of spoken word such as an audiobook or a podcast or recordings of the performance of musical works such as the singing of a song or the playing of musical instruments.

U.S. copyright law does not tell us what a "reasonable and limited" (17 U.S.C. § 110[2]) portion of a work might be. However, there are several other sources that can provide guidance to us on interpreting this language. A report put forward by the Senate in 2001 to accompany the passage of the TEACH Act states that "the performance of works [that can be made available under the TEACH Act] is limited, however, *to 'reasonable and limited portions' of less than the entire work*. What constitutes a "reasonable and limited" portion should take into account both the nature of the market for that type of work and the pedagogical purposes of the performance" (emphasis added) (S. Rep. 107-31, 7-8, 2001). This would seem to indicate that the performance of an entire work under the TEACH Act is not allowed. However, the Congressional Research Service, which is "a legislative branch agency within the Library of Congress" that provides "policy and legal analysis to committees and Members of both the House and Senate" released a report in that 2006 states that "the exhibition of an entire film may possibly constitute a 'reasonable and limited' demonstration if the film's entire viewing is exceedingly relevant toward achieving an educational goal; however, the likelihood of an entire film portrayal being 'reasonable and limited' may be rare" (Huber et al. 2006, 4). This language indicates that there could be situations where the sharing of an entire work under the TEACH Act could be allowed. Library staff will want to work with their institution's legal counsel to discuss how they will determine if requests put forward by instructors will constitute "reasonable and limited" portions, keeping in mind that such determinations will likely be tied closely to an instructor's pedagogical purposes, which could be explained on the reserve request form.

Displays of Works

Displays of copyrighted works occur when photographs, pages from literary works (such as a textbook or other reference work), or sheet music are made available for students to view via an e-reserves service. The TEACH Act allows for the "display of a work in an amount comparable to that which is typically displayed in the course of a live classroom session" (17 U.S.C. § 107). For example, if an instructor teaching an art appreciation lesson on Frida Kahlo displayed 30 images of her paintings as part of face-to-face instruction, then, under the TEACH Act, they could display the same 30 images if they began offering the course as a distance education course. The

2001 Senate report provided more clarity here in the amount of a work that could be displayed under the TEACH Act, stating that the "display of the entire work could be appropriate and consistent with displays typically made in a live classroom setting" and provided examples of such displays; "short poems or essays, or images of pictorial, graphic, or sculptural works, etc." (S. Rep. 107-31, 8, 2001).

Case Study: What Else the TEACH Act Allows to Be Shared

The TEACH Act allows for the "*full* performance of nondramatic literary works and nondramatic musical works" (emphasis added) (17 U.S.C. § 110[2]). To provide context for this option, a review of the definitions of some of these terms used here can be helpful.

Nondramatic literary works. The *Compendium of U.S. Copyright Office Practices, Third Edition* (Compendium) tells us that a nondramatic literary work is one that "explains, describes, or narrates a particular subject, theme, or idea through the use of narrative, descriptive, or explanatory text, rather than dialog or dramatic action" and that, "generally, nondramatic literary works are intended to be read; they are not intended to be performed before an audience" (Compendium [Third] § 703). Examples of nondramatic literary works that are likely to be used as part of course instruction include fiction and nonfiction, poetry, textbooks, and reference works.

Nondramatic musical works. Section 802.1 of the *Compendium* states that "musical works (which are also known as musical compositions) are original works of authorship consisting of music and any accompanying words." A nondramatic musical work "is a musical work that was not created for use in a motion picture or a dramatic work, such as a ballad intended for distribution solely on an album or an advertising jingle intended solely for performance on the radio" (Compendium [Third] § 802.2[A]). Examples of nondramatic musical works likely to be used as part of course instruction include symphony music and popular songs.

The TEACH Act also allows for "reasonable and limited" (17 U.S.C. § 102) performances of:

- Dramatic literary works, which are compositions "generally in prose or verse that portrays a story that is intended to be performed for an audience such as plays, musicals, or operas" (Compendium [Third] § 804.1).
- Dramatic musical works, which are "musical work[s] created for use in a motion picture or a dramatic work, [such as] musical plays and operas" (Compendium [Third] § 802.2[A]).
- Pantomime, which is "the art of imitating, presenting, or acting out situations, characters, or events through the use of physical gestures and bodily movements" (Compendium [Third] § Glossary).

- Choreography, that involves "the composition and arrangement of a related series of dance movements and patterns organized into a coherent whole. Choreography is not synonymous with dance" (Compendium [Third] § Glossary).

Under these two provisions of the TEACH Act, an instructor could read aloud to students from a nondramatic or dramatic literary work. They could also use an instrument to perform nondramatic or dramatic musical works from sheet music, and they could perform a work of pantomime or choreography for them. As such performances would be made live (e.g., as part of synchronous distance education where the instructor and students are meeting in a virtual classroom), this part of the TEACH Act will not apply to reserve services, where copies of works (e.g., an audio recording of a person reading from a book or a sound recording of a person performing music) are being made available for students to use. This case study is intended to highlight this option offered under the TEACH Act so that TEACH Act–compliant institutions let instructors seeking to make performances of nondramatic literary and musical works as part of distance education know about it.

Content That Cannot Be Made Available Under the TEACH Act

In seeking to promote the sharing of works "analogous to the type of performance or display that would take place in a live classroom setting" (17 U.S.C. § 110[11]), the TEACH Act includes prohibitions on sharing certain types of works such as those that traditionally used across "1 or more class sessions of a single course, such works as textbooks, course packs, or other material in any media, copies or phonorecords of which are typically purchased or acquired by the students in higher education for their independent use" (17 U.S.C. § 110[11]). The TEACH Act does not allow the sharing of "a work produced or marketed primarily for performance or display as part of mediated instructional activities transmitted via digital networks" (17 U.S.C. § 110[2]). This prohibition is intended to prevent the sharing of works under the TEACH Act from displacing the market for such works. The performance or display of works "given by means of a copy or phonorecord that is not lawfully made and acquired under this title, and the transmitting government body or accredited nonprofit educational institution knew or had reason to believe was not lawfully made and acquired" (17 U.S.C. § 110[2]) is also not allowed. This prohibition helps ensure that the use of illegal copies is not promoted or enabled. Fortunately, the library can facilitate compliance with this requirement by acquiring copies of works that will be made available under the TEACH Act for their collection, or obtaining copies through legitimate library lending services such as interlibrary loan.

Putting It All Together

The TEACH Act offer another option for libraries to consider when seeking to lawfully connect students with access to learning materials via electronic and media reserve. The TEACH Act does allow "a wide variety of uses of copyrighted works, without risk of copyright infringement" (Crews 2003, 35). However, a decision to utilize the TEACH Act cannot be made lightly, nor can compliance be ensured through the actions of a single individual. Compliance requires many members of a campus community coming together over the course of many months to ensure policies, educational practices, and technological measures are in place and then, after meeting these requirements initially, working together to continue to ensure they remain in place (Myers 2019, 162–163). Fortunately, there are tools and resources available that can assist members of the library staff and their campus partners in working through the requirements of the law. These include:

- American Library Association's Distance Education and the TEACH Act webpage: http://www.ala.org/advocacy/copyright/teachact
- The TEACH Act - Online Performances, a video lecture that is part of the Copyright for Educators & Librarians Massive Online Open Course (MOOC) created by Duke University, Emory University, The University of North Carolina at Chapel Hill: https://www.coursera.org/learn/copyright-for-education/lecture/4qRMU/the-teach-act-online-performances

Many institutions choose not to use the TEACH Act, either because they find the law to be too cumbersome or they are unable to get the engagement and support required from others across campus to meet all of the requirements set forth in the law. It is important for readers to understand that their institution is not required to use the TEACH Act. Rather, it is an option available along other user rights such as fair use that can be considered. Alternatively, if an institution is meeting all of the requirements of the TEACH Act, applications of it are not mutually exclusive. If an instructor places a reserve request that does not fit within the scope of the TEACH Act, library staff can apply another user right to the situation—for example, fair use—to see if they can lawfully make the work available to students that way.

CHAPTER TEN

Section 1201: The Digital Millennium Copyright Act

The Digital Millennium Copyright Act of 1998 (DMCA) is a law that was passed by Congress to meet treaty obligations under the World Intellectual Property Organization's Copyright Treaty. Article 11 of the treaty required that "Contracting Parties shall provide adequate legal protection and effective legal remedies against the circumvention of effective technological measures that are used by authors in connection with the exercise of their rights under this Treaty or the Berne Convention and that restrict acts, in respect of their works, which are not authorized by the authors concerned or permitted by law" (Art. 11). The DMCA added a new section to U.S. copyright law, Section 12, that has implications for libraries offering electronic and media reserve services. Often, digital works libraries may wish to make available through these services have technical protection measures (TPM), sometimes also referred to as digital rights management (DRM) software, that limits a user's ability to make copies of or modify the works. For example, a PDF (portable document format) copy of an article may have DRM protection that prevents library staff from deleting pages of the article or adding accessibility features like descriptive text to tables, charts, and pictures to it. A Digital Video Disc (DVD) or compact disc (CD) may have TPM that prevents copies of the media files stored on them from being made. There are ways to circumvent TPM; however, Section 1201(a)(1)(A) states that "no person shall circumvent a technological measure that effectively controls access to a work protected under this title." Here, "to 'circumvent a technological measure' means to descramble a scrambled work, to decrypt an encrypted work, or otherwise to avoid, bypass, remove, deactivate, or impair a technological measure [such as TPM], without the authority of the copyright owner" (17 U.S.C. § 1201[a][3][A]).

As written, it may seem that the anticircumvention prohibitions Section 1201(a)(1)(A) would fully prevent libraries seeking to make digital copies of works that have TPM applied available via reserve services, even when doing so may fall within the scope of user rights found in U.S. copyright law, such as fair use (17 U.S.C. § 107) or the TEACH (Technology, Education and Copyright Harmonization) Act (17 U.S.C. § 110[2]). However, there are exemptions to Section 1021(a)(1) that libraries can consider when seeking to make copies of works available via reserve services.

Exemptions Granted Through the Rulemaking Process

Sections 1201(a)(1)(C) and (D) requires that every three years the Registrar of Copyrights make a recommendation to the Librarian of Congress regarding "persons who are users of a copyrighted work are, or are likely to be in the succeeding 3-year period, adversely affected by the prohibition under subparagraph [1201(a)(1)](A) in their ability to make noninfringing uses under this title of a particular class of copyrighted works." Section 1201(a)(1)(C) requires that this rulemaking process take into account:

(i) the availability for use of copyrighted works;

(ii) the availability for use of works for nonprofit archival, preservation, and educational purposes;

(iii) the impact that the prohibition on the circumvention of technological measures applied to copyrighted works has on criticism, comment, news reporting, teaching, scholarship, or research;

(iv) the effect of circumvention of technological measures on the market for or value of copyrighted works; and

(v) such other factors as the Librarian considers appropriate. (17 U.S.C. § 1201[a][1][C])

Based upon information gathered in the rulemaking process and the recommendation of the Registrar of Copyright, the Librarian of Congress can choose to adopt limited exemptions to the anticircumvention prohibitions found in Section 1201(a)(1)(A) for the ensuing three-year period. The last rulemaking process concluded in 2021 and set forth a variety of exemptions for users, including some that may impact reserve uses, and these are outlined in the following sections. While it is now often the case that exemptions established in previous rulemaking sessions are renewed in future recommendations, readers should review the new rules set forth in the law every three years to ensure they are renewed verbatim, if they are renewed with revisions, or if new exemptions have been granted that may aid them in making digital copies of works available through reserve services. The 2021 Final Rule, which outlines exemptions renewed or granted as part of the *Eighth Triennial Rulemaking Process* is found in Title 37 of the *Code of Federal Regulations* (C.F.R.), Chapter 2, Section 201.40. Exemptions are also included in the law that address the making of accessible copies of works for patrons who may require an accommodation. These are discussed in Chapter 13.

DMCA Exemptions and Print Reserves

Many libraries make copies of DVDs and Blu-ray Discs available for checkout via print reserves. It is not unusual for these items to be damaged or deteriorate quickly from frequent use. Section 201.40(b)(3)(i) allows for the creation of a preservation or replacement copy of "motion pictures (including television shows and videos), as defined in 17 U.S.C. 101" by libraries. This can be a useful option for libraries who find that they need to make a copy of the work in order to ensure its continued availability for students and instructors utilizing reserve services.

Using the DMCA for Print Reserves

In order to take advantage of the exemption found in Section 201.40(b)(3)(i), libraries must meet eligibility requirements outlined in Section 201.40(b)(3)(ii):

(A) The collections of the library must be "open to the public and/or are routinely made available to researchers who are not affiliated with the library."
(B) The library must have "a public service mission."
(C) The staff of the library or its volunteers must "provide professional services normally associated with libraries."
(D) The collections of the library must be "composed of lawfully acquired and/or licensed materials."
(E) The library must implement "reasonable digital security measures as appropriate for the activities permitted by paragraph (b)(3)(i)" of the Section 201.40 of the C.F.R.

It is likely most libraries associated with institutions of higher education in the United States will meet these requirements. If reserve staff are uncertain of their library's eligibility, they should review these criteria with library administrators and their institution's legal counsel.

Before making a preservation or replacement copy, the library must put forth a "reasonable effort" to determine whether "an unused and undamaged replacement copy [can] be obtained at a fair price and that no streaming service, download service, or on-demand cable and satellite service makes the motion picture available to libraries, archives, and museums at a fair price" (37 C.F.R. § 201.40[b][3][i][C]). Much like Section 108 (Title 17, U.S. Code), this section of the law does not tell us what might be considered a reasonable effort in searching or what might be considered a fair price for a work. Here, libraries could consider following established institution procedures for acquiring copies of DVDs and Blu-rays for their collection as part of their search for a copy of the motion picture they are seeking to make a preservation or replacement copy of and discuss with those members of the staff who make acquisition decisions what reasonable pricing might look like in this area. If these efforts are not fruitful, then the library can proceed with making the replacement or preservation copy so long as the motion picture in question was "lawfully acquired on a DVD protected by the Content Scramble System, or on a Blu-ray disc protected by the Advanced Access Content System" (37 C.F.R. § 201.40[b][3][i]) and the making of the replacement or preservation copy must is "carried out without any purpose of direct or indirect commercial advantage" (37 C.F.R. § 201.40[b][3][i][B]). Section 201.40(b)(3)(i)(D) does require that the "preservation or replacement copies are not distributed or made available outside of the physical premises of the eligible library." This may mean that the library will need to provide viewing stations patrons can use on the physical premises to watch the motion picture.

DMCA Exemptions and Media Reserves

The Final Rule issued as part of the *Eighth Triennial Rulemaking Process* in 2021 includes an exemption found in Section 201.40(b) that can be utilized by library staff looking to make digital copies of "motion pictures (including television shows and videos), as defined in 17 U.S.C. 101" (37 C.F.R. § 201.40[b][1]) available via media reserve services. This exemption applies "where the motion picture [to be copied] is lawfully made and acquired on a DVD protected by the Content Scramble System, on a Blu-ray disc protected by the Advanced Access Content System, or via a digital transmission protected by a technological measure" (37 C.F.R. § 201.40[b][1]). Section 201.40(b)(1)(ii) allows for "short portions of the motion pictures" to be made "for educational purposes," and in subsections it identifies specific users who may take advantage of the exemption in specified situations.

Section 201.40(b)(1)(ii)(A)

Here, "employees acting at the direction of faculty" of colleges and universities can make short portions of motion pictures available "for the purpose of teaching a course, including of accredited general educational development (GED) programs, for the purpose of criticism, comment, teaching, or scholarship." In these situations, TPM applied to the DVD or Blu-ray may be circumvented so long as the user "reasonably believes" that a copy made using "screen-capture technology that appears to be offered to the public as enabling the reproduction of motion pictures after content has been lawfully acquired and decrypted" is "unable to produce the required level of high-quality content" needed for these instructional uses.

Using the DMCA for Media Reserves

The exemption found in Section 201.40(b) can be helpful for libraries seeking to make motion pictures available to instructors and students via media reserves. The options outlined in Section 201.40(b)(1) will likely cover many scenarios where instructors are looking to connect their students with learning resources via reserves. However, the limitations on only making available short portions of a motion picture may cause a problem when instructors are looking to have their students engage with a film in its entirety. Additionally, these exemptions may cause some confusion as to when screen-capture technology should be used to obtain the desired portions of the film to make available for use versus circumventing the TRM to obtain the clip. When screen-capture is used, circumvention of TPM many not actually take place, in which case a violation of Section 1201(a)(1)(A) would not occur. In both the current *Recommendation* report (2021) and the 2018 *Recommendation* report, the Registrar of Copyrights admitted that "it can be unclear to users as to whether screen-capture technology may in fact involve circumvention" (Perlmutter 2021, 34) and that rightsholders involved in the rulemaking process do assert that screen-capture is "an adequate alternative to circumvention for many of the proposed uses" (35). The 2021 report states that the exemptions it recommends "includes a screen-capture provision to address the possibility of circumvention when using this technology" (34). Because of this, the use of screen-capture technology may reduce legal risk, but it can result in a copy of the motion picture that does not have the same resolution and quality as the original. Also, as the film must be played for the screen-capture software to make the copy, this method does result in longer processing times. When deciding how to proceed, reserve staff may wish to discuss with the instructor making the copy what quality they are looking for in the copy. Screen-capture software has improved substantially over the years, so that now copies made using this technology can look good. However, there may be some classes, such as a film studies class, that is seeking to examine the film in a more detailed way and therefore do need the higher quality copy that can be made by circumventing the TPM. In these situations, this option is available under the current exemptions.

Other DMCA Considerations

The exemptions to the DMCA discussed above can help make the work of libraries and educational institutions looking to make copies of works available via print and media reserve of works a bit easier (there are no exemptions in the current rule expressly related to electronic reserve services). However, these exemptions last only for a three-year period. The exemptions outlined in this section were adopted in the *Eighth Triennial Rulemaking Process* and became effective on October 28, 2021, and they remain effective only until the *Ninth Triennial Rulemaking Process* is completed in 2024. While it is hoped that they will be renewed or, perhaps, even expanded upon in the *Ninth Triennial Rulemaking Process*, those who utilize them should pay close attention to the *Final Rule* issued by the Librarian of Congress in 2024 to see if they are. Those employees of libraries and educational institutions who use these exemptions should consider participating in the rulemaking process itself to help encourage their renewal. Information on the rulemaking process can be found on the U.S. Copyright Office's website at https://www.copyright.gov/1201/.

As discussed in earlier chapters, libraries can consider taking advantage of exemptions and user rights found in the law so long as they have not lawfully signed away their ability to do so when acquiring a copy of the item in question. Libraries should always be on the lookout for language that may limit their ability to exercise these rights and, when possible, request their removal from the contract.

The Scope and Reach of the DMCA

Text from a House Report that accompanied the passage of the DMCA states that the language found in paragraph (a)(1) of the DMCA prohibiting the circumvention of TPMs

> does not apply to the subsequent actions of a person once he or she has obtained authorized access to a copy of a work protected under Title 17, even if such actions involve circumvention of additional forms of technological protection measures. In a fact situation where the access is authorized, the traditional defenses to copyright infringement, including fair

> use, would be fully applicable. So, an individual would not be able to circumvent in order to gain unauthorized access to a work, but would be able to do so in order to make fair use of a work which he or she has acquired lawfully. (H.R. Rep. No. 105-551, pt. 1, 18, 1998)

Section 1201(c)(1) seems to support this assentation, stating that "nothing in this section shall affect rights, remedies, limitations, or defenses to copyright infringement, including fair use, under this title." However, U.S. courts have disagreed on when DMCA liability applies when users exercise rights granted to them under U.S. copyright law, such as fair use. For example, in *Chamberlain v. Skylink* (381 F.3d 1178 [2004]), the United States Court of Appeals for the Seventh Circuit seems to take the intent expressed in the House Report to heart, stating in its opinion that in passing the DMCA "Congress chose to create new causes of action for circumvention and for trafficking in circumvention devices" (1203); it "did not choose to create new property rights," a 'right of access' to exist alongside those rights found in Section 106 of U.S copyright law (e.g., the reproduction, the creation of derivative works, distribution, public performance, and public display). They argued that "the statutory structure and the legislative history both make it clear that the DMCA granted copyright holders additional legal protections, [it did not] rescinded the basic bargain granting the public noninfringing and fair uses of copyrighted materials" (1202). However, in *MDY Industries, LLC v. Blizzard Entertainment*, Inc. (629 F.3d 928 [2010]), the United States Court of Appeals for the Ninth Circuit stated in its option that in their reading of the DMCA, they believe that Congress was "extending a new form of protection, i.e., the right to prevent circumvention of access controls, broadly to works protected under Title 17, i.e., copyrighted works" (945) and that in passing the law, "that Congress intended to prohibit even non-infringing circumvention and trafficking in circumventing devices" (950). Similarly, in the case *Universal City Studios, Inc. v. Corley* (273 F.3d 429 [2d Cir. 2001]), the United States Court of Appeals for the Second Circuit stated that 1201(a)(1)(A) "targets the use of a circumvention technology" (441). They even address fair use considerations related to this interpretation of the language of Section 1201(a)(1)(A), arguing that "we know of no authority for the proposition that fair use, as protected by the Copyright Act, much less the Constitution, guarantees copying by the optimum method or in the identical format of the original. . . . The DMCA does not impose even an arguable limitation on the opportunity to make a variety of traditional fair uses of DVD movies, such as commenting on their content, quoting excerpts from their screenplays, and even recording portions of the video images and sounds on film or tape by pointing a camera, a camcorder, or a microphone at a monitor as it displays the DVD movie" (459).

The Impact of Court Decisions on Libraries

Given these decisions, how should libraries proceed when seeking to make digital copies of works for reserve services? They may wish to work with their institution's legal counsel to see if the courts have put forward any decisions related to the anticircumvention prohibitions applications of the DMCA and, if they have, how they might impact their interpretation of the text in this statute. District court opinions are generally not binding on other district courts, but opinions issued by an appellate court are only binding on the district courts in their jurisdiction and, even, then, only when the legal questions and facts of one case closely align with another; they are generally not binding on other appellate courts. So libraries located in the Seventh Circuit can look to the decision in *Chamberlain v. Skylink* as precedent for applications of the DMCA, but libraries in other Circuits, such as the Ninth, may need to look to *MDY v. Blizzard*. If a library is located in a circuit that does not yet have legal precedent set by a ruling from the courts, they can consider the merits of rulings from different circuit courts in deciding how to proceed. A map of the geographic boundaries of the U.S. courts of appeals and the U.S. district courts can be found in Figure 10.1.

Opinions issued by SCOTUS set a precedent for all lower courts; however, precedent set by the SCOTUS and circuit courts can be overturned, so it can be important to stay on top of these types of opinions issued by the courts.

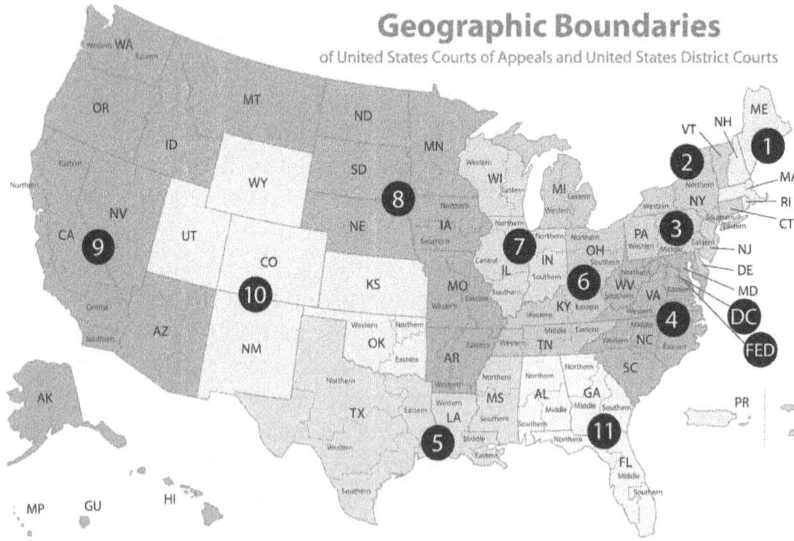

Figure 10.1 A map of the geographic boundaries of the U.S. Courts of Appeals and the U.S. District Courts, current as of publication of this book, published by the United States Department of Justice

Legal counsel can help library staff find relevant court opinions and decide how best to factor the decisions made in them to policies they develop in regard to the DMCA.

Putting It All Together

DMCA considerations can impact the processing of reserve requests, but they are manageable. Staff supporting these services should work closely with library administrators and their institution's legal counsel to identify where the DMCA may be implicated and how the various exemptions found in the current *Final Rule* may provide opportunities for connecting students and instructors with materials they are using as part of course instruction. They will also need to be cognizant of when new rules are issued as part of the triennial process and, if needed, revise their procedures accordingly. They may also wish to become active participants in the Rulemaking Process to help communicate to the Library of Congress the need for new exemptions, or the expansion of current ones, to help support teaching, research, and the creation of new scholarship at their institution.

CHAPTER ELEVEN

Permissions and Licensing

If a particular use of a work does not fall within the scope of user rights found in U.S. copyright law, then users can consider obtaining permission or a license from the rightsholder to exercise the desired rights, such as making and circulating works via reserve services. Legally speaking, the words permission and license have similar definitions, with permission meaning "to consent formally or to give opportunity for" (Garner 2009, 1255) and license meaning "a permission . . . to commit some act that would otherwise be unlawful" (1002). However, when talking about reserve services, the term 'permission' is often used when the library is given a free grant of rights by the rightsholder of a work to make a work available to patrons via these services, while the term 'license' is often used when a fee was paid to the rightsholder to make a portion of a work or, in some cases, an entire copy of a work available to students under very certain circumstances for a certain period of time. As both scenarios can be part of reserve workflow and have legal considerations, it is prudent to discuss them before moving on to reserve copyright workflows in the following chapters.

Permissions

Obtaining permission to make a work available via reserve services may seem like a daunting task. However, many individual rightsholders are often excited to hear that their works are being used for educational purposes and are willing to work with instructors and reserve staff to make them available to students. The steps involved with obtaining permission to use a work are outlined below.

Identifying the Rightsholder

The first step in the permissions process involves identifying the rightsholder of the work. Here, it is important to keep in mind that the creator of a work is not always necessarily the rightsholder. This is because for many types of works instructors may be interested in making available via reserve services (e.g., selections from books, journal articles, film, and music), creators often transfer some or all of their rights in a work to the publisher or film or music distributor as a condition of publication. Works may also be considered to be works made for hire depending on the circumstances of their creations (see Chapter 4 for more information on work made for hire situations). However, contacting the creator of the work is often a good place to start when seeking permission to reuse it. If the author can be reached, the person seeking permission will need to confirm they still retain the rights needed to grant permission for their intended reuses. Frustrations may arise if the author retained some rights in their work but not the rights the person seeing permission needs. However, with luck, the author may be able to direct them to the person who does hold these rights. If the author of the work cannot be identified (e.g., the work is published as an anonymous work or under a pseudonym), or if contact information for the author cannot be found, then contacting the publisher to see if they can provide contact information for the author or if they can provide the permission is the next logical step. Another place to look for rightsholder information look is in the records of the U.S. Copyright Office. Filing and renewal records can be searched online. Those covering 1891–1978 can be found online at https://www.archive.org/details/copyrightrecords/, and those for 1978 and after are accessible through the USCO's website at https://cocatalog.loc.gov/.

What Rights Do You Need?

Reserve staff will, at minimum, need permission to make copies of (reproduce) and distribute (circulate) copies of works via reserve services. As part of the request, rightsholders should also be informed of the following considerations. While this information is not directly related to any particular rights granted to the rightsholder under Section 106, knowing this information will allow the rightsholder to make a more informed decision about granting permission for reserve use.

How Many Copies Will Be Made?

A specific number of copies (e.g., three) can be identified in a permission request. However, it may be more prudent to ask for general permission to make *copies* available via reserves, rather than identifying a specific number.

Doing so offers several benefits. If permission is received to only make a certain number of copies, then once that limit is reached the rightsholder will need to be contacted again to obtain permission to make additional copies. Asking permission to make copies of the work available allows for more flexibility in addressing such situations.

What Format the Copies Will Be Made In?

For print reserve, photocopies of works will likely be made available to students, unless the library is considering circulating devices (e.g., a tablet or laptop) with the works preloaded on them. The benefits of making works such as articles and selections from books available to students via electronic reserve has been addressed in Part I. However, there could be situations when an instructor specifically asks that the library make photocopies of such works available to students via print reserves instead. If the library does offer an electronic reserves service, or is thinking about implementing this service in the future, then it may be prudent to request permission to make copies available *via reserve services* rather than specifying one particular service, as this can allow them to make the work available in a variety of formats to suit the format requirements of various reserve services.

Who the Copies Will Be Made Available To?

The permissions request should make it clear that students and instructors are the target users for print reserves. If members of the public are able to check out any print reserve item, then this information should also be made clear.

How Long Will Copies Be Made Available via Reserve Services?

Permission can be requested to make a work available for a particular period of time such as a certain semester or year. However, it may be prudent to request perpetual permission to make the work available, which can be helpful if the instructor decides to use the work in the future.

Who Is Work Being Made Available on Behalf Of?

It can be appealing to rightsholders to know what instructor is interested in using the work and for what class. However, when it comes to drafting a permissions request for a work to be made available via reserve services, it may be useful to ask that the permission be granted to the academic institution or library to make the copies rather than a particular instructor or for a particular class This is because an instructor may leave for a position at another institution or retire, and if the permission is granted solely for this particular person to use the work, then the rightsholder will need to be contacted again when that person is no longer affiliated with the institution. Alternately, rather than granting permission for a work to be copied and distributed in connection with a particular course, it can be wise to ask permission to make copies available for educational purposes. For example, if permission is received for a work to be copied and distributed to students in association with a particular class, say, History 101, and then an instructor is interested in using it for a History 201 course, permission will need to be obtained from the rightsholder in order to do so. When it comes to drafting permission requests, using more general language should not be seen as an attempt to be vague but rather an effort to make things easier for both the instructor, the library, and the rightsholder down the road.

Drafting the Permissions Request

A good permissions request includes the following information:

- An introduction. The person sending the permission request should start off by sharing their name and affiliation.
- Identification of the work in question. Information should be provided that, very specifically, identifies the work being used. This can include the title; source (e.g., the title of a journal or edited volume); author or editor; publisher; publication date or copyright date; edition; and, if applicable, information such as page numbers.
- How the work will be used. Here is where information about the class or assignment can be shared.
- Who copies will be made available to, and how they will be made available.
- A grant of permissions statement. This language outlines the specific permission the requestor is asking for.
- Rightsholder certification. This statement will ask the person being contacted to confirm that they are the rightsholder.
- Contact information. Information that the rightsholder can use to seek additional information about the permission request should be included.

A template for a permissions request staff can use for a work they are seeking to make available via reserve services can be found below. Readers are encouraged to speak with their Office of General Counsel (OGC) to approve the use of the template or draft their own template language for such requests in conjunctions with their OGC.

Dear [insert name of author/rightsholder]

My name is [insert name] and I am [insert job title] at [insert name of institution]. I am reaching out to you as I would like to obtain your permission to use the following work:

> [insert as much identifying information as possible, e.g., the title, source, publisher, publication/copyright date, edition, and page numbers].

This work will be used by [insert name of instructor] in their [insert name of course] as part of [include brief description of the use, e.g., the discussion topic or assignment]. We are seeking your nonexclusive, perpetual, irrevocable, and royalty free permission for [name of institution] to make copies of the work identified above, and to make those copies available to students via our reserve service. I am contacting you because I believe you are the rightsholder of the copyright in this work. If you are not the rightsholder, please provide me with the name and contact information of the person to whom permissions requests should be directed.

If you are willing to grant the permission outlined above, please reply confirming that you are the rightsholder and are able grant these rights to us.

I appreciate your kind consideration of this request. If I can answer any questions that may aid you in making a decision regarding this request please do not hesitate to contact me at [insert phone number, email address, and address.]

Here is an example of what a completed permission request might look like:

Dear Mrs. Buck,

My name is Susan Smith and I am the course reserves manager at De Smet College (South Dakota). I am reaching out to you as I would like to obtain your permission to use the following work:

> Buck, Rebecca. 2017. *Flora and Fauna of South Dakota* (pp. 74–201). Silver Lake Press.

This work will be used by Caroline Swanzey in in her Environmental History of South Dakota course as part of an assignment and class discussions that explore plant and animal life in the state. We are seeking your nonexclusive, perpetual, irrevocable, and royalty-free permission for De Smet College to make copies of the work identified above, and to make those copies available to students via our reserve service. I am contacting you because I believe you are the rightsholder of the copyright in this work. If you are not the rightsholder, please provide me with the name and contact information of the person to whom permissions requests should be directed.

If you are willing to grant the permission outlined above, please reply confirming that you are the rightsholder and are able grant these rights to us.

I appreciate your kind consideration of this request. If I can answer any questions that may aid you in making a decisions regarding this request please do not hesitate to contact me at 605-555-1879, ssmith7@desmet.edu, or Ingalls Library, 127 Main Street, Room 103, De Smet, South Dakota 57231.

Reaching out to the Rightsholder

Requests for permission can be sent to the person who created the work, such as the author of a book, or they can be directed to those who make the work available to the public, such as a book or journal publisher or a film or music distributer. It has been the author's experience that permission to use a work is more likely to be freely granted when reaching out to the person who created the work; however, this process often tends to be time consuming. Many publishers and film and music distributors have websites with entire sections or pages devoted to submitting permissions requests, which often speed up this process. However, permission requests submitted this way often morph into formal licensing situations where payment is required for use under very specific terms that are nonnegotiable (e.g., how long the work can be used and who it can be made available to). The person who will be pursuing permission will need to decide which option they will pursue or, if both will be, in what order. Often these decisions can be driven by time and funds available to pay licensing fees, when they are requested.

Thanks to the internet, finding contact information for permission requests is easier than it was 30 years ago. Many authors, publishers, and filmmakers have a website where contact information for them can be found. These content creators also often have a presence on social media, such as Facebook, Twitter, Instagram, and so on that can be used to find contact information, or even to begin a conversation about obtaining permission to make a work available via reserve services. As permissions requests like these are a nonexclusive grant of rights, a topic addressed in Chapter 4, they do not need to be secured in writing. However, there are many benefits to doing so, including documenting the terms upon which the permission was granted. This can be useful to have should the library's copying and circulation of a work via reserve services ever later be questioned by the rightsholder.

Today, most permissions requests are initiated by email, which is an efficient way to send such requests and provides the advantage of documenting all conversations between the person seeking permission and the rightsholder. Contacting a rightsholder by phone is often a quick way to get a response to a permission request. It can be helpful to have the template outlined above populated with all of the information related to the request prior to making the call so it can serve as a script for the conversation. Sometimes the rightsholder will be amenable to discussing the request over the phone, or they may request that it be submitted via email or a form found on their website. It is ideal to follow such instructions as they will often facilitate the processing of the request. If the rightsholder is willing to grant permission over the phone, it is advisable to ask for their email address and send them an email with the text of the drafted permission request, modified to thank them for their time and asking that they please confirm the agreed upon terms. There is little to prevent permission requests from being sent by mail so long as the person preparing the request knows the rightsholder's address. However, pursuing permission in this manner could add significant delays to the process, and, unless tracking or delivery confirmation is used, it may not be known whether the rightsholder chose to ignore the request or whether it never reached them. However, if a rightsholder has indicated or, after a phone or email conversation, has asked that permission requests be submitted this way, the requestor should comply.

Negotiation

While initial terms may be put forward, the individual requesting permission should be prepared to negotiate with the rightsholder. For example, language may be used in the initial request that indicates that the requestor would like to have the permission granted to the institution, for any educational use, and for perpetual permission to use the work. However, the rightsholder may be more comfortable only granting permission to a specific instructor, or a specific course, and for use for a certain period of time (e.g., two or three years) after which they would like to renegotiate the permission. The requestor should be prepared to consider such terms and, barring any situations where the terms put forward by the rightsholder would prevent their intended use, consider accepting them.

Licensing Considerations for Reserve Services

There are several situations where reserve staff may engage with licenses when making works available via reserve services. These include works licenses by the library as part of their collections, works created with an open license, and licenses obtained on a case-by-case basis for particular works instructors wish to make available via reserve services.

Works Licensed by the Library

Most physical copies of works libraries acquire will not be restricted by a license that prohibits them being circulated via print reserves, though, when having to sign a license agreement as part of a purchase of physical copies of works, staff should carefully review the contract to make sure such terms do not exist and, when possible, strike them from the document if such terms are present. They should also seek to strike any language that might prohibit copies being made of the physical work and then being made accessible to students and instructors via electronic or media reserve. Libraries may be able to place printed copies of works from their electronic collections (e.g., electronic journal collections, electronic book collections, etc.) so long as the license agreement the library signed when acquiring these resources does not expressly forbid doing so. These works can also be made available via electronic or media reserve so long as the license agreement does not also forbid it. Often, instructors will ask if PDF (portable document format) copies of articles and book chapters from electronic collections can be made available to their students via electronic reserve. Some licenses allow reserve staff to do this, while other licenses allow only links or citations to works in these online collections to be shared. An advantage of linking to library resources even when PDF copies can be shared is that it promotes user engagement with the library's online resources, raising student and instructor awareness of them and allowing the library to use data about views, downloads, and so on when making collection development decisions about online resources. Additional considerations tied to linking are discussed in the section "Is the Item Available Electronically?" found in Chapter 3. Alternatively, instructors may ask if a copy of a film found in one of the library's online databases can be embedded in the page for the course found in the institutions' learning management system (LMS), for example, Blackboard or Canvas. Here, not only will reserve staff need to check to see if the license agreement the library signed when acquiring these resources allows for this, but also if the LMS will support the embedding of these films.

Openly Licensed Work

Open license works, often referred to as open access (OA) works, are "digital, online, free of charge, and free of most copyright and licensing restrictions" (Suber 2012, 4). Over the past few decades, OA publishing has emerged as a way for individuals, especially scholars, to make their articles and books more readily available to the public. Most OA works are published under a license that supports the *5R's of Openness* identified by David Wiley:

- Retain a copy of the work for their use
- Reuse the work in a variety of ways

- Revise the work to suit their particular need
- Remix the work with other works to create a new work
- Redistribute the original work or their revised or remixed version to others

As OA works are published digitally, there are many benefits to making them accessible to students via electronic and media reserve services, if the library offers them. This includes having access to a digital copy that can be used across devices and that can easily be revised, remixed, and shared with others. However, if the instructor or students wish to have a copy of an OA work made available via print reserves, the nature of the licenses should allow this.

Some people who publish OA works author their own license terms outlining what uses users may take advantage of when looking to retain, reuse, revise, remix, or redistribute the work. However, most OA works use Creative Commons (CC) licenses to communicate reuse rights to users, a topic discussed in depth in the next section. Works shared under CC licenses are still protected by copyright. CC licenses provide creators with "simple, standardized way to give your permission to share and use [their] creative work—on conditions of [their] choice (Creative Commons, n.d.-a). Creative Commons provides six standard licenses for authors to choose from. They are identified in Table 11.1. All of these licenses would allow works to be circulated to students via print, electronic, and media reserves.

Creative Commons also makes available an instrument known as CC0 that allows "scientists, educators, artists and other creators and owners of copyright- or database-protected content to waive those interests in their works and thereby place them as completely as possible in the public domain, so that others may freely build upon, enhance and reuse the works for any purposes without restriction" (Creative Commons, n.d.-b). The Public Domain Mark is a tool offered by Creative Commons that "enables works that are no longer restricted by copyright to be marked as such in a standard and simple way, making them easily discoverable and available to others" (Creative Commons, n.d.-c). As works with CC0 and the Public Domain mark attached to them are considered to be fully in the public domain in the United States, they can be made available to students via reserve services. More information about the CC0 instrument and the Public Domain Tool can be found in Table 11.2.

Licenses Obtained on a Case-by-Case Basis

For those items not available in the library's online collections or freely and legally available online and whose use does not fall within the scope of user rights found in U.S. copyright law, a special license can may be obtainable

Table 11.1 The Standard Creative Commons Licenses

License Logo	Name	Description
CC BY	Attribution	This license lets others distribute, remix, adapt, and build upon [the original] work, even commercially, as long as they credit [the creator] for the original creation.
CC BY-SA	Attribution-ShareAlike	This license lets others remix, adapt, and build upon [the original] work even for commercial purposes, as long as they credit [the creator] and license their new creations under the identical terms.
CC BY-ND	Attribution-NoDerivatives	This license lets others reuse the work for any purpose, including commercially; however, it cannot be shared with others in adapted form, and credit must be provided to [the creator].
CC BY-NC	Attribution-NonCommercial	This license lets others remix, adapt, and build upon [the original] work non-commercially, and although their new works must also acknowledge [the creator] and be non-commercial, they don't have to license their derivative works on the same terms.
CC BY-NC-SA	Attribution-NonCommercial-ShareAlike	This license lets others remix, adapt, and build upon [the original] work non-commercially, as long as they credit [the creator] and license their new creations under the identical terms.
CC BY-NC-ND	Attribution-NonCommercial-NoDerivatives	This license allows others to download works and share them with others as long as they credit [the creator], but they can't change them in any way or use them commercially.

License descriptions provided by the Creative Commons (https://creativecommons.org/licenses/), and is licensed under a Creative Commons Attribution 4.0 International license (https://creativecommons.org/licenses/by/4.0/).

Table 11.2 Information about the CC0 and Public Domain Mark

License Logo	Name	Description
	CC0	The CC0 mark creators a way to waive all their copyright and related rights in their works to the fullest extent allowed by law.
	Public Domain Mark	The Public Domain Mark enables works that are no longer restricted by copyright to be marked as such in a standard and simple way, making them easily discoverable and available to others.

Mark description provided by the Creative Commons (https://creativecommons.org/share-your-work/public-domain/cc0/) and is licensed under a Creative Commons Attribution 4.0 International license (https://creativecommons.org/licenses/by/4.0/).

from the publisher, film or music service, or an organization like the Copyright Clearance Center (CCC) to make the work available via reserve services. In these situations the terms of the license agreement are often not negotiable and, as such, must be carefully reviewed before the purchase to ensure they allow for the work to be made available via the requested reserve service. Licenses granted in these ways are rarely offered in perpetuity. Instead, they are often for a very specific time period such as a few months. In these cases, reserve staff will need to identify ways to ensure reserve access to the work is suspended and the end of the period the license is granted for.

Special Considerations for Permission and Licensing

The following topics are special considerations for staff and administration to consider when seeking permission or a license to make works available via reserve services.

Who Will Be Responsible for Securing Permission or a License?

Staff may decide that they will obtain permission or a license when it is needed to make and circulate copies of works via reserve services. Alternately, they may require that instructors placing the work on reserve be responsible for obtaining permission or a license for their use when needed. In these situations, it can be helpful for the library to provide instructors with information about the process and template permission forms. Not only can this help facilitate the process, but it can also ensure that the permission the instructor receives addresses all relevant issues identified in this section.

Paying for Licenses

Reserve staff will need to work with library administrators to decide how license fees will be paid. Some libraries establish a budget line for these fees. In these situations, the amount allotted to cover these fees should be reviewed on a regular basis to ensure adequate funding is made available to support the service. In these situations, to help ensure that funds are spent equitably, reserve staff may wish to discuss with administrators if caps will be placed on how much will be paid in fees per request or for a particular course or per instructor. Some libraries pay licensing fees for reserve requests each semester but then bill the department the instructor who placed the request is employed by to be reimbursed. In these situations, library administrators should speak with deans and directors of the various departments around campus to ask if they wish to place any caps on how much will be paid in fees per request or for a particular course or per instructor so they can ensure they have funds to pay this bill when it arrives. Finally, when license fees need to be paid, some libraries require that the instructor who placed the request work with administrators in their department to pay for them and share a copy of the receipt with reserve staff before they will make the work available via reserve services.

Tracking Grants of Permission and Licenses

It is important to keep a record of the permission and licenses received from rightsholders. Any permissions or licenses received by email should not be solely archived with the person who received it. This person should consider forwarding it to a general email account (e.g., a departmental email account) that can be accessed by others, or saving the email as a PDF to a shared file folder that can be accessed by others. This can ensure that anyone who needs to review the grant of permission or license can access it at any time or, in the event the person who obtained the permission or license leaves the institution, the agreement can still be accessed by others. Any grants of permission or licenses that are obtained in a print format (e.g., if the permission form was sent by mail) could be scanned and kept in a digital format to serve as a back-up should the original be lost or damaged.

It will also need to be decided how long copies of the permission and licenses will be kept. At minimum, they need to be kept for the duration the permission or license is granted for. They should not be disposed of once the work is no longer made available via print reserve as the statute of limitations for civil infringement claims is three years (a topic discussed in Chapter 14).

Planning Appropriately

The process of obtaining permission or a license can take time. As discussed above, when working with some publishers or the CCC, a license to make a work available via reserve services can be obtained in a matter of minutes. Sometimes rightsholders will respond to such requests within a day or two, but is not uncommon for the process to take weeks or months, especially for permissions requests. Whoever is responsible for securing permission or a license to make a work available via reserve services should begin doing so well before the work needs to be made available for students. If reserve staff will be responsible for securing permission or licenses, then it is advisable to add information to the procedures for instructors seeking to place items on reserve letting instructors know that requests should be submitted in a timely manner that allows them to do so.

When No Response Is Received, or the Response Is 'No'

There will be times when no acknowledgment or response is received to a permission or license request. In these situations, the person seeking permission should follow up with the rightsholder in a timely manner, and it may be prudent for them try an alternate method of communication from the initial inquiry. For example, if the requestor had called and left a message with the rightsholder about wanting to obtain permission to use a work, they may choose to follow up via email, or vice versa.

If a rightsholder does respond to the request but refuses to give permission for the use or says they are unable to provide a license for the work, all is not lost. In these situations, reserve staff and the instructor placing the request can consider the following options.

Alternative Access Options

There will be times where an item an instructor wishes to make available via reserve services cannot be licensed by the library. For example, now some books are only published in electronic formats, and the vendor refuses to license the work to libraries. Media companies like Netflix, Hulu, HBO (Home Box Office), and Amazon Prime are producing their own original content such as feature films, documentary films, and television shows, and some musicians will only make their music available via platforms that libraries cannot obtain licenses to, such as Spotify or iTunes. Often the only way this type of video content can be accessed is via a subscription to these services. In these situations, students may need to purchase content from or pay for a subscription to these vendors and services, as libraries are unable to make them available based upon the restrictive distribution model. Some instructors have embraced subscription models in place of assigning textbooks—for example, having students in a film class subscribe to Netflix for a semester and teaching films available through the platform. Sometimes these vendors will begin to distribute physical copies of the books, DVDs (Digital Video Discs) or Blu-ray Discs of the films, and CDs (compact discs) of music after an embargo period where they are only available via the subscription service. In these situations, the library can consider obtaining physical copies to circulate via print reserve. Otherwise, in these restrictive licensing situations, if the instructor is not comfortable directing students to buy or subscribe to these services on their own, they may need to identify alternative materials to use as part of course instruction that could be made available via reserve services.

Modifying Their Use of the Work

Generally, permission is going to be sought to make a work available via reserve services when doing so does not fall within the scope of user rights found in U.S. copyright law. If permission or a license to use a work is denied, then the staff supporting reserve services can consider working with the instructor to see if the original request can be modified so that it does fall within the scope of user rights found in U.S. copyright law.

Reevaluating Fair Use

If no response is received from this rightsholder for a permission or license request, fair use can be reconsidered as "reaching a dead end [with the permission process] may suggest that [a] use will cause little or no harm to the market for . . . the work. Armed with the new information, a new fair use analysis may now have a different result" (Crews 2020, 257). The person seeking permission or a license can also incorporate the denial of permission into a new determination of fair use to see if they feel that their use would be considered fair or infringing under the new circumstances. Courts have supported such claims. For example, in the case of *Campbell v. Acuff-Rose Music, Inc.*, the band 2 Live Crew had originally asked Acuff-Rose Music, Inc., which holds the copyright for the song "Oh, Pretty Woman," for their permission to make a parody of the song. Acuff-Rose denied the permission; however, 2 Live Crew still released their song, relying on fair use for their reuse of the first line of lyrics and the opening bass riff of "Oh, Pretty Woman." This resulted in Acuff-Rose bringing a copyright infringement suit against the band and its record company, Luke Skyywalker Records. The case made its way to SCOTUS, and 2 Live Crew's reuse of parts of the original song was found to be a fair use. Justice Souter, in writing the opinion of the court, stated that "being denied permission to use a work does not weigh against a finding of fair use" (Campbell v. Acuff-Rose Music 1994, 585). In the case of *Bill Graham Archives v. Dorling Kindersley, Inc.* (F.3d 605 [2d Cir. 2006]), Dorling Kindersley (DK) originally sought permission from the Bill Graham Archives to reproduce images of seven concert posters in a coffee table book they were publishing that explored the history of the band the Grateful Dead. Talks between the two fell apart, and DK proceeded with the publication of the book without having obtained permission or a license for their use. In the opinion for the U.S. Court of Appeals for the Second Circuit, which found DK's use of the images to be a fair use, Judge Restani wrote that DK's "willingness to pay license fees for reproduction of images does not establish that [they] may not, in the alternative, make fair use of those images" (Bill Graham Archives v. DK 2006, 615).

Finding an Alternative Work to Use

If neither of the proceeding options work, then the staff supporting reserve services can work with the instructor who originally places the request and others, such as a subject librarian, to see if an alternative work can be identified to use in its place.

Putting It All Together

In situations where user rights found in U.S. copyright law do not allow for making and distributing copies of works via print, electronic, or media reserve, then seeking permission or a license to use the work can be considered. Drafting the permissions request is often not difficult; however, identifying the rightsholder, if it is not the author of the work, finding their contact information, and receiving a timely response to requests can all pose various challenges. The biggest challenges associated with obtaining licenses can be reaching terms that are satisfactory for both the library and the rightsholder and the fund available to pay the associated fees. In the rare case neither of these options prove fruitful, there are other considerations the reserve staff can review with the instructor, such as placing the request to make some type of learning materials available to students enrolled in the course, even if it might be an alternative work.

PART III

Additional Legal Considerations for Reserve Services

CHAPTER TWELVE

A Copyright Workflow for Reserve Services

This chapter will outline workflows for addressing copyright considerations associated with making works available via print, electronic, and media reserves. Library staff supporting these services can use the framework and flowcharts found in this chapter to help ensure they are making thoughtful decisions regarding the options available for making requested works available in compliance with the law.

A Copyright Workflow for Print Reserves

Works can lawfully be made available via print reserves if they fall into one of the following categories:

1) The work can be circulated under the first sale doctrine (17 U.S.C. § 109).
2) The work is in the public domain.
3) The person placing the request to circulate the work on print reserve is the rightsholder.
4) The item is licensed in a way that allows it to be circulated via print reserve.
5) A copy of the item can be made and circulated under user rights found in U.S. copyright law, such as fair use (17 U.S.C. § 107) or the reproduction by libraries and archives exception (17 U.S.C. § 108).
6) Permission or a special license is received to circulate the item through print reserve.

If the library is only making physical copies of works such as books, DVDs (Digital Video Discs), and CDs (compact discs) available via print reserves, then reserve staff just need to ensure they are lawfully made copies so they can be circulated under option 1, the first sale doctrine, and that items were not acquired under a license that may preempt the right of first sale (see Chapter 8 for more information on this). If the library will also be circulating photocopies of works such as selections from books or journal articles via print reserves, then the copyright review process becomes more complex, but is manageable. The following framework will help those supporting print reserve services work through these options in a thoughtful and thorough manner. This framework is based upon the *Framework for Analyzing any U.S. Copyright Problem*, developed by Kevin L. Smith and Lisa Macklin (their original version can be found online at http://hdl.handle.net/1808/22723). Smith and Macklin (2014) advise users to proceed through the questions presented "in the order they are presented . . . to identify which of the parts of copyright law apply to the specific problem or fact pattern" that needs to be addressed, and readers of this book are encouraged to do the same with the workflow provided here.

A Framework for Reviewing Print Reserve Copyright Considerations

1. Is the work to be circulated on print reserve a lawfully made copy?
    a. Physical works such as books, DVDs, and CDs can be circulated via print reserve under the first sale doctrine (17 U.S.C. § 109) so long as it was lawfully made under U.S. copyright law and the owner of the copy of the physical work (here, the library or the instructor placing the request) has not entered into any type of binding contract with the rightsholder preempting these rights.
        i. Does the library currently own a lawfully made physical copy of the work? If yes, circulate this copy.
        ii. Can the instructor loan or donate their lawfully made personal copy of the work to the library to circulate to students? If yes, this copy can be circulated via print reserves.
        iii. Would the library be willing to acquire a lawfully made copy of the work? If yes, this copy can be circulated via print reserves.
        iv. Answer 'no' to options i, ii, and iii? If so, proceed to question 2.

    Note: If the library feels the copy to be circulated is not a lawfully made copy (e.g., an instructor brings you a DVD they burned on a computer), they should seek to purchase a lawfully made copy of the work.
2. Is the work in the public domain?
    a. Works in the public domain do not have copyright protection and can be made freely available via print reserve. Works fall into the public domain when their term of copyright has expired, when they contain

no copyrightable content, or when they have been created "by an officer or employee of the United States Government as part of that person's official duties" (17 U.S.C. § 101).

   i. If the work is in the public domain, an original physical copy of the work (e.g., a book, DVD, or CD) or a photocopy of it can be circulated via print reserve.

   ii. If the work if not in the public domain or if you are uncertain of its copyright status, proceed to question 3.

3. If the work is protected by copyright, who owns the rights?

   a. If the person submitting the reserve request is the rightsholder, they can authorize the library to copy and circulate the work on their behalf.

   b. If the person submitting the reserve request is not the rightsholder, then proceed to question 4.

   Note: The instructor will want to ensure they have not signed these rights away via a publication agreement or the work was not created as part of a work made for hire situation.

4. Is the work licensed in a way that allows copies to be made and circulated via print reserve?

   a. For works made available through the library's electronic holdings, is there a license that governs how it can be accessed and used (e.g., do these terms allow for the downloading and printing a copy of an article to circulate via print reserve)? If so, be sure to comply with the license terms.

   b. For works published under an open access (OA) or a Creative Commons (CC) license, make them available in compliance with the license requirements.

   c. If the work is not licensed in a way that allows copies to be made and circulated via print reserve, proceed to question 5.

   Note: OA and CC licenses will likely allow the library to post a copy of the work to the electronic or media reserve platform, but staff should review the terms to be certain.

5. Can making and circulating of copies of the work via print reserve be done under user rights found in U.S. copyright law?

   a. Is the use covered by fair use (17 U.S.C. § 107)?

      i. If the making of a copy of a work might not be considered a fair use, can a physical copy of the original work (e.g., the book the chapter came from or the issue the journal article came from) be placed on print reserve? If so, this work can be lawfully circulated via print reserve under the first sale doctrine.

   b. Could a copy of the work be made and circulated under the reproduction by libraries and archives (17 U.S.C. § 108) right?

   c. If the making and circulating of copies of the work via print reserve cannot be done under user rights found in U.S. copyright law, proceed to question 6.

6. Can permission be obtained to make and circulate a copy of the work via print reserves?
   a. Locate the copyright owner and fully explain your intended use in your permission request.
   b. If no response is received or the answer is no, reconsider your use of this work to see if you can make a fair use.
   c. If permission cannot be obtained to make the work available via print reserve, proceed to question 7.
7. Can a license be obtained to make and circulate a copy of the work via print reserves?
   a. See if the publisher or a rights granting agency can provide a license to make the work available via print reserve.
   b. If no response is received or the answer is no, reconsider your use of this work to see if you can make a fair use of it. If you feel the use would still not be fair, help the person placing the request find an alternative work to use in its place

These options can also be presented in flowchart form. Figure 12.1 outlines the basics of this process. Figure 12.2 breaks these steps down in detail.

A Copyright Workflow for Electronic and Media Reserves

Works can lawfully be made available via electronic reserves (e-reserves) or media reserves if they fall into one of the following categories:

1) The work is in the public domain.
2) The item is licensed in a way that allows it to be circulated via electronic or media reserve.
3) You can link to a version made freely and legally available online.
4) The person placing the request to circulate the work on electronic or media reserve is the rightsholder.
5) A copy of the item can be circulated under user rights found in U.S. copyright law, including fair use (17 U.S.C. § 107) or the reproduction by libraries and archives exception (17 U.S.C. § 108) or the TEACH Act (Technology, Education and Copyright Harmonization Act) (17 U.S.C. § 110[2]).
6) Permission or a special license is received to make the item available via electronic or media reserve.

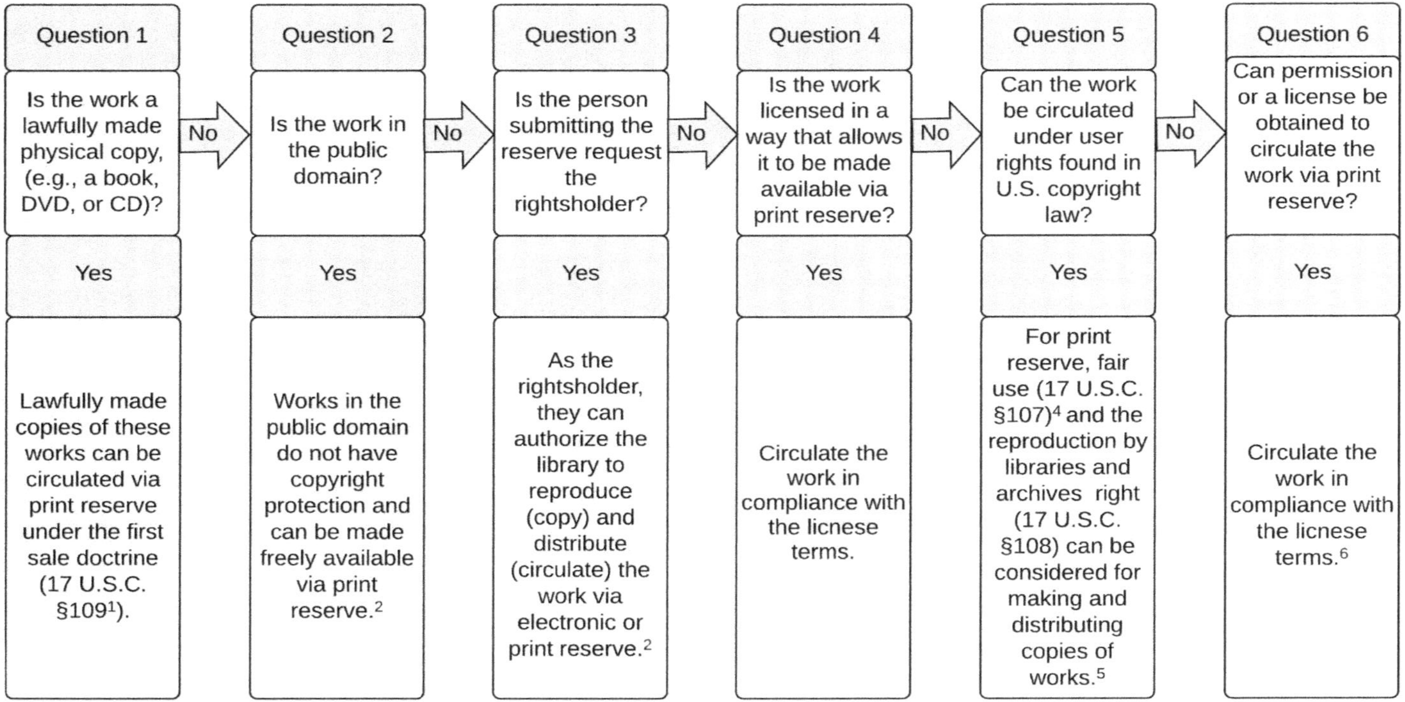

1. Special requirements for circulating copies of computer programs can be found in 17 U.S.C. § 109(2)(b)(2)(A).
2. Public domain works can also be digitized and made freely available via electronic or media reserve, if this might help facilitate access and use.
3. The instructor should make sure they did not sign away their rights via a publication agreement or the copyright belongs to an employer as a result of a work make for hire situation.
4. In situations where fair use may not apply, lawfully made copies of the original work (e.g. the book a chapter is found in or the issue an article is in) can be circulated via print reserve under the first sale doctrine (17 U.S.C. § 109).
5. Consider using a tool like the fair use or Section 108 checklist to aid you in making these determinations.
6. It is recommended that the library have the terms of the permission agreement documented in writing.

Figure 12.1 Making works lawfully available via print reserves: the basics

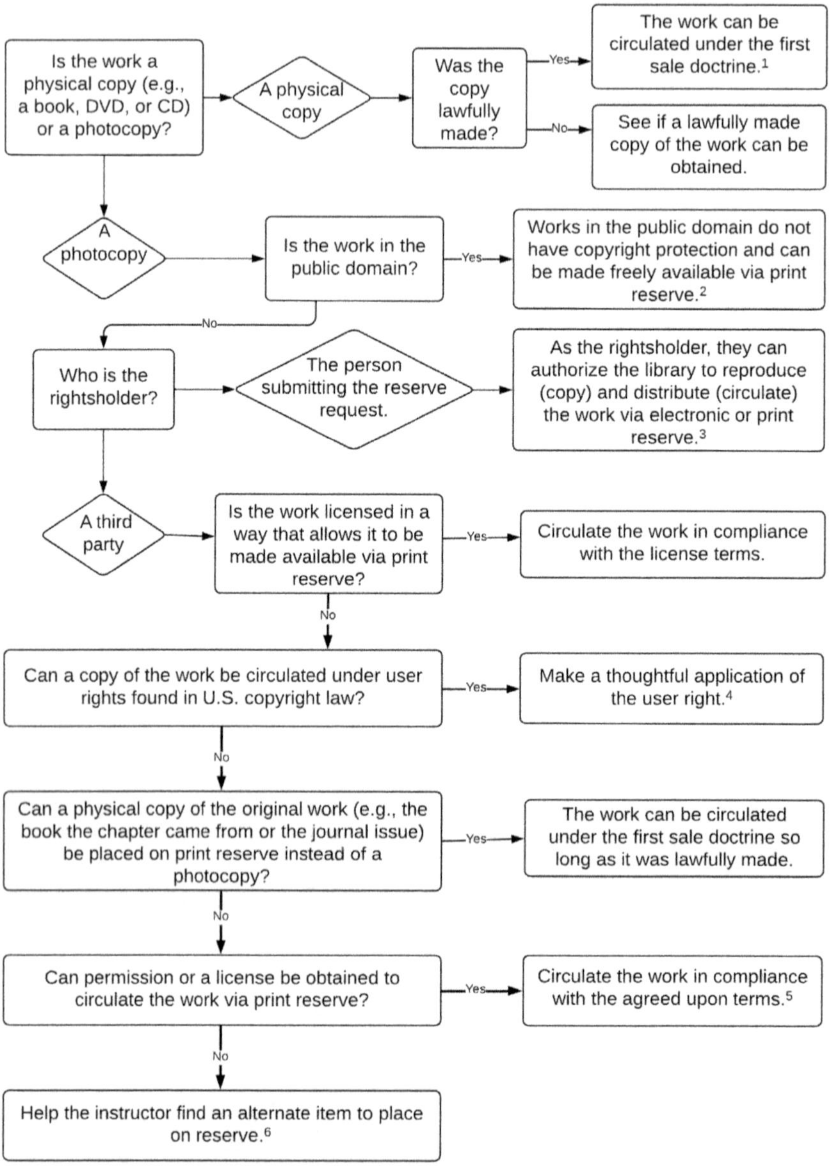

1. Special requirements for circulating copies of computer programs can be found in 17 U.S.C. § 109(2)(b)(2)(A).
2. Public domain works can also be digitized and made freely available via electronic or media reserve, if this might help facilitate access and use.
3. Instructors could sign away their rights via a publication agreement or the copyright could belong to an employer as a result of a work make for hire situation.
4. Consider using a tool like the fair use or Section 108 checklist to aid you in making these determinations.
5. It is recommended that the library have the terms documented in writing.
6. In some situations, the inability to obtain permission or a license can be reconsidered in the application of one of the exceptions, e.g. fair use.

Figure 12.2 Making works lawfully available via print reserves: detailed review

The following framework, which is also a modified version of the *Framework for Analyzing any U.S. Copyright Problem* developed by Kevin L. Smith and Lisa Macklin, will help those managing electronic and media reserve services work through these options in a thoughtful and thorough manner. Reserve staff using the *Framework* should proceed through the questions presented "in the order they are presented . . . to identify which of the parts of copyright law apply to the specific problem or fact pattern that you need to address" (Smith and Macklin 2014).

A Framework for Reviewing Electronic and Media Copyright Considerations

1. Is the work in the public domain?
    a. Works in the public domain do not have copyright protection and can be made freely available via electronic and media reserve. Works fall into the public domain when their term of copyright has expired, when they contain no copyrightable content or when they have been created "by an officer or employee of the United States Government as part of that person's official duties" (17 U.S.C. § 101).
        i. If the work if not in the public domain or if you are uncertain of its copyright status, proceed to question 2.
2. Is the work licensed in a way that allows copies to be made available via electronic and media reserve?
    a. For works made available through the library's electronic holdings, is there a license that governs how it can be accessed and used? For example, does the license allow a copy of the work be downloaded from a database and posted to the library's electronic or media reserve platform, or does it only allow links to the work to be shared via these platforms? If so, be sure to comply with the license terms.
    b. For works published under an OA or a CC license, make them available in compliance with the license requirements.
    c. If the work is not licensed in a way that allows copies to be made available via electronic and media reserve, proceed to question 3.

    Note: OA and CC licenses will likely allow the library to post a copy of the work to the electronic or media reserve platform, but staff should review the terms to be certain.
3. Can you link to a version made legally and freely available online?
    a. Generally, there are no infringement considerations with linking to works made freely and legally available online by the rightsholder. This could include providing a link to:
        i. A post on a blog
        ii. A story made freely accessible on a news website

iii. A film made freely available on a documentary film makers website or an a free on demand streaming service such as Tubi

iv. Music made available via a musician's personal website or YouTube Channel

b. If you are uncertain if a work is made legally available online, proceed to question 4.

4. If the work is protected by copyright, who owns the rights?

   a. If the person submitting the reserve request is the rightsholder, they can authorize the library to make a copy and circulate it via electronic or media reserve.

   b. If the person submitting the reserve request is not the rightsholder, proceed to question 5.

   Note: The person submitting the request will want to ensure they have not signed these rights away via a publication agreement or the work was not created as part of a work made for hire situation.

5. Can making and circulating copies of the work via electronic or media reserve be done under user rights found in U.S. copyright law?

   a. Is the use covered by fair use (17 U.S.C. § 107)?

   b. Could a copy of the work be made available under the reproduction by libraries and archives (17 U.S.C. § 108) right?

   c. Could a copy of the work be made available under the TEACH Act (17 U.S.C. § 110[2])?

   d. If the making and circulating of copies of the work via electronic and media reserve cannot be done under user rights found in U.S. copyright law, proceed to question 6.

   Note: If copies of a work are being made from a source protected by digital rights management (DRM) that limits a user's ability to make copies of or modify the works such as the Content Scramble System employed on many commercially produced DVDs, then considerations tied to the Digital Millennium Copyright Act may also need to be addressed before the copy is made.

6. Can permission be obtained to make and circulate a copy of the work via electronic or media reserve?

   a. Locate the copyright owner and fully explain your intended use in your permission request.

   b. If no response is received or the answer is no, reconsider your use of this work to see if you can make a fair use.

   c. If permission cannot be obtained to make the work available via electronic or media reserve, proceed to question 7.

7. Can a license be obtained to make and circulate a copy of the work via electronic or media reserve?
   a. See if the publisher or a rights granting agency can provide a license to make the work available via electronic or media reserve.
   b. If no response is received or the answer is no, reconsider your use of this work to see if you can make a fair use of it. If you feel the use would still not be fair, help the person placing the request find an alternative work to use in its place.

These options can also be presented in flowchart form. Figure 12.3 outlines the basics of this process. Figure 12.4 breaks these steps down in detail.

Reviewing Requests

Staff will need to determine who will be responsible for reviewing submitted reserve requests to see under which option they may be able to circulate the item. Depending on staffing in the department and the volume of requests, one person may be responsible for this, or multiple people may be. With proper training, staff should be able to confidently handle the review of copyright considerations for the majority of reserve requests submitted. They should work with library administration, though, to establish a process through which they can seek advice on decisions that may involve elevated legal risk. This could include having someone available, such as a copyright librarian or member of the institution's legal counsel, who can help them find additional information about the law that can aid them in making thoughtful applications of it. It could also include having someone from the administrative staff make the final decision regarding which option the will make the work available under. Additional information about developing these processes can be found in Chapter 14.

Addressing Copyright Concerns with Instructors

If staff determine a work cannot be made available to students as originally submitted (e.g., it falls outside the scope of user rights found in U.S. copyright law), then they can share the *Framework* with the instructor who submitted the request to determine what alternate options may be available. For example, staff may determine they are unable to make a photocopy of a selection from a book available via print or electronic reserve but could make a physical copy of the book available via print reserve for students to borrow. If library staff find they are unable to take advantage of any of these options outlined in this chapter to make works available via print, electronic, or media reserve, then they should work with the instructor and other staff

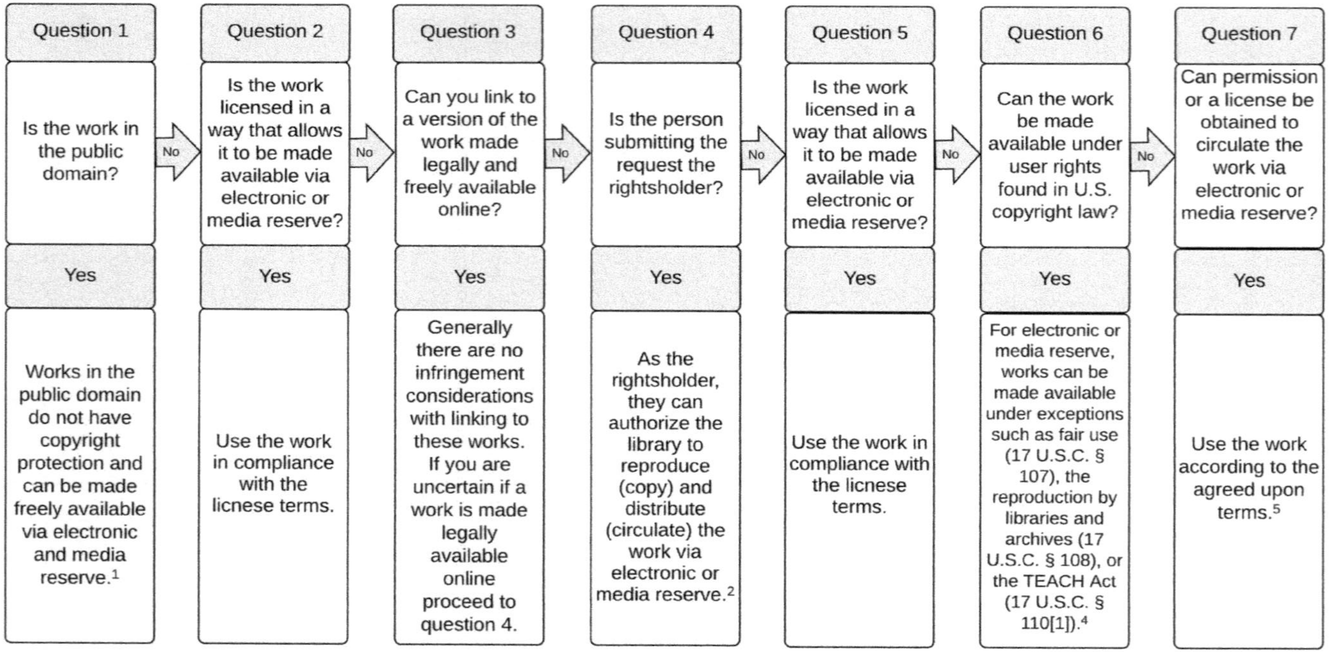

1. Public domain works can also be digitized and made freely available via the library's catalog or the World Wide Web, if this might help facilitate access and use.
2. The instructor should make sure he or she did not sign away their rights via a publication agreement or under a work make for hire contract.
3. Remember that exceptions such as fair use may be considered in situations where an intended use exceeds the bounds of a CC license.
4. If copies of a work are being made from a source protected by digital rights management software that limits a user's ability to make copies of or modify the works such as the Content Scramble System employed on many commercially produced DVDs, then considerations tied to the Digital Millennium Copyright Act may also need to be addressed before the copy is made.
5. It is recommended that the library have the terms of the permission agreement or license documented in writing.

Figure 12.3 Making works lawfully available via electronic and media reserves: the basics

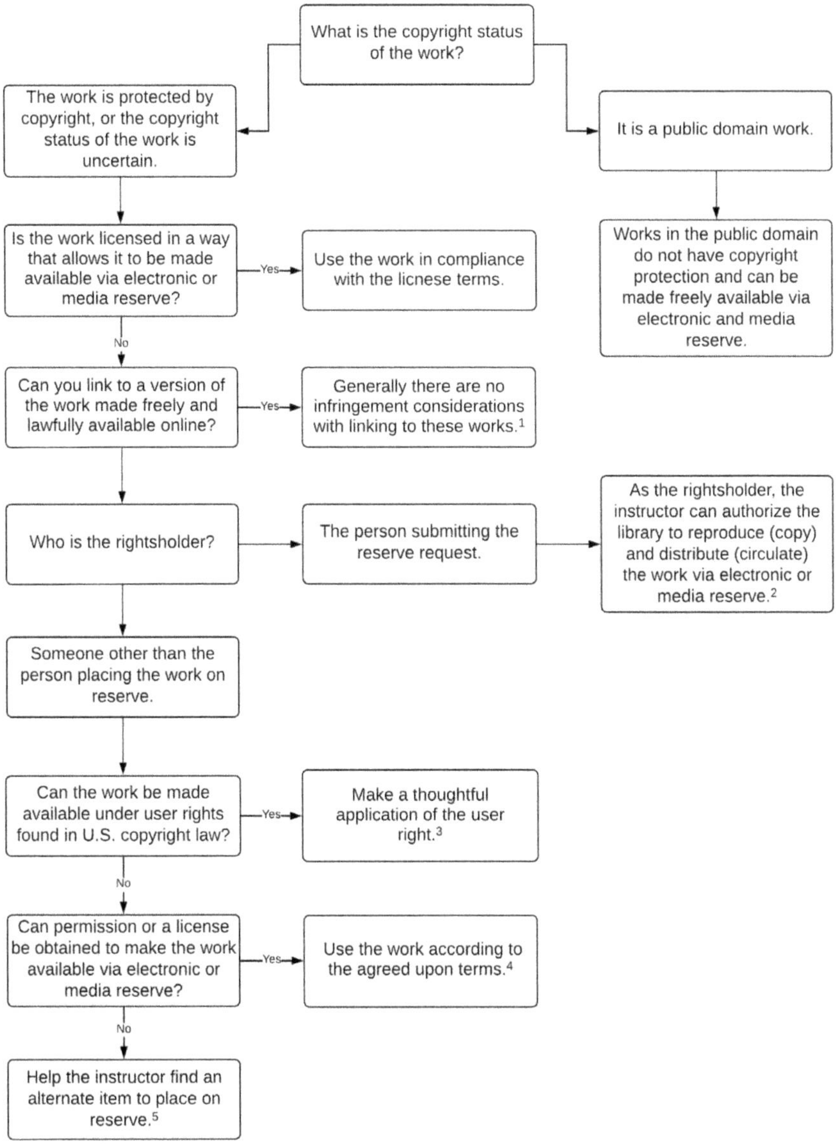

1. If you are uncertain if a work is made legally available online proceed to question 4.
2. Instructors could away their rights via a publication agreement or the copyright could belong to an employer as a result of a work make for hire situation.
3. If copies of a work are being made from a source protected by digital rights management software that limits a user's ability to make copies of or modify the works such as the Content Scramble System employed on many commercially produced DVDs, then considerations tied to the Digital Millennium Copyright Act may also need to be addressed before the copy is made.
4. It is recommended that the library have the terms documented in writing.
5. In some situations, the inability to obtain permission or a license can be reconsidered in the application of one of the exceptions, e.g. fair use.

Figure 12.4 Making works lawfully available via electronic and media reserves: detailed review (e.g., a subject specialist librarian) to identify other works that could be lawfully available to students that would serve as a quality substitute for the original item. Staff can also consider making copies of the workflow or the flowcharts provided in this chapter to instructors as it may aid them in working through these options, helping to ensure their request can be quickly processed and made available via reserve services.

Putting It All Together

There are many options available for lawfully making works available to students through reserve services. Staff can use the *Framework* found in this chapter and the associated flowcharts to determine which option is the best fit for submitted requests. Having a strong copyright policy based upon the law and working carefully through the options above will not guarantee that the library will never receive inquiries from a rightsholder about making a work available via these services; however, it will help demonstrate the library's intent to balance the rights granted to creators of copyrightable works with the rights granted to users, the processes used to make thoughtful determinations, and their efforts to "promote the Progress of Science and useful Arts" (U.S. Const. art. I, § 8, c8) through research, education, and the creation of new copyrightable works.

CHAPTER THIRTEEN

Accessibility Considerations Related to Reserve Services

The *Code of Ethics* of the American Library Association (ALA) emphasizes the responsibility of staff to "provide the highest level of service to all library users through appropriate and usefully organized resources; equitable service policies; equitable access; and accurate, unbiased, and courteous responses to all requests" (Committee on Professional Ethics, 2021). Promoting equitable access to information requires libraries to ensure that resources and services they make available to patrons can be accessed by people with disabilities.

The term disability can be defined in a variety of ways. Medically, it means "any condition of the body or mind that makes it more difficult for the person with the condition to do certain activities and interact with the world around them" (Center for Disease Control, 2020). Legally, it can mean a "physical or mental impairment that substantially limits one or more major life activities, a record of such an impairment, or being regarded as having such an impairment" (ADA National Network, n.d.-a), though various laws define the term differently.

Ensuring that resources and services made available through the library are accessible to patrons with disabilities is not just an ethical obligation. There are federal laws and international standards that prohibit discrimination against people with disabilities, such as:

- The Rehabilitation Act of 1973, Section 504. Any institutions of higher education that receive federal funding (e.g., Pell Grants or federal work study funding) must abide by this law. It states that "no otherwise qualified individual with a disability in the United States . . . shall, solely by reason of his or her disability, be excluded from the participation in, be denied the benefits of, or be subjected to discrimination under any program or activity receiving Federal financial assistance" (29 U.S.C. § 701).

- The Rehabilitation Act of 1973, Section 508. This section of the Rehabilitation Act applies "to all Federal agencies when they develop, procure, maintain, or use electronic and information technology" (U.S. Access Board, n.d.). It requires these agencies to ensure that employees with disabilities or members of the public with disabilities can access electronic resources and information technology in ways comparable to those who do not. Section 508 also addresses accessibility standards for webpages. While most institutions of higher education are not federal agencies, "many states have codified Section 508 to be state law, which requires state institutions to comply with these requirements" (Bazeley 2018).
- The Americans with Disabilities Act (ADA) of 1990. "The ADA is a civil rights law that prohibits discrimination against individuals with disabilities in all areas of public life, including jobs, schools, transportation, and all public and private places that are open to the general public," and provides baseline requirements intended "to make sure that people with disabilities have the same rights and opportunities as everyone else" (ADA National Network, n.d.-b). Title I of the act requires both public and private employers to "provide reasonable accommodations to qualified applicants or employees," allowing people with disabilities to "access the same employment opportunities and benefits available to people without disabilities" (ADA National Network, n.d.-b). Title II "prohibits discrimination against qualified individuals with disabilities in all programs, activities, and services of public entities," and Title III "prohibits private places of public accommodation from discriminating against individuals with disabilities" (ADA National Network, n.d.-b).
- Assistive Technology Act (ATA) of 2004. This law, which reauthorized and amended the Assistive Technology Act of 1998, among other things, provides states with grant funding to provide assistive technology to people with disabilities so they can more fully participate in educational opportunities, employment, and other life activities. The concept of universal design is addressed in the ATA and involves "designing and delivering products and services that are usable by people with the widest possible range of functional capabilities, which include products and services that are directly accessible (without requiring assistive technologies) and products and services that are interoperable with assistive technologies" (29 U.S.C. § 3002).
- The Twenty-First Century Communications and Video Accessibility Act (CVAA). Signed into law in October 2010 by President Barak Obama, the CVAA updated "federal communications law to increase the access of persons with disabilities to modern communications . . . including new digital,

broadband, and mobile innovations" (Federal Communications Commission 2019).

- The Web Content Accessibility Guidelines (WCAG). These are a series of web accessibility guidelines published by the World Wide Web Consortium (W3C). The guidelines are the international standards of organization for the internet and apply to anyone designing web content such as websites, applications, and Web content. The first set of guidelines, WCAG 1.0 was published by W3C in 1999. Version 2.0 was published in 2008 and was updated in version 2.1, published in 2018. Version 2.2 is currently being drafted and scheduled to be finalized in the summer of 2022. Some states have regulations in place requiring that state government websites comply with a version of these standards, or have implemented their own web accessibility standards based upon them. This means public educational institutions in these states would have to ensure they are complying with them.

Butler et al. (2019, 10) tell us that failure to comply with the law exposes libraries and educational institutions "to risk of enforcement actions that can be brought by multiple federal agencies as well as by affected individuals and associations committed to disability rights." The University of Minnesota Duluth maintains a listing of institutions of higher education that have faced liability over complaints for inaccessible web content and technologies. As of the writing of this book (2022), this list, found online at https://www.d.umn.edu/~lcarlson/atteam/lawsuits.html, identifies over 40 institutions that have been involved in accessibility lawsuits, complaints, and settlements.

Unfortunately, most resources libraries may be looking to acquire for their collection are not accessible or created with the principles of universal design in mind, and, as a result, libraries often to struggle to provide patrons with disabilities with access to resources they can easily engage with. This is because of:

- The small percentage of published works that are made available in formats that can be used by people with disabilities (e.g., large print books for use by people who have visual impairments, audio versions of books that can be used by people who have dyslexia) and shrinking library budgets that affect the funding available to acquire these items when they actually are available for purchase.
- Vendor platforms that do not meet web accessibility standards.
- Resources included in vendor platforms that are not accessible. For example, a PDF (portable document format) copy of a journal article that is not machine-readable or a film posted to a streaming video database that does not have subtitles for the deaf and hard of hearing (SDH).

- Restrictions set forth by vendors when licensing resources to libraries that limit the ways staff and users can apply technology to overcome accessibility issues.

Staff try to respond to these challenges by making accessible copies of these resources. This could include:

- Making a digital copy of a print book so that someone who is blind or who has visual impairment can engage with it using a Braille terminal or screen reader
- Making an audio version of a print work or digital document (e.g., PDF copies of newspapers, magazine, and scholarly articles) so that someone who is blind or who has a visual impairment can listen to the text or so that it can be used by those with learning disabilities (e.g., dyslexia)
- Adding SDH to a video, allowing a person who is deaf or has a hearing impairment to follow the words being spoken on screen and identifying for them background noises and other sounds taking place as part of the action
- Adding audio description to a video to provide people who are blind or who have visual impairments with "narrative descriptions of a program's key visual elements such as actions, graphics and scene changes . . . carefully blended into natural pauses in the program soundtrack" (Harris Family Center for Disability and Health Policy n.d.)
- Adding descriptive text (also sometimes called alternate text) to pictorial and graphical works included on websites and digital documents so that those who are blind or who have visual impairments can gain an understanding of what is being represented

Copyright considerations come into play when staff make these accessible copies as this often involves exercising rights granted to rightsholders in Section 106. For example, creating a Braille copy of a textbook involves reproducing the original work and the creation of a derivative.

An entire book would be needed to explore the considerations associated with libraries ensuring that all their services and resources are fully accessible to patrons with disabilities. Given the nature of this book, this chapter will focus on the administrative considerations involved with ensuring that library reserve services are accessible. Information will also be provided on options available under U.S. copyright law for making accessible copies of works for people with disabilities. Combined, readers will be able to use their knowledge of these administrative and legal issues to better identify barriers to access for people with disabilities and work with others at their institution to find solutions for them.

Administrative Considerations

To comply with the accessibility requirements found in the law, many institutions of higher education have established a disability services office (DSO) dedicated to ensuring that employees and students with disabilities receive appropriate accommodations when engaging with institutional services and resources. Employees of the DSO will be key allies in helping staff identify and address accessibility issues related to the services and resources they provide. When it comes to reserve services, areas that should be evaluated for accessibility are outlined below.

Reserve Service Platforms

The platforms that are used to provide access to print, electronic, and media reserves should be evaluated to ensure they meet the accessibility standards outlined in the law. For print reserves this may be the online public access catalog. It could also include the discovery layer, if reserve materials are indexed there. For electronic and media reserves this will involve evaluating the platform used to host these services. If electronic and media reserve services are made available through the institution's learning management system, it is likely that the institution has done some work in evaluating it for accessibility. If these services are being offered via a home-grown platform, then DSO staff can help staff determine if it meets accessibility standards. If electronic and media reserves are made available through a commercial platform, the library should request a VPAT (Voluntary Product Accessibility Template) from the vendor to determine its level of accessibility. A VPAT is a "document that explains how . . . products such as software, hardware, electronic content, and support documentation meet (conform to) the Revised 508 Standards for IT accessibility" (Office of Government-wide Policy 2018). The VPAT will help the library determine if the platform they use for reserve services will meet the accessibility needs of their users. Having copies of the VPAT will be especially important if a library is shopping for a platform when launching reserve services or when switching platforms, as it will allow them to make a more informed decision about which platform to choose.

Reserve Request Procedures

Staff need to determine if the procedures put into place for the submission of reserve requests can be fully accessed by everyone. Staff can work with the DSO to ensure that information posted to the library's website about reserve services and any electronic copies of reserve request forms posted there comply with accessibility standards. If the library posts online request forms in a document format (e.g., a Word document or PDF document), it should also be confirmed that these forms are formatted in a way that allows people with disabilities to fully engage with them.

Library Spaces

It is likely that a lot of time and attention has already gone into ensuring that the library itself is accessible to people with disabilities, but it is important for staff to reevaluate their spaces on a regular basis to see if any short-term barriers to access have appeared or if accessibility features can be improved upon. Short-term barriers to access that could impact users looking to use print reserve items or wishing to speak with staff in person about any type of reserve service can include wet, muddy, or icy walkways leading into the building that can make it difficult for people who have mobility issues to get inside or aisles and pathways that do not have appropriate clearance or that may be temporarily obstructed. Staff should perform periodic sweeps of the building throughout the day to identify and remove these short-term barriers to access. In situations where a library may be looking to remodel a space or redesign a service point, staff from the DSO and a qualified architect can ensure changes are made with accessibility considerations in mind.

The Accessibility of Library Resources

Any item in the library's print and electronic collections may pose accessibility issues for people with disabilities. However, many of these issues can be overcome through the use of assistive technology or the making of accessible copies of works. Assistive technology is "any item, piece of equipment, or product system that is used to increase, maintain, or improve functional capabilities of individuals with disabilities. Examples include message boards, screen readers, refreshable Braille displays, keyboard and mouse modifications, and head pointers" (ADA National Network, n.d.-a). Many libraries have some assistive technology that patrons with disabilities can use in-house to engage with resources. The DSO will also likely have assistive technology available for use by those members of the campus community with disabilities.

In some situations, print or electronic library resources will need to be remediated for a person who has a disability. As mentioned previously, when an accessible copy of a copyrightable work needs to be made for patrons who have a disability, there are copyright considerations that must be addressed. These considerations will be explored in the next section of this chapter, and then suggestions and recommendations for collaborating with the DSO to make accessible copies will be addressed after.

Copyright and the Making of Accessible Copies for Reserves

It may seem that in situations where an accessible version of a copyrightable work needs to make for use by a patron, copyright law and accessibility laws are at odds with each other. Copyright law can be used to restrict access to works and the ways they are shared with others, while accessibility laws require libraries to make works in their collection accessible to people with disabilities. Fortunately, user rights found in U.S. copyright law can be utilized by libraries and educational institutions looking to make accessible copies of works available to people with disabilities. These include Section 121, reproduction for blind or other people with disabilities; Section 121A, reproduction for blind or other people with disabilities in Marrakesh Treaty countries; and Section 107, fair use. There are also Digital Millennium Copyright Act (DMCA) exemptions libraries and educational institutions can take advantage of when making accessible copies of works.

Limitations on Exclusive Rights: Reproduction for Blind or Other People with Disabilities (17 U.S.C. § 121)

Section 121 (also known as the Chafee Amendment) was added to U.S. copyright law in 1996 to address the making accessible copies of copyrightable works for the blind or other people with disabilities. In October 2018, President Donald Trump signed the Marrakesh Treaty Implementation Act (MTIA), which revised Section 121. It also created Section 121A to comply with the Marrakesh Treaty to Facilitate Access to Published Works for Persons Who Are Blind, Visually Impaired, or Otherwise Print Disabled (Marrakesh Treaty), and in February 2019 the United States' ratification documents were deposited with the World Intellectual Property Organization (WIPO), officially making the United States one of the treaty ratifiers. The Marrakesh Treaty is an international treaty that "requires Contracting Parties to introduce a standard set of limitations and exceptions to copyright rules in order to permit reproduction, distribution and making available of published works in formats designed to be accessible to VIPs [visually impaired persons], and to permit exchange of these works across borders by organizations that serve those beneficiaries" (World Intellectual Property Organization, n.d.-b).

Changes Made to Section 121 Under the MTIA

With the passage of the MTIA, Section 121(a) now reads, "Notwithstanding the provisions of section 106, it is not an infringement of copyright for an *authorized entity* to reproduce or to distribute in the United States copies or phonorecords of a previously published literary work or of a previously published musical work that has been fixed in the form of text or notation if such copies or phonorecords are reproduced or distributed in *accessible formats* exclusively for use by *eligible persons*" (emphasis added).

Section 121 contains three key definitions readers should be familiar with.

Authorized entities. Section 121(d)(2) tells us this term "means a nonprofit organization or a governmental agency that has a primary mission to provide specialized services relating to training, education, or adaptive reading or information access needs of blind or other persons with disabilities." The opinion of the United States District Court for the Southern District of New York in *Authors Guild, Inc. v. HathiTrust* (755 F.3d 87 [2014]) confirmed that academic libraries can be authorized entities. It states, "The ADA requires that libraries of educational institutions have a primary mission to reproduce and distribute their collections to print-disabled individuals, making each library a potential "authorized entity" under the Chafee Amendment" (Authors Guild v. HathiTrust 2012, 465). Nonprofit academic institutions will generally fall within the scope of this definition as well.

Accessible formats. According to Section 121(d)(1) an accessible format "means an alternative manner or form that [permits] an eligible person . . . to have access [to a copyrighted work] as feasibly and comfortably as a person without such disability as described in paragraph [d](3)."

Eligible persons. Under the Section 121(d)(3) an eligible person is defined as an individual who, regardless of any other disability—

(A) is blind;

(B) has a visual impairment or perceptual or reading disability that cannot be improved to give visual function substantially equivalent to that of a person who has no such impairment or disability and so is unable to read printed works to substantially the same degree as a person without an impairment or disability; or

(C) is otherwise unable, through physical disability, to hold or manipulate a book or to focus or move the eyes to the extent that would be normally acceptable for reading. (17 U.S.C. § 121[d][3])

Butler et al. (2019) tell us the language found in this statute "helps clarify that the provision is meant to apply not only to physical disabilities specifically affecting vision, but also to any disability (including learning disabilities and mobility impairments) that affect the ability to read text in a standard format" (30).

Eligible works. The MTIA greatly expanded the categories of works covered under Section 121(a) by striking the word "nondramatic" from the original text and adding the words "or of a previously published musical work that has been fixed in the form of text or notation." As a result, the rights granted under Section 121(a) now apply to previously published musical works and any type of previously published literary work, with the exception of "standardized, secure, or norm-referenced tests and related testing material, or to computer programs, except the portions thereof that are in conventional human language (including descriptions of pictorial works) and displayed to users in the ordinary course of using the computer programs" (17 U.S.C. § 121[b][2]).

Section 121 compliance requirements. When making accessible copies of a "previously published literary work or of a previously published musical work that has been fixed in the form of text or notation" under Section 121(a), authorized entities must abide by three rules that are outlined in Section 121(b)(1):

(1) Copies or phonorecords to which this section applies shall—
- (A) not be reproduced or distributed in the United States in a format other than an accessible format exclusively for use by eligible persons;
- (B) bear a notice that any further reproduction or distribution in a format other than an accessible format is an infringement; and
- (C) include a copyright notice identifying the copyright owner and the date of the original publication.

If the authorized entity does not comply with these rules, their making of the accessible copy would not be covered under this section of the law.

Sharing Copies of Accessible Works Across Borders

In addition to revising the text of Section 121, the MTIA established Section 121A, which addresses the importing and exporting of copies of accessible literary and musical works for use by eligible persons. When it comes to exporting works, this section of the law allows

> an authorized entity, acting pursuant to this section, to export copies or phonorecords of a previously published literary work or of a previously published musical work that has been fixed in the form of text or notation in accessible formats to another country. These exports are allowed when the exportation is made either to—
>
> (1) an authorized entity located in a country that is a Party to the Marrakesh Treaty; or
> (2) an eligible person in a country that is a Party to the Marrakesh Treaty,

> if prior to the exportation of such copies or phonorecords, the authorized entity engaged in the exportation did not know or have reasonable grounds to know that the copies or phonorecords would be used other than by eligible persons. (17 U.S.C. § 121[A][a])

Section 121A(f)(1) makes it clear that "the terms 'accessible format', 'authorized entity', and 'eligible person'" as used in Section 121A "have the meanings given those terms in sections" 121(d)(1), 121(d)(2), and 121(d)(3), respectively. A list of countries that are party to the Marrakesh Treaty can be found on WIPO's website: https://www.wipo.int/treaties/en/ip/marrakesh/.

In regards to the importing of accessible copies of literary and musical works, Section 121(A)(b) states that "is not an infringement of copyright for an authorized entity or an eligible person, or someone acting on behalf of an eligible person, acting pursuant to this section, to import copies or phonorecords of a previously published literary work or of a previously published musical work that has been fixed in the form of text or notation in accessible formats."

As part of the requirements for outlined in Section 121(A)(c) for making accessible copies of works available across borders, authorized entities must

(1) establish that the persons the authorized entity serves are eligible persons;
(2) limit to eligible persons and authorized entities the distribution of accessible format copies by the authorized entity;
(3) discourage the reproduction and distribution of unauthorized copies;
(4) maintain due care in, and records of, the handling of copies of works by the authorized entity, while respecting the privacy of eligible persons on an equal basis with others; and
(5) facilitate effective cross-border exchange of accessible format copies by making publicly available—
    (A) the titles of works for which the authorized entity has accessible format copies or phonorecords and the specific accessible formats in which they are available; and
    (B) information on the policies, practices, and authorized entity partners of the authorized entity for the cross-border exchange of accessible format copies. (17 U.S.C. § 121[A][c])

Section 121A will allow for time savings and costs savings in getting accessible copies of works into the hands of eligible persons in the United States by importing accessible copies made in other countries. It will also benefit those eligible persons living in the United States who do not speak English as a primary language as it will allow for the importing of accessible copies of works in foreign languages from countries that are a party to the Marrakesh Treaty where their primary language is spoken. Just as important, under Section 121A authorized entities located in the United States will now have more flexible options for sharing accessible copies of works they make with an authorized entity or eligible person living in a country that is a party to the Marrakesh Treaty. For libraries and educational institutions, this could include students who are studying abroad or distance learners based in a Marrakesh country as well as international students who are home over breaks.

Using Section 121 and 121A

While the MTIA has made significant improvements to Section 121, there are some aspects of the law that libraries and educational institutions should be aware of when utilizing it.

Under the revised Section 121(a), authorized entities are empowered "to reproduce or to distribute" works in accessible formats to eligible persons in the United States. Other rights outlined in Section 106, including the right to publicly perform or display a work, are not covered here. The making and distributing of accessible copies or phonorecords of unpublished literary and musical works are still not covered under Section 121. The making and distributing of accessible copies of other types of copyrightable works, such as dramatic works; pantomimes and choreographic works; pictorial, graphic, and sculptural works; motion pictures and other audiovisual works; sound recordings; and architectural works, is also not covered under Section 121. Not all is lost, though, as nothing in Section 121 restricts the application of other user rights found in U.S. copyright law when making copies of these categories of works for people with disabilities. Libraries and educational institutions can consider fair use when looking to make accessible copies of these types of works. If the making of such a copy falls outside the scope of fair use, libraries and educational institutions can consider obtaining permission from the rightsholder to make the accessible copy.

Under Sections 121 and 121A, authorized entities can and should include illustrations from literary works or published musical works in the accessible copy being made. A report published by the Senate in conjunction with the passage of MTIA makes this clear, stating:

> In keeping with the [Marrakesh Treaty], it is Congress' intent that accessible format copies made pursuant to section 121 and/or section 121A include illustrations that are integrated with the text or notation being rendered into an accessible format. For example, where a textbook includes graphs, maps, or tables of information, the accessible format version of the textbook may include presentations of that information in as accessible a way as possible; where a book includes photographs or illustrations accompanying the text, the accessible format copy may

> include suitable descriptions of the photographs and illustrations. If illustrations, graphs, maps, tables, or photographs included in a text subject to sections 121 and/or 121A are also separately copyrighted works, they are subject to section 121 and/or section 121A to the same extent as the copyrighted works in which they are embodied. (S. Rep. No. 115-261, 3, 2018)

Should a library or educational institution, acting as an authorized entity looking to import or export an accessible copy of a work under Section 121A, it must be careful to abide by the rules outlined in Section 121(A)(c). These rules may seem a bit overwhelming; however, Section 121A(c) states that "in conducting activities under subsection (a) or (b), an authorized entity shall establish and follow *its own practices, in keeping with its particular circumstances*" (emphasis added). A report published by the Senate in conjunction with the passage of MTIA emphasizes that there are no formal or federalized standards that each authorized entity must adhere to. Instead, "the practices required under section 121A(c) can be established by each authorized entity to meet that provision's stated objectives in whatever manner is suitable to the authorized entity's own particular circumstances . . [and] an organization that establishes the required practices to qualify for section 121A is under no obligation to apply the practices to the organization's other activities in relation to copyrighted works and section 121A(c) implies no new obligations in relation to the organization's other activities" (No. 115-261, 4).

Fair Use (17 U.S.C. § 107)

As readers will recall from the discussion of fair use in Chapter 6, making a fair use determination involves the balancing of the four factors found in Section 107:

(1) the purpose and character of the use, including whether such use is of a commercial nature or is for nonprofit educational purposes;

(2) the nature of the copyrighted work;

(3) the amount and substantiality of the portion used in relation to the copyrighted work as a whole; and

(4) the effect of the use upon the potential market for or value of the copyrighted work. (17 U.S.C. § 107)

The application of fair use in making accessible copies of works for people with disabilities is supported by legislative reports, judicial opinions, and community practice.

Legislative Reports

The House Committee on the Judiciary addressed the making of accessible copies in a report they issued to coincide with the passage of the Copyright Act of 1976. It states:

> A special instance illustrating the application of the fair use doctrine pertains to the making of copies or phonorecords of works in the special forms needed for the use of blind persons. These special forms, such as copies in Braille and phonorecords of oral readings (talking books), are not usually made by the publishers for commercial distribution. The making of a single copy or phonorecord by an individual as a free service for blind persons would properly be considered a fair use under section 107. (H.R. Rep. No. 94-1476, 73, 1976)

Though this statement focuses on the making of copies of accessible works for blind persons, it is not unreasonable to think the argument it makes regarding the application of fair use could extend to the making of copies for those with other disabilities. While this report does not hold the force of law, it can help staff better understand that in codifying fair use into U.S. copyright law as part of the Copyright Act of 1976, Congress was looking to support uses that help promote equitable access to copyrighted works, especially in those situations where publishers are not meeting this need.

Judicial Opinions

The case that is most applicable to the making of accessible copies of works for reserve services may be *Authors Guild v. HathiTrust* (755 F.3d 87 [2014]). The HathiTrust Digital Library (HDL) is "a digital preservation repository and highly functional access platform . . . [that] provides long-term preservation and access services for public domain and in copyright content from a variety of sources, including Google, the Internet Archive, Microsoft, and in-house partner institution initiatives" (HathiTrust Digital Library n.d.). HathiTrust, the organization set up to operate the HDL, was formed by a group of academic libraries that had allowed Google to digitize books in their collection as part of the Google Books Project. The digital copies of the books included in the HDL allowed for the preservation of these works, enable users to perform full text searchers for specific words in the digitized text found there, and allows patrons at member libraries who have print disabilities to access the full text "to the contents of works in the digital library using adaptive technologies such as software that converts the text into spoken words, or that magnifies the text" (Authors Guild v. HathiTrust 2014, 91). In 2011 the Authors Guild sued HathiTrust, claiming that, among other things, that their digitization of the works in the library violated the rights granted to them under Section 106.

The 2012 opinion issued by Judge Harold Baer of the U.S. District Court for the Southern District of New York in this case supported the application of fair use and Section 121 when making copies of works for people with disabilities. On appeal, the United States Court of Appeals for the Second Circuit also ruled in favor of the HDL, finding, among other things, that providing access to digitized HDL works for the print-disabled falls within the scope of the fair use doctrine. When considering the first factor of fair use, the appellate court stated that "providing access to the print-disabled is . . . a valid purpose under Factor One" (102). For the second factor it concluded that because "the disabled can obtain access to copyrighted works of all kinds . . . Factor Two weighs against fair use [but] this does not preclude a finding of fair use" (102). When considering the third factor of fair use the court stated that "it is reasonable for the Libraries to retain both text and image copies" from the books they had scanned as it "is necessary" for individuals with disabilities to have access to both in order "to perceive the books fully" (103). For the fourth factor of fair use, the court found that "the present-day market for books accessible to the handicapped is . . . insignificant" primarily because publishers often do not make their books available in the specialized formats needed by those who do have print disabilities. The court concluded this part of its analysis by holding that, "weighing the factors together, we conclude that the doctrine of fair use allows the Libraries to provide full digital access to copyrighted works to their print-disabled patrons" (103).

Community Practice

In addition to addressing the application of fair use to reserve practices, the *Code of Best Practices in Fair Use for Academic and Research Libraries* (the Code) also addresses, in Principle Five, Reproducing Material for use by Disabled Students, Faculty, Staff, and Other Appropriate Users. The Code emphasizes the importance of equitable access to information, stating:

> [M]aking library materials accessible serves the goals of copyright, not to mention the goals of a just and inclusive society, and has no negative consequence for rightsholders who have not entered the market to serve these users. Such uses add value to a work by making it available to communities that would otherwise be excluded, presenting the work in a format the rights holder has not provided and to an audience that the rights holder is not serving. (ARL 2012, 21–22)

In exploring the application of fair use to the making of accessible copies, the Code finds that "when fully accessible copies are not readily available from commercial sources, it is fair use for a library to (1) reproduce materials in its collection in accessible formats for the disabled upon request, and (2) retain those reproductions for use in meeting subsequent requests from qualified patrons" (22). The Code identifies two steps staff can take to help support the application of fair use when making accessible copies of works available for students with disabilities.

(1) "Claims for fair use may well be further reinforced if technological protection measures are applied to assure that limitations on the use of accessible copies are observed" (22).
(2) "The fair use case will be enhanced by programs that are well publicized to the affected communities together with policies that are widely and consistently applied" (22).

The Code also encourages libraries to provide those patrons receiving accessible copies made under the auspices of fair use with information about their own reuse rights and responsibilities regarding the copies they receive. This practice can be supported by the library by providing copyright education where requests for accessible copies of works are submitted and by making quality copyright information available for users online through their website or via books and resources created by reputable authors for checkout in their collection.

Using the Code

Fair use determinations must be made for each individual accommodation request received, and fair use tools can be used to ensure that a thoughtful application of the four factors is being made. As stated previously, the Code does not hold the force of law, but it does describe "a carefully derived consensus within the library community about how those rights should apply in certain recurrent situations" and "it enhances the ability of librarians to rely on fair use" (ARL 2012, 3). Therefore, staff looking to make copies of accessible work for patrons should carefully consider its application.

While this document is framed as the *Code of Best Practices in Fair Use for Academic and Research Libraries*, the considerations it puts forward can be taken into account by DSO staff when they are making accessible copies of works on the library's behalf. As the DSO often only provides accommodation services for institutional staff and currently enrolled students, community patrons who use the library may not be able to take advantage of their services. In these situations, staff may need to consider making the accessible copy of the work for the patron, and here the Code can provide them with guidance in considering their options for doing so in compliance with U.S. copyright law.

Digital Millennium Copyright Act Considerations

As discussed in the section on the Digital Millennium Copyright Act (DMCA) in Chapter 10, Section 1201(a)(1)(A) prohibits users from circumventing "a technological measure that effectively controls access to a [copyrighted] work." In those situations where a library or educational institution needs to circumvent a technological measure put into place by a rightsholder to control access to a copyrighted work to make an accessible copy of that work for a person who has a disability, the DMCA could be seen as another barrier to access. Fortunately, as part of the *Eighth Triennial Proceeding to Determine Exemptions to the Prohibition on Circumvention*, previously established exemptions to the DMCA regarding the circumvention of technology for the making of accessible copies of audiovisual and literary works were renewed and broadened. Codified in the Code of Federal Regulations (C.F.R.), the law states that "the prohibition against circumvention of technological measures that effectively control access to copyrighted works set forth in 17 U.S.C. § 1201(a)(1)(A) shall not apply to persons who engage in noninfringing uses of the following classes of copyrighted works" These categories include "motion pictures (including television shows and videos), as defined in 17 U.S.C. 101, where the motion picture is lawfully acquired on a DVD [digital video disc] protected by the Content Scramble System, on a Blu-ray disc protected by the Advanced Access Content System, or via a digital transmission protected by a technological measure" (37 C.F.R. § 201.40[b][2][i]). In these situations, the technological protection measures (TPM) can be circumvented when it is

> undertaken by a disability services office or other unit of a . . . college, or university engaged in and/or responsible for the provision of accessibility services for the purpose of adding captions and/or audio description to a motion picture to create an accessible version for students, faculty, or staff with disabilities. (37 C.F.R. § 201.40[b][2][i][A])

Here, the law tells us that here an "accessible version of sufficient quality means [the creation of] a version [of the work] that in the reasonable judgment of the educational institution unit has captions and/or audio description that are sufficient to meet the accessibility needs of students, faculty, or staff with disabilities and are substantially free of errors that would materially interfere with those needs" (37 C.F.R. § 201.40[b][2][ii][B]). Before circumventing the TPM to make the accessible copy, the law requires that the unit at the educational institution must have "a reasonable belief that the motion picture will be used for a specific future activity of the institution and, after a reasonable effort, has determined that an accessible version of sufficient quality cannot be obtained at a fair market price or in a timely manner, including where a copyright holder has not provided an accessible version of a motion picture that was included with a textbook" (37 C.F.R. § 201.40[b][2][i][B]) and, once an accessible version has been made, that they "accessible versions are provided to students or educators and stored by the educational institution in a manner intended to reasonably prevent unauthorized further dissemination of a work" (37 C.F.R. § 201.40[b][2][i][C]). If academic libraries or academic institutions find they need to take advantage of this section of the law to make an accessible copy, they should have procedures established in their workflow to perform the searches as outlined here, to securely distribute the accessible copies to those who need them and to securely store them for future use. To help facilitate the work of this unit, the law allows that "accessible materials created pursuant to this exemption and stored pursuant to paragraph (b)(2)(i)(C) of this section may be reused by the educational institution unit to meet the accessibility needs of students, faculty, or staff with disabilities pursuant to paragraphs (b)(2)(i)(A) and (B) of this section" (37 C.F.R. § 201.40[b][2][ii][C]).

Section 201.40(b)(6) of Section 37, Chapter 2 of the C.F.R. addresses the circumvention of TPM applied to "Literary works or previously published musical works that have been fixed in the form of text or notation, distributed electronically," and says that when they "are protected by technological measures that either prevent the enabling of read-aloud functionality or interfere with screen readers or other applications or assistive technologies," the TPM may be circumvented:

(A) When a copy or phonorecord of such a work is lawfully obtained by an eligible person, as such a person is defined in 17 U.S.C. 121; provided, however, that the rights owner is remunerated, as appropriate, for the market price of an inaccessible copy of the work as made available to the general public through customary channels; or

(B) When such a work is lawfully obtained and used by an authorized entity pursuant to 17 U.S.C. 121. (37 C.F.R. § 201.40[b][6])

Section 37 C.F.R. § 201.40(b)(6)(ii) does place one caveat here, stating that "for the purposes of paragraph (b)(6)(i) of this section, a 'phonorecord of such a work' does not include a sound recording of a performance of a musical work unless and only to the extent the recording is included as part of an audiobook or e-book (electronic book)."

Using the DMCA Exemptions

These exemptions to the DMCA can help make the work of libraries and educational institutions looking to make accessible copies of works a bit easier. However, these exemptions last only for a three-year period. The exemptions outlined in this section were adopted in the *Eighth Triennial* rulemaking and became effective on October 28, 2021, and they remain effective only until the *Ninth Triennial* rulemaking process is completed in 2024. While it is hoped that they will be renewed or, perhaps, even expanded upon in the *Ninth Triennial* rulemaking process, those who utilize them should pay close attention to the *Final Rule* issued by the Librarian of Congress in 2024 to see if they are. Those employees of libraries and educational institutions who use these exemptions should consider participating in the rulemaking process itself to help encourage their renewal. Information on the rulemaking process can be found on the U.S. Copyright Office's website at: https://www.copyright.gov/1201/.

Developing a Game Plan to Address Accessibility

While accessibility considerations are important and must be addressed when providing reserve services, it is not practical or feasible for libraries to make all resources in their collection fully accessible in any format in anticipation of someone with a disability accessing it. Instead, staff should consider accessibility as items are acquired for their collections and then have a plan in place for obtaining or making accessible copies should an accommodation be requested by a person who has a disability.

Accessibility Considerations During the Acquisitions Process

There are steps staff can take to help support and facilitate access for people with disabilities when purchasing and licensing items for their collections.

Book Purchases

The World Blind Union (2020) estimates that "[m]ore than 90% of all published material is not accessible to the blind or partially sighted." While libraries can frequently purchase copies of newly released, popular works of fiction in accessible formats (e.g., audiobooks), finding scholarly monographs, textbooks, and print journal publications produced in accessible formats can be challenging. Libraries will need to develop a collection development plan to identify in what situations they will purchase accessible copies of book for their collections, when they are available.

DVD and Blu-ray Purchases

Commercial DVD and Blu-ray vendors are now often selling copies of popular films and television shows that have closed-captioning. While SDH provides the most accessibility for people with disabilities, closed-captioning does "communicate all audio information, including sound effects, speaker IDs, and non-speech elements . . . [as] required by law for most video programming in the United States" (Lewis 2021). While not as common, versions of popular films with audio description tracks are also made available for purchase. When acquiring physical copies of popular films and television shows, staff should look to see if there are versions available that have SDH, closed-captions, and audio description tracks and, when possible, purchase them.

While many documentary films are released with closed-captions, some are not as it can be a challenge for small, independent filmmakers to cover the costs of having SDH, closed-captioning, or audio description added to a film. Staff can check with these filmmakers to see if SDH, closed-captions, or audio description tracks are available for their titles. If not, they can look to user rights found in U.S. copyright law for adding them when patrons with disabilities need to engage with these films.

Purchasing Electronic Resources

When purchasing electronic resources, staff should ask the vendor for a VPAT and review it with staff from the DSO to determine is level of accessibility. Bazeley (2018) encourages staff to have a frank and open dialogue with vendors about their products. Questions she recommends asking about include:

- "Known accessibility issues and associated workarounds.
- Administrative settings or add-ons that provide additional accessibility features for a resource. These are not always fully documented by vendors, so [staff should] ask the vendor about these possibilities.
- Accessibility roadmap or enhancements: Many vendors make continuous improvements to their resources or products. Some vendors are willing to work with taff or the organization's accessibility staff to create an accessibility roadmap or remediation plan, which creates a timeline on which the vendor commits to making their resource more accessible."

Licensing Considerations

When entering into a license with a vendor for the purchase of an electronic resources or, sometimes, physical resources such as DVDs, staff should review the document carefully to see if it addresses accessibility considerations. If they are addressed, but not in a way that meets accessibility standards, then the person negotiating the license on behalf of the library should request that language be added to the license addressing accessibility or that they revise the unfavorable terms. The Big Ten Academic Alliance Libraries has drafted model license language that libraries can use:

> Licensor shall comply with the Americans with Disabilities Act (ADA), by supporting assistive software or devices such as large print interfaces, text-to-speech output, voice-activated input, refreshable braille displays, and alternate keyboard or pointer interfaces, in a manner consistent with the Web Accessibility Initiative Web Content Accessibility Guidelines 2.1 AA (http://www.w3.org/WAI/guid-tech.html). Licensor shall ensure that product maintenance and upgrades are implemented in a manner that does not compromise product accessibility. Licensor shall provide to Licensee a current, accurate completed Voluntary Product Accessibility Template (VPAT) to demonstrate compliance with accessibility standards (https://www.itic.org/policy/accessibility). If the product does not comply, the Licensor shall adapt the Licensed Materials in a timely manner and at no cost to the Licensee in order to comply with applicable law. Nothing in this Agreement shall limit the Licensee or any end user from making lawful, noninfringing uses to facilitate access to the Licensed Materials by users who have disabilities. For the avoidance of doubt, the Licensor authorizes such uses. (Big Ten Academic Alliance Libraries, n.d.)

In reviewing the license, staff should also be on the lookout for any copyright restrictions the vendor may seek to impose upon the library and its users. For example, a license for an electronic database may state that users cannot make derivative versions of the works it contains, or it may prohibit users from overriding TPM attached to works. As stated in previous chapters, contract agreements may trump other rights granted under the law, so if the library agrees to such terms, then staff and patrons may not be able to take advantage of the user rights such as Section 121, Section 121A, or fair use to make accessible copies. If any such restrictions exist, the person negotiating the license on behalf of the library should request that it be struck from the license agreement. Alternately, language could also be added to the license agreement stating that the licensor shall not "restrict, abrogate or circumvent the rights of the licensee or its user community permitted under copyright law, including the fair use provisions of Section 107 of the U.S. Copyright Act (17 U.S.C. 107)" (American Association of Law Libraries Executive Board 2018, 6).

Ensuring Access to Reserve Resources for People with Disabilities

When a work made available via library reserve services needs to be modified for a person with a disability, the library should work closely with the DSO to accommodate the request. To be eligible for the services DSOs offer, many institutions of higher education require that students and instructors register with them so they are aware of the person's disability and can work with them to determine what accommodations will best suit their needs. The DSO will usually notify the course instructor when a student who will be receiving an accommodation through them registers for the class so they can work together to ensure that all course resources and materials can be made accessible for the student. In these situations, when the course instructor has placed materials on print, media, and electronic reserve for students to use, staff should also be brought into the conversation DSO so they too can collaborate with them to ensure that the student can fully engage with these materials.

Using Accessible Technology as an Accommodation

Some students may only need to use assistive technology to engage with reserve works. For these situations, libraries should ensure that information regarding what assistive technology they have and where it is located in the library. Staff should be trained in its use so they can teach patrons how to operate the equipment and, if necessary, help troubleshoot problems that may arise with it. If the DSO has a lab with assistive technology that students can use, the library should have a listing of what assistive technology is available there and their hours of operation so they can direct students there, if needed.

Making Accessible Copies

While staff could make accessible copies of inaccessible works to provide for patrons with disabilities, it is likely that the DSO has remediation hardware and software and staff trained in making accessible copies of works. There will be some considerations in these situations that staff and DSO staff will need to work through together.

Purchasing considerations. There will be situations where accessible copies of reserve works are available for purchase from rightsholders or their representatives. Staff and the DSO will need to determine how purchasing these copies might be considered as part of the process of making accessible copies of works available to students. Considerations here include:

- At what part of this process will someone check to see if an accessible copy is available for purchase?
- Who will check to see if a copy is available for purchase, and what will the search procedures be?
- If an accessible copy is available for purchase and the decision is made to purchase it, who will be responsible for making the purchase—the DSO, the

library, or the person with the disability? Here, much may depend on the format of the accessible copy, how it is sold or licensed, the price of the work, and how quickly the accessible copy can be delivered to the user who needs it. For example, if an SDH copy of DVD is needed and one can be obtained for a reasonable price, the library may consider purchasing it for their collection. However, if the accommodation needed involves the making of a digital copy of a print copy of a textbook that is being circulated on reserve and the publisher makes an accessible copy available for purchase but will only sell it to students or only license it for single use, then the library may not be in a position to acquire the item; the student may have to. Alternately, some DSOs have a budget from the institution to purchase accessible copies of such works on behalf of students. Given the complexity of this issue, staff will want to work with DSO staff to have procedures established regarding who might purchase what and under what circumstances.

If an accessible copy of a work is available for purchase, then this fact may need to be factored into applications of fair use if these sections of the law are being considered in making an accessible copy of a work. It is important for those utilizing these sections of the law to understand that the fact that an accessible version of a work is for sale is not, generally, dispositive to the application of them (though it is often easier and more time efficient to purchase an accessible copy). Rather, this fact should be worked carefully into the application of these user rights to the situation. Butler, Adler, and Cox (2019, 14) counter the common misconception that libraries, DSOs, and students often feel compelled to purchase a copy of an inaccessible work "as a predicate for receiving accessible ones." They point out this is not the case, noting that "Section 121 makes no mention of a purchase" and the "fair use analysis in HathiTrust is premised on the importance of accessibility as an objective, and failure of the market to meet it [and] makes no mention of additional purchases by either users or fulfilling institutions" (17). They also state that "this arrangement—permitting copying without purchase, and with the assumption that the copy will be retained by the recipient—is not unique to Section 121; the Copyright Act similarly provides in Section 108 that libraries may provide patrons with copies of portions or, where they are not commercially available, copies of entire works, with one condition being that the copy 'becomes the property' of the requestor" (31).

Amount consideration. Another consideration for libraries and educational institutions looking to make accessible copies of works is whether an accessible copy of the entire work needs to be made, or just a portion. There will be situations where a student needs an entire copy of a work made in an accessible format, and Sections 107, 121, and 121A support this, but there will also be times when students are required to engage only with a portion of a work (e.g., a few chapters from a book or a clip from a film), and this information should be factored into application of user rights to these situations (e.g., the third factor of fair use). Given the time and expense that can be involved in making accessible copies of works, when only a portion of the work is needed, the library or DSO may wish to only convert that portion of the work.

Time considerations. Having staff from the DSO make an accessible copy of a work can be a great service, but staff will need to consider how long they will need to have the library's copy of the item for in order to make the accessible copy. For example, if a digital copy of a print book needs to be made for a student who has a disability, then the DSO staff many need to have the copy of the book in their office for several days to make a scanned copy of it. If it is reserve item, this could impact those other students enrolled in the course, so the library will need to work with the DSO to have plans in place to address these situations.

Delivery considerations. Some sections of the law (e.g., Section 121 and 121A) promote the giving of accessible copies directly to the user they are made for. When making a fair use determination, staff will need to decide whether they are going to give the accessible copy of the work made directly to the patrons who requested it for their own use or, when appropriate, if they will make it available to all users via a reserve platform. An example of this would be a copy of an audiovisual work that has closed-captions added to it as an accommodation. If the instructor has asked that the film be made available to students enrolled in their class via media reserve, then the library and DSO may decide to make the closed-captioned copy available for all students via the media reserve platform (if doing so falls within the scope of user rights such as fair use or the Technology, Education and Copyright Harmonization [TEACH] Act), as closed-captions can be useful to those who do not have hearing impairments. For example, closed-captions are useful to those who are not native speakers of the language being spoken in the film and can be used when the film is being watched in a noisy environment (e.g., the student is watching the film on their computer while eating lunch in the student center) or when dialogue in the film is being mumbled by the actor, is obscured by other noise in the background of the shot, or if the actor has or is speaking with a heavy accent.

Storage consideration. Once an accessible copy of a work is made, the library and the DSO will need to decide if a copy of it will be kept for use in future situations where people with a similar disability can use it. Doing so makes sense given the time and expense needed to make accessible versions of works. Storing copies of such works is clearly supported by judicial opinions on fair use and "is one of the primary lessons of the HathiTurst decision"

(Butler et al. 2019, 19). In these situations, DSO and staff will have to determine who will have ready access to the secured folder or server where these works are stored.

Ongoing Assessment and Review

Understanding the ways in which accessible copies of copyrightable works can be made in compliance with U.S. copyright law is just one aspect of the accessibility considerations associated with reserve services. Administrative considerations must be addressed as well, and staff from the DSO will be able to help staff perform a full and comprehensive evaluation of all accessibility considerations associated with reserve services. Both groups should work together to review services procedures and procedures for making accessible copies of work on a regular basis. Conversations about the accessibility of library spaces, services, and resources should not be limited to DSO staff and course instructors. Staff should actively seek feedback from patrons with disabilities and encourage an open dialogue on the services, tools, and resources that are most beneficial to them.

Putting It All Together

Staff have an ethical and legal obligation to ensure that people with disabilities are able to access and engage with services and resources they offer. Dealing with any legal situation can be daunting: however, the complimentary nature of accessibility laws and the user rights found in U.S. copyright law allow staff to balance their ethical obligations to provide equitable access to all users while at the same time showing "respect [for the] intellectual property rights" of content creators (Committee on Professional Ethics, 2021). The next steps in resolving resource accessibility issues must involve getting rightsholders and vendors to embrace the idea of universal design to help eliminate the delays caused by converting the nonaccessible resources into accessible ones. By seeking input from patrons with disabilities and maintaining an open dialogue on the services, tools, and resources that are most beneficial to them, staff can help set a positive example for others regarding the importance of accessibility in all facets of our society.

CHAPTER FOURTEEN

Mitigating Legal Risk

Staff may be uncomfortable working with copyright because of the perceived legal risk involved with making applications of the law. Actually, many aspects of librarianship require staff to engage with and make applications of the law, such as:

- The privacy rights that protect access to patron information, including those resources patrons have checked out from the library's collection or accessed through the library's online databases
- Employment law and its impact on employee hiring and termination processes
- The legal liability associated with injuries or accidents that may occur on library property
- First Amendment issues that may arise if a resource in the library's collection is challenged by a patron who disagrees with its content or message or if a patron feels they have been unjustly denied access to library services and resources due to behavioral issues

Smith and Davis (2013, 59) wisely state, "[W]e do not forbid our users from entering our buildings, stop hiring employees, and so forth because we are afraid of what might happen. Copyright should not be treated any differently, but most libraries back away in fear of running the risk of a lawsuit." Instead of avoiding copyright considerations related to their work, staff and administrators should be prepared to handle copyright issues related to reserve services with the same confidence and competence used when addressing other legal issues like privacy and employment law. This process will involve:

- Learning about the law
- Identifying the areas of legal risk associated with reserve services
- Establishing copyright policies to help mitigate this risk
- Identifying allies across the institution who can help address copyright questions
- Having plans in place to address issues, if they arise

To be successful, staff must be prepared to work through this process in an open and thorough manner.

Step 1: Learning About U.S. Copyright Law

All library employees should have some knowledge of U.S. copyright law. However, those employees supporting reserve services will likely need to have advanced knowledge of it. At a minimum, these staff members should be aware of how copyright is secured, what works are and are not eligible for copyright protection, the duration of copyright, and the rights granted to the creators of copyrightable works under the law. This knowledge will help these library employees better understand when they are engaging with copyrighted works and what issues need to be addressed if instructors are looking to make a work available through reserve services. They will also need to have advanced knowledge and understanding of user rights found in U.S. copyright law that can be utilized for reserve services so they can explain them to instructors looking to place items on print, electronic, and media reserve and confidently answer questions they may have about them. It will also allow them to make thoughtful and thorough applications of the user rights when processing items to be placed on reserves.

Staff supporting reserve services should also have knowledge of other options available for making copyrightable works available in compliance with the law (e.g., obtaining permission to use a work), so when the use of a copyrightable work falls outside the scope of the user rights they are prepared to explain these options to instructors.

Given all of this, copyright education must be provided to staff supporting reserve services continually over time. Workshops on the law should be provided on a regular basis by a copyright librarian or an attorney from the institution's Office of General Counsel (OGC). If the institution does not have a copyright librarian, or if someone from the OGC is not available to provide copyright education, the library can look into options for bringing a copyright librarian from another institution or a local intellectual property (IP) attorney to campus to present.

RECOMMENDED RESOURCE

Bar Association Directories. The Bar Association for each state usually has a *Find an Attorney* search feature on its website that can be used to identify practicing attorneys in the state by specialty. The may also have an IP section, where users can find information on the law or identify local attorneys who specialize in this area. The American Bar Association's *Bar Directories and Lawyer Finders* web page also provides resources that allow users to find an attorney near them who is practicing in a specific area of law: https://www.americanbar.org/groups/legal_services/flh-home/flh-bar-directories-and-lawyer-finders/. Before bringing a copyright or IP attorney to campus, the library should ensure they have knowledge and experience addressing library copyright issues and are aware of current case law and legislative updates that may impact library services.

There are numerous books written on copyright law as it applies to libraries and academic institutions that can be ordered for the library's collection to serve as reference resources for the reserve services staff. Staff should also look for sessions on copyright offered online or at conferences, and financial support should made available by administrators for them to engage in these in-person educational opportunities.

Beware of Misinformation

When seeking out information on copyright, staff should ensure the resources they identify are authored by (or presented by) knowledgeable individuals and that the information being shared is based upon the law itself. Unfortunately, many resources put forward information that is based upon common misconceptions related to copyright law. The continued promotion of the *Agreement on Guidelines for Classroom Copying in Not-For-Profit Educational Institutions with Respect to Books and Periodicals* as law, as discussed in the case study in Chapter 6, is an example of this. These guidelines hold no force of law, yet they are frequently represented as the law online, in publications, and by speakers. If staff internalize this misinformation and then make decisions based off it, they risk making the wrong decision, because they are operating without regard to the law itself.

Additionally, those looking to learn about the law may wish to proceed with caution around resources that purport to be informational but instead place their primary emphasis on legal liability. In a 2017 interview, Peter Jaszi, Professor of Law Emeritus and Faculty Director of the Glushko-Samuelson Intellectual Property Clinic, stated that "whenever you read something or are given something to read which is offered [as] copyright guidance that begins by talking about how much trouble you could get in to if you get it wrong . . . that begins by saying you could be subject to so much damage or lose your car or whatever it is, put that down and look for something else to read" (Jaszi et al. 2017, 6). He warns that resources like this could "lead [users], best case, to make decisions that are radically over conservative and, worst case, it will actually lead [them] to make decisions which although over conservative, may be wrong enough to actually get [them] into affirmative trouble. So leave it behind and look for sources of guidance that talk to you about the reasoning process that goes into making your own good and robust decisions about what is and isn't acceptable [copyright] practice" (6).

Continuing Education

Lawyers and copyright librarians often say there is always something new to learn about the law and those working with it should continually seek out opportunities to expand their knowledge. They should also keep abreast of pending copyright infringement lawsuits and jury verdicts or opinions issued by the courts on these cases as they can have an impact on how the law is interpreted an applied. Staff will also want to pay close attention as new legislation is passed that amends the law.

RECOMMENDED RESOURCE

The U.S. Copyright Office's (USCO) *Legislative Developments* web page. This web page provides links to copyright legislation proposed in the current congressional term as well as links to legislation and studies that explore possible revisions to the law. It can be found online at: https://www.copyright.gov/legislation/. The USCO also has a web page that identifies active policy studies and past policy reports that can be useful for staying informed of trends and issues the office is exploring or recommending that Congress consider as part of legislative updates. It can be found online at: https://www.copyright.gov/policy/.

Staff should seek to develop a network of colleagues in the profession who can help them learn about the law and with whom they can discuss copyright questions. Jaszi emphasizes the importance of networking, stating, "[T]here are more and more supporting networks for people who are doing copyright jobs in various libraries to take advantage of, and they really should do that. [They] will learn an enormous amount from [their] peers and from the opportunity to be in touch with [their] peers" (Jaszi et al. 2017, 7). These networks can be built by engaging with those who are also attending copyright workshops and conference sessions, identifying and reaching out to colleagues in the profession who work with U.S. copyright law, and by following and contributing to listserves, blogs, and social media accounts that address library copyright issues. Staff should also look for ways they can identify and engage with copyright allies at their institution, a topic that will be discussed more in the *Identifying Allies* section of this chapter.

Step Two: Identifying Area of Legal Risk

For reserve services, there will be two primary areas of risk: copyright infringement and the violation of contract terms.

Copyright Infringement

Copyright infringement occurs when a person exercises one of the exclusive rights granted under Section 106 without the authorization of the rightsholder in ways that does not fall under the user rights found in U.S. copyright law. It has been established in previous chapters that when offering reserve services libraries will, among other things, regularly make copies of (reproduce) and circulate (distribute) copyrightable works. These actions are included in Section 106, which outlines the rights of the copyright holder. However, user rights such as the first sale doctrine (17 U.S.C. § 109) and fair use (17 U.S.C. § 107) offer opportunities for libraries to provide these services in compliance with U.S. copyright law. The legal risk associated with offering reserve services will be reduced if staff are making thoughtful applications of the law and, when appropriate, exploring alternate options for making works available, such as obtaining permission or a license, when a request exceeds the scope of user rights. If staff are making incorrect applications of the law or ignoring the law entirely, then the legal risk for the library will increase.

The Three Types of Infringement

Under common law, which is "the body of law derived from judicial decisions, rather than from statutes or constitutions" (Garner 2009, 313), there are three types of liability for copyright infringement: direct, contributory, and vicarious. *Direct liability*, which can also be referred to as *primary liability*, attaches to the person who commits the infringement. For example, a person makes and distributes a copy of a copyrighted work without the permission of the rightsholder and in a way that does not fall within the scope of user rights found within U.S. copyright law. With *contributory liability*, which is also referred to as *secondary liability*, a person or entity (like a library) may not actually be committing the infringing acts themselves yet has "knowledge of the infringing activity [and] induces or causes or materially contributes to the infringement" (Lipinski 2006, xxviii). In the case of *A&M Records,*

Inc. v. Napster, Inc. (114 F. Supp. 2d 896 [2000]), the U.S. District Court for the Northern District of California issued an injunction compelling Napster to stop "engaging in, or facilitating others in copying, downloading, uploading, transmitting, or distributing plaintiffs' copyrighted musical compositions and sound recordings, protected by either federal or state law, without express permission of the rights owner" due to infringement considerations (A&M Records v. Napster 2000, 927). Among other things, the court found that Napster could be held liable for contributory copyright infringement because "executives knew Napster users were engaging in unauthorized downloading and uploading of copyrighted music" (903) and had received "actual notice of direct infringement because the RIAA [Recording Industry Association of America] informed [Napster] of more than 12,000 infringing files" (918). Upon appeal to the Ninth Circuit Court of Appeals (239 F.3d 1004 [2001]), it was found "that sufficient knowledge exists to impose contributory liability when linked to demonstrated infringing use of the Napster system" and that "the record supports the district court's finding that Napster has actual knowledge that specific infringing material is available using its system, that it could block access to the system by suppliers of the infringing material, and that it failed to remove the material" (A&M Records v. Napster 2001, 1022).

According to Peters (2004), *vicarious liability*, which is also a form of secondary liability, "requires two elements: (1) the right and ability to supervise or control the infringing activity; and (2) a direct financial benefit from that activity" even if the person supervising or controlling and benefiting from the infringement are not the ones committing the infringing act themselves. For example, in the case of *Gershwin Pub. Corp. v. Columbia Artists Management, Inc.* (443 F.2d 1159 [1971]), Columbia Artists Management, Inc. (CAMI) was sued for, among other things, the performance of a musical work at a concert venue without a license. The Second Circuit Court of Appeals upheld the lower courts ruling that found CAMI liable for vicarious infringement because "CAMI knew that copyrighted works were being performed at [concerts they helped coordinate] and that neither [CAMIs] local association [who helped plan the concerts] nor the performing artists would secure a copyright license" (Gershwin v. Columbia 1971, 1163). Additionally, they found "that CAMI was in a position to police the infringing conduct of its artists, and that it derived substantial financial benefit from the actions of the primary infringers" by making "money through the reimbursement of its expenses, plus a percentage for-profit for the nurturing of local associations; and [from] artists who . . . pay a commission to CAMI for management" (1163), among other fees and charges. Therefore, CAMI was vicariously liable for the infringing performances.

Having sound copyright policies and practices can help libraries reduce the risk of their employees committing direct or vicarious infringement that can, in turn, reduce legal risk for the library itself. By providing reserve services that are offered in compliance with U.S. copyright law, the library can also help mitigate risk of infringement against the larger academic institution that may come as a result of instructors making copies of copyrightable works available to students on their own outside the scope of the law.

Case Study: Section 108 and Limited Liability for Library Duplication Equipment

Sometimes students will check out a print reserve item and then head over to the library's photocopier or scanner to make a copy of the work. Students can make copies of works placed on reserve when they are in the public domain, are licensed for reproduction, or when doing so would fall within the scope of user rights found in the law, such as fair use. There may be times when patrons use library duplication equipment to make copies of works that are infringing. Under Section 108(f)(1), a library and its employees are released from liability for copyright infringement "for the unsupervised use of reproducing equipment located on its premises: Provided, That such equipment displays a notice that the making of a copy may be subject to the copyright law." Often, Section 108(f)(1) is spoken of in terms of photocopiers, but the immunity in this section could apply to all reproducing equipment located on the premises of the library, including printers, scanners, VHS (video home system) and DVD (Digital Video Disc) duplication equipment, and 3D (three-dimensional) printers. The immunity applies only to unsupervised use. Decades ago, library staff often operated photocopies and printers on behalf of patrons because the equipment and its supplies were costly, and mediated services were used as a way to mitigate damage or the wasting of supplies. In these situations, as library employees were responsible for supervising the use of the equipment, Section 108(f)(1) would not have applied. Times have changed, though, and today many patrons are trusted to operate much of the library's duplication equipment on their own. Patrons may ask staff to train them to use the equipment, which they should do as, generally, this will not be considered to be supervision of the duplication of works itself.

While libraries can enjoy the immunity offered by Section 108(f)(1), this immunity does not apply to patrons, a fact addressed in Section 108(f)(2), which states that "[nothing in this section] excuses a person who uses such reproducing equipment [as identified in Section 108(f)(1)] . . . from liability for copyright infringement for any such act, or for any later use of such copy or phonorecord, if it exceeds fair use as provided by section 107." It is not unusual for student, when checking out works from print reserve to ask staff, "Can I make a copy of this and, if so, how much can I copy?" When dealing with works that are licensed for reuse such as open access or Creative Common works, staff can review the license with students to help them understand how much of the work they can copy. When students are asking the question about works such as books, DVDs, or CDs, staff can explain to patrons that they may consider user rights like fair use when looking to make copies of protected works for their own personal use and should refer them to quality educational materials that help them understand their rights and responsibilities when considering such user rights. Having the required notice placed on all duplication equipment in the library means that the legal liability for any copying that falls outside the scope of user rights found in the law becomes the responsibility of the user. The law does not specify what text this notice should contain. Crews (2020, 175) states that many libraries choose to use the following text: "Notice: The copyright law of the United States [Title 17, U.S. Code] governs the making of photocopies or other reproductions of copyrighted material. The person using this equipment is liable for any infringement." In compliance with the language found in Section 108(f)(1), staff should place these notices directly on the equipment. Lipinski (2006) notes that these copyright notices often "populate the photocopying area of many libraries" however, "the statute does not state the notice can be on or near the equipment" (119) (e.g., on a nearby wall or on the table the equipment is placed on). Rather the notice should be placed directly on the equipment itself.

Contract Law

Violating the terms of a contract can also place an institution at risk. When it comes to reserves services, a violation of contract terms could arise when:

- Staff make licensed items available through reserve services in violation of contract terms agreed upon by the vendor and the institution. For example, the terms of use for a database may state that its contents cannot be shared via electronic reserves (e-reserves), used in electronic course packs, or shared via persistent links in course syllabi or by any other means connected to course resources. If staff provided instructors and students with a copy of or a link to an article covered by these terms via the library's e-reserves platform, they would be in violation of these license terms.
- Exceeding the terms of an agreed-upon license entered into for making a particular item available through reserves. For example, a library may acquire a license from a vendor to make a film available via media reserves for a particular semester. Making the film available to via media reserves for more than the agreed-upon time period would be a violation of this license.

Staff can help reduce risk in this area by carefully reading all license agreements and negotiating for terms that allow the licensed resources to be made available via reserve services.

Step 3: Establishing Sound Copyright Practices

The development of copyright policies specific to each type of reserve service has been discussed in previous chapters. Libraries may also wish to establish an institutional copyright policy that outlines the scope and intent of its application of the law to all library services and sets the tone for the reuse of copyrighted works by employees and patrons. It is critically important that this policy be rooted in the law as this helps mitigate legal risk. In its simplest form, a library's institutional copyright policy can be fairly straightforward: *In support of the teaching and learning mission of the library and the educational institution, library services will be offered in compliance with U.S. copyright law.* A policy like this highlights the importance of reusing copyrighted works as part of the educational process and allows for flexibility in developing policy and practice documents that address specific library services.

Library employees should always be made to feel comfortable approaching their supervisor or administrator with any job-related questions, but creating an atmosphere of collaboration and open communication is especially important when it comes to interpreting copyright policies and finding answers to legal questions, especially in situations where the application of the law may create increased risk for the institution. For example, an instructor may wish to place a DVD copy of a television program they recorded off-air on print reserve. The staff, hesitating to circulate a homemade DVD on print reserve, first check to see if this television program is available for purchase and discover it is not. Knowing this, staff may think that a fair use argument could be made for the circulation of the DVD but realize that there could be some legal risk for the institution in doing so and decide they would like additional input and guidance on this particular situation. It should be established in advance who staff should bring such questions to. This could be a supervisor, a staff member in another library department who has advanced knowledge of copyright law, or a member of the administrative team, or it could be an attorney who represents the institution. It should also be established in advance who will have the final decision-making authority regarding the application of the user rights in situations such as these. Library administrators should also work to ensure that, in these situations:

- Staff receive a timely answer to their requests for assistance.
- The legal reasoning behind these decisions are made to staff so they can apply this reasoning to similar situations in the future.
- When a decision may negatively impact a patron (e.g., a work will not be made available via e-reserve as it exceeds the user rights found the law), staff are offered assistance in explaining the situation to the

person who submitted the reserve request and an administrator is available to further explain the situation or hear complaints if the patron is upset by the news.

Staff are often eager to connect a patron to a resource or service, but this eagerness should not extend to breaking the law. Jaszi (Jaszi et al. 2017, 6) stated that "the truth of the matter is that the main reason libraries and librarians want to be good copyright citizens is because they want to be good 'everything' citizens." When it comes to providing reserve services in a way that promotes student and instructor access to resources, staff can be good copyright citizens and, in the process, help mitigate legal liability for their institution, by making thoughtful application of the law and by saying "no" to those uses that may constitute infringement.

Case Study: How to Avoid Giving Legal Advice to Patrons

Hickey (2011, 10) tells us that "copyright occupies a vexed place when it comes to reference work. There are two camps: some [staff] view answering copyright questions as an integrated part of everyday operations, while others classify them as untouchable legal questions." Staff may hesitate to answer copyright questions for patrons out of fear that the information they share could be construed legal advice, bringing upon them liability for practicing law without a license, or putting the library at risk, with the patrons claiming that staff told them that their infringing behavior was in fact legal. However, Healey (1995, 516) argues that while "articles that warn of the dangers of potential liability for reference librarians are quite common in the library literature . . . none of these claims to be based on actual experiences." Rather, many of these articles "create a hypothetical situation with dire warnings that the scenario could easily become a reality" though they lack "either legal precedent or solid legal theory to back up such predictions" (517). Staff should not let the fear of litigation prevent them from communicating information about copyright law to patrons. Instead, they should identify and follow best practices for handling these situations. The easiest way that staff can avoid the perception of giving legal advice is to simply provide information to patrons, allowing them to interpret the law for themselves, and not trying to interpret it for them. This is actually a common scenario in libraries. When patrons approach the reference desk to ask for information on a medical issue, staff will direct them to books, journal articles, and other quality informational resources on the topic. They do not attempt to provide a diagnosis for the patron or tell them how their medical issue should be treated. Instead, if patrons ask such questions, staff would encourage them to speak with their physician or another trained medical professional to obtain advice on the issue. Questions staff receive pertaining to all legal issues, including copyright, should be handled in a similar way. Staff can direct patrons to quality information about the law, and if patrons have questions about how the law should be interpreted, they should encourage them to speak with an attorney to obtain legal advice on how the information applied to their particular situation. At a college or university, staff may be able to direct the patron to the institution's OGC for assistance, though much will depend on the nature of their question. OGCs usually exist to protect the interests of the institution, and while they may be able to provide legal advice to a member of the campus community if their issues are related to an institutional policy or service, they will general not provide legal advice on issues of a more personal nature. For example, the OGC will likely be able to advise staff on crafting copyright policies regarding applications of fair use for reserve services, but would likely not provide advice to an instructor asking if their reuse of a third-party photograph in a book they are writing would be considered fair use. The state and national Bar Association resources identified easier in this chapter can also be used to help patrons identify attorneys who can help them with their personal legal issues.

Patrons may try to compel staff to provide them with more direct answers on interpretations of the law. In these situations, staff should calmly yet clearly state that, as they are not attorneys, they cannot interpret the law for the patron but would be happy to assist them in identifying an attorney who specializes in the area of law they have questions about. Often, after these interactions, it can be helpful for staff to make a few personal notes about what was discussed with the patron that they can refer to later or, if possible, send the patron an email recapping the conversation, reiterating the information that was shared, and reminding them of resources that can help them identify an attorney who can provide them with legal advice.

When it comes to reserve services, the legal question staff are most likely to receive will be in relation to applications of user rights such as fair use. For example, an instructor may ask staff, "How much of this book I can have scanned and posted to electronic reserve?" In these situations, it is best to share the applicable reserve service's copyright policy with the instructor and walk them through factors staff will likely consider when they make applications of user rights to determine whether works can lawfully be made available through reserves. If it seems that the work the instructor wishes to use will fall within the scope of one of the options available for making works lawfully available via reserve services, the staff member can tell them, "It appears that your request will fall within the scope of the policy, and it is likely we will be able to make it available for you and your students to access via reserves."

Identifying Allies

Chances are that there are individuals who can assist staff in addressing copyright questions and issues. These allies may include a copyright librarian, campus legal counsel, and other members of the campus community.

The Copyright Librarian

Some academic libraries employ librarians who are responsible for helping members of the campus community understand their rights and responsibilities under U.S. copyright law, who can provide guidance on finding answers to copyright questions, and who can help develop copyright policies that promote compliance with U.S. copyright law. If an academic library has such a person on staff, they should be directly involved in developing reserve copyright policies and answering questions staff may have about options for making works lawfully available through reserve services. As the copyright librarian positions are a fairly new development in the library profession, chances are that a library has been offering reserve services and had reserve copyright policies in place long before they have had a copyright librarian on staff. In these situations, the copyright librarian can review the library's copyright policies and practices and, if needed, work with administration and staff to make changes that can ensure that the library is acting in a way that effectively takes advantage of the user rights found in the law.

RECOMMENDED RESOURCE

Additional Readings. If a library is thinking about hiring a copyright librarian or launching a copyright services program for their campus, Donna Ferullo's guest column in *Reference & User Services Quarterly* titled "Managing Copyright Services at a University" (Volume 51, issue 2, Winter 2011, 111–114) outlines key considerations that can aid administrators in deciding what the responsibilities of this position may be, the scope of services that will be offered, and how they will be provided. Ferullo has also written a useful book, *Managing Copyright in Higher Education: A Guidebook*, published by Rowman & Littlefield Publishers (Lanham, Maryland, 2014) that can aid libraries and copyright librarians in providing copyright services to their campus community. Another useful resource is the article "Making the Transition as the New Copyright Librarian," authored by Emilie Regina Algenio, who serves as the Copyright and Fair Use librarian for the Texas A&M University Libraries. The article can be found in volume 2, issue 1 (2018) of the *Journal of Copyright in Education and Librarianship* (https://doi.org/10.17161/jcel.v2i1.6579).

Campus Legal Counsel

Most institutions of higher education employ attorneys who work in the OGC and provide a wide range of legal services that can include assisting with policy development and providing legal opinions on IP issues. Library administrators should work with their campus attorneys when developing copyright policies for reserve services, ask them to help provide training to staff on U.S. copyright law, and inquire if they may be available to answer questions about the law when complex scenarios arise. Having an established relationship with the institution's legal counsel will be exceedingly important if a rightsholder should ever reach out to the library objecting to the use of their work on reserve. While these situations are exceedingly rare, should a rightsholder contact the library with questions, the campus attorneys will be key allies in deciding how best to respond.

Other Allies

There may be employees with knowledge of copyright law that can be found in various office and departments around campus. For example, many institutions of higher education have offices dedicated to supporting researchers and helping them find grant funding. These offices may have an employee who has knowledge of IP issues as a result of addressing them when they arise in research projects. Some academic institutions have positions or offices dedicated to helping secure and manage patents for the institution. Frequently, these offices will employ an IP attorney, and while this person may specialize in patent law, if they concentrated in IP law while in law school, they may be able to provide information and guidance for staff on copyright law. Library administrators may already be aware of individuals working for the educational institution who have experience working with copyright law and can also reach out to deans, directors, and department heads across campus to see whether they are aware of individuals on their staff who have knowledge of copyright and can serve as allies when addressing copyright issues.

When Issues Arise

It is best for staff and administrators to be proactive in developing a plan for addressing complex legal questions that arise regarding the application of copyright law to reserve services, or for responding to inquiries from rightsholders.

Anticipating Inquiries from Rightsholders

Smith (2012, 18) tells us that the legal risk associated with library services can be managed by "first, trying to reduce the number of risky items that a collection contains [and] second, try to reduce the number of people who are likely to want to sue you." The number of risky items made available through reserve services can be reduced by:

- Circulating lawfully obtained items through print reserve
- Linking to works made legally and freely available to instructors and students whenever possible for electronic and media reserve services
- Using works that are licensed for reuse, such as open access or open educational resources distributed under Creative Commons licenses
- Making thoughtful and thorough applications of the user rights found in U.S. copyright law when processing reserve requests

The library can reduce the number of people who may wish to sue them by recognizing those instances when obtaining permission or a license to make a work available through print, electronic, or media reserve is necessary, and then making works available through reserve services in accordance with the agreed-upon terms.

Addressing Inquiries from Rightsholders

At some point, a rightsholder or their representative may reach out to a library to express concern over a work that is made available through reserve services. These inquiries may range from polite emails or letters asking about the use of a work on reserve to a cease-and-desist letter demanding that the work stop being made available by the library or a lawsuit will be brought against the institution for copyright infringement. Inquiries may be directed to staff, library administrators, or to attorneys employed by the institution.

Inquiries from rightsholders should never be ignored. If one is received, library administrators, the institution's attorneys, and staff should meet to decide:

- Is the request legitimate? It will be important to establish if the request actually comes from the rightsholder of the work in question or their representative.
- What are they asking for? Are they asking that the library stop making the work available via reserve services: are they asking for payment of a license fee: or are they threatening to bring a lawsuit against the institution?

- What might the library's legal liability be? Here, it will be important for those involved in the discussion to determine whether the rightsholder's requests (or threats) are reasonable. For example, a rightsholder may ask for the payment of a license fee for use of the work or threaten to bring a copyright infringement lawsuit against the institution, but if staff, administrators, and institution's attorneys feel that a strong fair use claim could be made for the use of the work on reserve, they may choose to reject the rightsholder's request for payment of a fee or state their intent to continue making the work available under the user rights found in the law. However, if those discussing the matter conclude that the rightsholder may have a strong claim of infringement against the institution, they may be willing to pay the requested fee or stop making the work available to users through reserve.

In the case of a civil infringement claims, the institution will want to determine whether it is within the statute of limitations outlined in Section 507(b), which is "within three years after the claim accrued." Otherwise, the court, barring special circumstances, can dismiss the claim. It is important for libraries to realize though that these terms can be difficult to calculate as they can apply to a series of infringements that may take place. For example, if a selection from a book was copied and then made available to students via print reserve, the rightsholders could bring claims of infringement for the reproduction and the distribution of the work against the institution. The statute of limitations for the reproduction would expire three years after the copying took place; however, each semester the copies are circulated to students via reserves a distribution of the work is taking place, "a new offense is created, and the three-year tolling period begins anew" (Lipinski 2006, 326).

Receiving an inquiry, a cease-and-desist letter, or a threat of a lawsuit can be a nerve-wracking experience, but in these situations having a plan for responding to them can help assuage much of the initial anxiety.

How Much Is at Stake If the Library Is Sued?

Courts can impose penalties on those found liable for copyright infringement. Remedies available to rightsholders that are outlined in Sections 504 and 505 include:

- Actual damages, which can include revenue lost by the rightsholder as a result of the infringement as well as the profits the infringer might have made from their reuse of the original work, or statutory damages, which are financial penalties established by the law that range from $750 to $30,000 per infringement or, in the case of willful infringement, can run to $150,000
- Requiring the infringer to pay the costs and attorney fees of the party (e.g., the rightsholder) that sued them

A remedy is a "means of enforcing a right or preventing or redressing a wrong" (Garner 2009, 1407).

Knowing the potential consequences for infringement may make some staff hesitant to provide services and resources that have copyright considerations, even if they feel comfortable in their knowledge of the law. Their anxiety can be reduced somewhat by knowing that allowances are made in the law that can reduce or remit (pardon or forgive) some damages in certain situations.

Limited Liability for State Institutions

Sovereign Immunity is "a government's immunity from being sued in its own courts [state and federal] without its consent" (Garner 2009, 818). The concept of sovereign immunity comes from the 11th Amendment to the U.S. Constitution and states, "The Judicial power of the United States shall not be construed to extend to any suit in law or equity, commenced or prosecuted against one of the United States by Citizens of another State, or by Citizens or Subjects of any Foreign State" (U.S. Constitution. Art./Amend. XI).

It is a common misconception that sovereign immunity protects state agencies like a public college or university and their employees from being sued, but this is not the case. Rightsholders can still pursue an injunction, asking the court to compel the institution to stop infringing behavior. If it is established that a state agency is responsible for copyright infringement, sovereign immunity prevents them from having to pay actual and statutory damages; however, the agency could be held responsible for covering costs and the attorney fees of the prevailing party. In extreme cases, officials at state institutions could also be sued as individuals if their actions exceed the scope of their job duties to the point that they violate federal law. In these situations, the 11th Amendment would not provide these individuals with protection.

Case Study: Sovereign Immunity and the Copyright Remedy Clarification Act

Section 501(a) was added to Title 17 in 2001 with the passage of Copyright Remedy Clarification Act (CRCA) and seemed to negate sovereign immunity in regard to claims of copyright infringement. It states:

> [A]nyone who violates any of the exclusive rights of the copyright owner as provided by sections 106 through 122 or of the author as provided in section 106A(a), or who imports copies or phonorecords into the United States in violation of section 602, is an infringer of the copyright or right of the author, as the case may be. . . . As used in this subsection, the term "anyone" includes any

State, any instrumentality of a State, and any officer or employee of a State or instrumentality of a State acting in his or her official capacity. Any State, and any such instrumentality, officer, or employee, shall be subject to the provisions of this title in the same manner and to the same extent as any nongovernmental entity. (17 U.S.C. § 501[a])

In 2019, SCOTUS granted certiorari to review the case *Allen v. Cooper* (139 S.Ct. 2664 [June 03, 2019]), in which the petitioner, Frederick Allen, sued the state of North Carolina over its use of photographs and video he took of the shipwreck of *Queen Anne's Revenge*. In this case, the district court ruled in Allen's favor, saying that the state could be sued for copyright infringement under Section 501(a). However, the Fourth Circuit reversed the decision, citing the SCOTUS decisions in the cases of *Seminole Tribe of Florida v. Florida* (517 U.S. 44 [1996]), which held that Congress does not have the power to abrogate [abolish] a state's sovereign immunity under Article I of the U.S. Constitution, and *Florida Prepaid Post-Secondary Education Expense Board v. College Savings Bank* (527 U.S. 627 [1999]), which held that Congress cannot abrogate state sovereign immunity under the 14th Amendment.

In March 2020, the SCOTUS unanimously ruled that "Congress lacked authority to abrogate the States' immunity from copyright infringement suits in the CRCA," preserving sovereign immunity for states (Allen v. Cooper 2020, 1). However, the court warned that their ruling "need not prevent Congress from passing a valid copyright abrogation law in the future" (16). Until Congress does so, state institutions should not view sovereign immunity as a get out of jail free card for claims of infringement as rightsholders can still pursue an injunction, asking the court to compel them to stop infringing behavior and, if they are found to be responsible for copyright infringement, could be held responsible for covering costs and the attorney fees of the prevailing party.

Remittance of Damages Provided by the Law for Applications of Fair Use

The third sentence of Section 504(c)(2) states:

[T]he court shall remit statutory damages in any case where an infringer believed and had reasonable grounds for believing that his or her use of the copyrighted work was a fair use under section 107, if the infringer was: (i) an employee or agent of a nonprofit educational institution, library, or archives acting within the scope of his or her employment who, or such institution, library, or archives itself, which infringed by reproducing the work in copies or phonorecords. (17 U.S.C. § 504[c][2])

Essentially, this means that if an employee of a nonprofit library or educational institution reproduces protected works under the auspices of fair use and it is later determined by the courts that those copies or phonorecords are infringing, statutory damages must be remitted in full so long as the employee was "acting within the scope of his or her employment" and had "reasonable grounds for believing that his or her use of the copyrighted work was a fair use under section 107" (17 U.S.C. § 504[c][2])). Libraries should not assume this provision provides complete protection from claims of infringement as there are some nuances to the law that affect its application.

Making copies. Here, it is important to note that the relief provided by this section does not extend to any of the other rights granted under Section 106, including the distribution of works. As reserve services involve the distribution of protected works, this statute's application in a lawsuit related to reserve services may be limited.

Statutory damages versus actual damages. This section of the law applies to statutory damages only. A library or educational institution could still be held liable for actual damages, costs, and attorney fees if their use of a work is not found to be a fair use.

Acting within the scope of employment. Lipinski (2006, 88) tells us that "the statutory damages subject to remission . . . must be the result of infringement that is work related, not just committed by an employee." For example, if an academic librarian were to use the library's scanning equipment to make a PDF (portable document format) copy of a short story from an anthology under the auspices of fair use to make it available through e-reserve, this section of 504(c)(2) shall remit damages for the reproduction of the work should it later be found to be infringing. However, if a librarian were to send the PDF copy of the same short story to members of their book group to read for their next discussion, considering this to be a fair use as well, this act would not be covered under this section of 504(c)(2) as it was a personal pursuit rather than one done within the scope of their employment.

Reasonable grounds. To take advantage of this section of 504(c)(2), a library employee will need to be able to prove they "believed and had reasonable grounds for believing that his or her use of the copyrighted work was a fair use." It could be difficult to prove what a person's mindset was at a particular moment in time, but there are methods that can employed to help demonstrate that thoughtful applications of fair use are encouraged. This could include providing staff with training in the law, encouraging them to think carefully through the four factors of fair use, and having them record as part of the request review process that use was determined to be a fair use.

Administrators should emphasize to staff that if they ever feel uncertain in making a fair use determination they should reach out to their allies for assistance.

Reduction of Damages Provided by the Law

The second sentence of Section 504(c)(2) allows for the reduction of statutory damages and may provide some relief to libraries and educational institutions in those situations not covered by the third sentence. These can include:

- Fair use applications other than reproductions in copies and phonorecords, for example, distributions of works of works
- Applications of Sections 108 (Reproduction by libraries and archives), 109 (first sale), or 110 (Exemption of certain performances and displays), which are other user rights that can be used in delivering reserve services

The second sentence of Section 504(c)(2) states that in "a case where the infringer sustains the burden of proving, and the court finds, that such infringer was not aware and had no reason to believe that their acts constituted an infringement of copyright, the court in its discretion *may reduce* the award of statutory damages to a sum of not less than $200" (emphasis added). Essentially, this means that if anyone accused of copyright infringement (this portion of the law is not limited to employees of a nonprofit educational institution, library, or archives), and can successfully prove in court they were "not aware and had no reason to believe that his or her acts constituted an infringement of copyright" then statutory damages, if assessed, may be reduced down to $200 (17 U.S.C. § 504[c][2]). While this provision of the law can substantially reduce fiscal penalties under the law, it is important for administrators to note that:

- Here it is not required that the statutory damages be reduced. Rather, the law states that they may be reduced.
- It too applies to statutory damages only. Actual damages, costs, and attorney fees could still be awarded to the prevailing party if it is proven that infringement occurred.
- It does not apply in situations where works have been published with a properly formatted copyright notice attached to it, "except as provided in the last sentence of section 504(c)(2)" (17 U.S.C. § 401[d]).

Innocent infringement. It is a common misconception that innocent infringement relieves users from being sued for copyright infringement or from any legal liability under the law. However, much in the same way that claiming not to know the speed limit down a particular stretch of road will not get a driver out of a speeding ticket, claiming that one was not aware of copyright law and how it works will not relieve someone from claims of infringement. Instead, users will have to prove that there was no reason to believe the way they used a protected work amounted to copyright infringement. For example, a novel may have been published in 1990, but due to a mistake with the printing of the book, the publication date on the title page is listed as 1970. A theater instructor purchases the novel at a used bookstore and enjoys it so much she considers developing it into a play. She checks online and discovers that works published in 1970 without a copyright notice are in the public domain so, feeling free from copyright infringement considerations, she decides to write a script based upon the work and have the local community theater perform the work. The rightsholder comes across a notice for the play posted to social media and sues the instructor for making an unauthorized derivative work. The instructor is found liable for copyright infringement. However, she may be eligible for reduced damages under this portion of Section 504(c)(2) as the erroneous copyright date led her to believe that the work was in the public domain.

Going to Court

While trials are often made to look very glamorous, dramatic, and suspenseful on television and in movies, the fact is that bringing a lawsuit against another and going to court can be stressful, time consuming, and expensive for all of those involved. Given these complexities, lawsuits brought against libraries for copyright infringement, while not unheard of, are exceedingly rare. Instead, in cases where rightsholders believe that copyright infringement has occurred, the first course of action usually involves the rightsholder or their representative reaching out to the library or academic institution to try to resolve the situation. The rightsholder may ask the library or educational institution stop using their work and pay a fee for the use. The library can choose to do so if they think the rightsholder may have a strong infringement claim, but the library can also choose to stand behind their use of a work if they feel it falls within the scope of the law. Either way, as discussed in the *When Issues Arise* section of this chapter, libraries should have a plan in place for responding to such inquiries from rightsholders. Should a library actually find themselves in court over claims of copyright infringement, the institution will need to invest significant human and financial resources to defend itself. However, it is important for administrators to realize that the awarding of costs and attorney's fees under Section 505 works both ways. If a library is found liable for of copyright infringement, they may be compelled by the courts to pay the costs and attorney fees of the prevailing party. However, if the library's use of the work if found not to be an infringement of copyright, then the party that brought the suit against them may be compelled by the courts to pay their costs and attorney fees.

Case Study: The CASE Act

In 2020, Congress passed the Copyright Alternative in Small-Claims Enforcement (CASE) Act, adding a new chapter to U.S. copyright law, Chapter 15, establishing a Copyright Claims Board (CCB). The CCB is intended to "serve as an alternative forum" to federal court where "parties may voluntarily seek to resolve certain copyright claims regarding any category of copyrighted work" (17 U.S.C. § 1502[a]). A rightsholder can file a claim against another with the CCB for the "infringement of an exclusive right in a copyrighted work provided under section 106" (17 U.S.C. § 1504[c][1]). Claims can also be brought for "a declaration of noninfringement of an exclusive right in a copyrighted work provided under section 106" (17 U.S.C. § 1504[c][2]) or for "misrepresentation under Section 512(f)" of U.S. copyright law (17 U.S.C. § 1504[c][2]).

Three Copyright Claims Officers (CCOs) will "render determinations on the civil copyright claims, counterclaims, and defenses" (17 U.S.C. § 1503[a][1][A]) filed with the CCB. Participation in CCB proceedings is voluntary, though those who receive a notice of a claim filed against them must actively op out of the proceedings within 60 days. If they do not, the CCB proceeding will then move forward, with or without their participation, and they "shall be bound by the determination in the proceeding" (17 U.S.C. § 1506[i]).

As part of the proceedings, CCOs will review documents and testimony submitted by the parties and then issue a determination of the claim in which they will, among other things, provide an explanation of the factual and legal basis of their decision and damages and other relief awarded to the prevailing party. These can include actual or statutory damages, though "a party that pursues any 1 or more claims or counterclaims in any single proceeding before the Copyright Claims Board may not seek or recover in that proceeding a total monetary recovery that exceeds the sum of $30,000, exclusive of any attorneys' fees and costs that may be awarded under section 1506(y)(2)" (17 U.S.C. § 1504[e][1][D]).

CCB proceedings are scheduled to begin in the summer of 2022. Libraries and archives that do "not wish to participate in proceedings before the Copyright Claims Board [can] preemptively opt out of such proceedings," (]). This opt-out "extends to a library's or archives' employee acting within the scope of their employment," though it "does not apply to employees acting outside the scope of their employment" (37 C.F.R. § 223[a][5]). An example of acting outside the scope of employment is discussed in the *Acting Within the Scope of Employment* section of this chapter. Information about procedures for opting out can be found in Section 223(a) of

Chapter 37 of the *Code of Federal Regulations*. This opt-out should be submitted by a "person with the authority to take legally binding actions on behalf of a library or archives in connection with litigation," (37 C.F.R. § 223[c]), which could be an administrator or legal counsel. Claims may be able to be filed with the CCB against employees of federal and state governmental institutions, though, under Section 1504(d)(3), claims may not be filed with the CCB against a "Federal or State governmental entity." Readers working at state educational institutions will want to pay close attention to see how this situation is addressed by the CCB. They can do so by visiting this website, hosted and maintained by the USCO: https://www.copyright.gov/about/small-claims/.

Putting It all Together

Having an understanding of U.S. copyright law, user rights found in it, and ways to mitigate legal risk and respond to inquiries from rightsholders should help staff and administrators proceed more confidently when offering reserve services. Understanding that the courts can recognize and provide allowances for good faith behavior are an added incentive for making thoughtful and thorough applications of the law.

Unfortunately, when it comes to U.S. copyright law, there are rarely easy answers. For example:

- The copyright status of a work can be in question.
- The person who thinks they own rights in a particular work may not actually be the rightsholder.
- Applications of the user rights found in the law are not always clear.
- Sometimes when an individual reaches out to try to obtain permission or a license for the reuse of a work, they get no response from the rightsholder or the license fee requested far exceeds what libraries can pay.

To build upon these complexities, patrons may vent their frustrations on staff when they are unable to provide them with a quick and direct yes or no answer when they ask about applications of the law and how works can legally be shared through reserve services. Those who work with copyright law often find themselves replying to questions about copyright with the phrase "it depends." Rather than seeing this as an incomplete answer, staff should embrace it as an informed and practical response to many copyright situations they encounter. Saying "it depends" allows staff the opportunity to pause and consider how U.S. copyright law applies to the situation before them. It should also be seen as an opportunity to reflect on those values and ethical principles that form the core of the profession. There will be times when staff need to say, "We can't make this work available through reserves," as doing so would be a violation of copyright law. However, there will be many situations where staff will be able to say, "We can make works available to patrons by utilizing user rights found in the law, and we also have an ethical obligation to do so in support of our mission and that of our educational institution." In these situations, if staff truly seek to provide patrons with access to services and resources that strikes a balance between rightsholders and users, they will not only be mitigating legal risk, but they will also be modeling the ethics and values that are at the core of librarianship.

APPENDIX A

Copyright Term and the Public Domain in the United States Charts

The following charts, which were developed by Peter B. Hirtle and published in his article "Recent Changes to the Copyright Law: Copyright Term Extension," *Archival Outlook* (January/February 1999), are a valuable resource when working to determine the copyright status of a work. Readers should note that these charts are accurate for the year of publication of this book, 2022, and that certain dates such as the public domain date will change on a yearly basis. For example, barring any legislative action by Congress, this date will move progressively forward year by year. This means that on January 1, 2023, unpublished works first registered with the USCO or works published in the United States prior to January 1, 1928, will also pass into the public domain; on January 1, 2024, unpublished works first registered with the USCO or works published in the United States prior to January 1, 1929, will also pass into the public domain; and so forth. Readers should make sure they are taking this information in to account when using the charts. They can also view the most up-to-date charts online at https://guides.library.cornell.edu/copyright/publicdomain.

Copyright Term and the Public Domain in the United States Charts[1]

Never Published, Never Registered Works[2]

Type of Work	Copyright Term	In the public domain in the U.S. as of 1 January 2022[3]
Unpublished works	Life of the author + 70 years	Works from authors who died before 1952
Unpublished anonymous and pseudonymous works, and works made for hire (corporate authorship)	120 years from date of creation	Works created before 1902
Unpublished works when the death date of the author is not known[4]	120 years from date of creation[5]	Works created before 1902[5]

Works Registered or First Published in the U.S.

Date of Publication[6]	Conditions[7]	Copyright Term[8]
Before 1927	None	None. In the public domain due to copyright expiration
1927 through 1977	Published without a copyright notice	None. In the public domain due to failure to comply with required formalities
1978 to 1 March 1989	Published without notice, and without subsequent registration within 5 years	None. In the public domain due to failure to comply with required formalities
1978 to 1 March 1989	Published without notice, but with subsequent registration within 5 years	70 years after the death of author. If a work of corporate authorship, 95 years from publication or 120 years from creation, whichever expires first

(continued)

(continued)

Date of Publication[6]	Conditions[7]	Copyright Term[8]
1927 through 1963	Published with notice but copyright was not renewed[8]	None. In the public domain due to copyright expiration
1927 through 1963	Published with notice and the copyright was renewed[8]	95 years after publication date
1964 through 1977	Published with notice	95 years after publication date
1978 to 1 March 1989	Created after 1977 and published with notice	70 years after the death of author. If a work of corporate authorship, 95 years from publication or 120 years from creation, whichever expires first
1978 to 1 March 1989	Created before 1978 and first published with notice in the specified period	The greater of the term specified in the previous entry or 31 December 2047
From 1 March 1989 through 2002	Created after 1977	70 years after the death of author. If a work of corporate authorship, 95 years from publication or 120 years from creation, whichever expires first
From 1 March 1989 through 2002	Created before 1978 and first published in this period	The greater of the term specified in the previous entry or 31 December 2047
After 2002	None	70 years after the death of author. If a work of corporate authorship, 95 years from publication or 120 years from creation, whichever expires first
Anytime	Works prepared by an officer or employee of the United States Government as part of that person's official duties.[19]	None. In the public domain in the United States, unless the employee was a civilian member of the faculty of one of 15 service academies and the work in question is a literary work intended for scholarly publication. (17 U.S.C. § 105)

Works First Published Outside the U.S. by Foreign Nationals or U.S. Citizens Living Abroad[9]

Date of Publication	Conditions	Copyright Term in the United States
Before 1927	None	In the public domain (But see first special case below)
	Works Published Abroad Before 1978[10]	
1927 through 1977	Published without compliance with U.S. formalities, and in the public domain in its source country as of 1 January 1996 (but see special cases)[20]	In the public domain
1927 through 1977	Published in compliance with all U.S. formalities (i.e., notice, renewal)[11]	95 years after publication date
1927 through 1977	Solely published abroad, without compliance with U.S. formalities or republication in the U.S., and not in the public domain in its home country as of 1 January 1996 (but see special cases)	95 years after publication date
1927 through 1977	Published in the U.S. less than 30 days after publication abroad	Use the U.S. publication chart to determine duration
1927 through 1977	Published in the U.S. more than 30 days after publication abroad, without compliance with U.S. formalities, and not in the public domain in its home country as of 1 January 1996 (but see special cases)	95 years after publication date

	Works Published Abroad After 1 January 1978	
1978 to 2002	Created before 1978 and first published in a country that is a signatory to the Berne Convention or other 17 USC § 104A(h)(3) treaties[20]	The greater of 70 years after the death of author (or if work of corporate authorship, 95 years from publication) or 31 December 2047
2003–	Created before 1978 and first published after 2002 in a country that is a signatory to the Berne Convention or other 17 USC § 104A(h)(3) treaties[20]	70 years after the death of the author, or if work of corporate authorship, 95 years from publication
1 January 1978– 1 March 1989	Published without copyright notice, and in the public domain in its source country as of 1 January 1996 (but see special cases)[18]	In the public domain
1 January 1978– 1 March 1989	Published without copyright notice in a country that is a signatory to the Berne Convention or other 17 USC § 104A(h)(3) treaties and is not in the public domain in its source country as of 1 January 1996 (but see special cases)[18]	70 years after the death of author, or if work of corporate authorship, 95 years from publication
1 January 1978– 1 March 1989	Published with copyright notice in a country that has copyright relations with the U.S. (but see special cases)[13]	70 years after the death of author, or if work of corporate authorship, 95 years from publication
After 1 March 1989	Published in a country that has copyright relations with the US[13]	70 years after the death of author, or if work of corporate authorship, 95 years from publication

(continued)

(continued)

Date of Publication	Conditions	Copyright Term in the United States
After 1 March 1989	Published in a country with which the United States does not have copyright relations under a treaty	In the public domain
	Special Cases	
1 July 1909 through 1978	In Alaska, Arizona, California, Hawaii, Idaho, Montana, Nevada, Oregon, Washington, Guam, and the Northern Mariana Islands ONLY. Published in a language other than English, and without subsequent republication with a copyright notice[12]	Treat as an unpublished work until such date as first US-compliant publication occurred
Anytime	Created by a resident of Eritrea, Ethiopia, Iran, Iraq, Marshall Islands, and published in one of these countries. Works from Palau, Somalia, South Sudan, or Timor-Leste may also be included.[13]	Not protected by U.S. copyright law until they become party to bilateral or international copyright agreements
Anytime	Works whose copyright was once owned or administered by the Alien Property Custodian, and whose copyright, if restored, would as of January 1, 1996, be owned by a government[14]	Not protected by U.S. copyright law
Anytime	If fixed or solely published in one of the following countries, the 1 January 1996 date given above is replaced by the date of the country's membership in the Berne Convention or the World Trade Organization, whichever is earlier: Afghanistan, Algeria, Andorra, Angola, Armenia, Azerbaijan, Belarus, Bhutan, Cambodia, Cape Verde, Cook Islands, Comoros, Equatorial Guinea, Grenada, Haiti, Jersey, Jordan, Kiribati, Democratic People's Republic of Korea, Kuwait, Kyrgyzstan, Laos, Malaysia, Micronesia, Mongolia, Montenegro, Nauru, Nepal, Niue, Oman, Panama, Papua New Guinea, Qatar, Samoa, San Marino, São Tomé and Príncipe, Saudi Arabia, Solomon Islands, Sudan, Syria, Taiwan, Tajikistan, Tonga, Turkmenistan, Tuvalu, United Arab Emirates, Uzbekistan, Vanuatu, Vietnam, Yemen	

Sound Recordings

(Note: The following information applies only to the sound recording itself, and not to any copyrights in underlying compositions or texts.)

Date of Fixation/ Publication	Conditions	Copyright Term in the United States
	Unpublished Sound Recordings, Domestic and Foreign	
Prior to 15 Feb. 1972	Indeterminate	Subject to state common law protection. Enters the public domain on 15 Feb. 2067
After 15 Feb. 1972	Life of the author + 70 years. For unpublished anonymous and pseudonymous works and works made for hire (corporate authorship), 120 years from the date of fixation	Nothing. The soonest anything enters the public domain is 15 Feb. 2067
	Sound Recordings Published in the United States	
Before 1923	None	1 January 2022
1923 to 1946	None	100 years from publication
1947 to 1956	None	110 years from publication
1957 – 14 Feb 1972	None	15 Feb 2067
15 Feb 1972 to 1978	Published without notice (i.e, ©, year of publication, and name of copyright owner)[15]	In the public domain
15 Feb. 1972 to 1978	Published with notice	95 years from publication. 2068 at the earliest

(continued)

(continued)

Date of Fixation/ Publication	Conditions	Copyright Term in the United States
1978 to 1 March 1989	Published without notice, and without subsequent registration	In the public domain
1978 to 1 March 1989	Published with notice	70 years after death of author, or if work of corporate authorship, the shorter of 95 years from publication, or 120 years from creation. 2049 at the earliest
After 1 March 1989	None	70 years after death of author, or if work of corporate authorship, the shorter of 95 years from publication, or 120 years from creation. 2049 at the earliest
	Sound Recordings Published Outside the United States	
Before 1923	None	1 January 2022
1923 to 1946	None	100 years from publication
1947 to 1956	None	110 years from publication
1957 to 14 Feb 1972	None	15 Feb. 2067
15 Feb 1972 to 1 March 1989	In the public domain in its home country as of 1 Jan. 1996 or there was U.S. publication within 30 days of the foreign publication (but see special cases)	Subject to state common law protection. Enters the public domain on 15 Feb. 2067
15 Feb. 1972 to 1978	Not in the public domain in its home country as of 1 Jan. 1996. At least one author of the work was not a U.S. citizen or was living abroad, and there was no U.S. publication within 30 days of the foreign publication (but see special cases)	95 years from date of publication. 2068 at the earliest

1978 to 1 March 1989	Not in the public domain in its home country as of 1 Jan. 1996. At least one author of the work was not a U.S. citizen or was living abroad, and there was no U.S. publication within 30 days of the foreign publication (but see special cases)	70 years after death of author, or if work of corporate authorship, the shorter of 95 years from publication, or 120 years from creation
After 1 March 1989	None	70 years after death of author, or if work of corporate authorship, the shorter of 95 years from publication, or 120 years from creation
	Special Cases	
Fixed at any time	Created by a resident of Eritrea, Ethiopia, Iran, Iraq, Marshall Islands, San Marino, or Timor-Leste and published in one of these countries. Works from Nauru, Palau, Somalia, or South Sudan may also be included.[13]	Not protected by U.S. federal copyright law because they are not party to international copyright agreements
Fixed prior to 1996	Works whose copyright was once owned or administered by the Alien Property Custodian, and whose copyright, if restored, would as of 1 January 1996 be owned by a government[14]	Not protected by U.S. federal copyright law
Fixed at any time	If fixed or solely published in one of the following countries, the 1 January 1996 date given above is replaced by the date of the country's membership in the Berne Convention or the World Trade Organization, whichever is earlier: Afghanistan, Algeria, Andorra, Angola, Armenia, Azerbaijan, Belarus, Bhutan, Cambodia, Cape Verde, Cook Islands, Comoros, Equatorial Guinea, Grenada, Haiti, Jersey, Jordan, Kiribati, Democratic People's Republic of Korea, Kuwait, Kyrgyzstan, Laos, Malaysia, Micronesia, Mongolia, Montenegro, Nauru, Nepal, Niue, Oman, Panama, Papua New Guinea, Qatar, Samoa, San Marino, São Tomé and Príncipe, Saudi Arabia, Solomon Islands, Sudan, Syria, Taiwan, Tajikistan, Tonga, Turkmenistan, Tuvalu, United Arab Emirates, Uzbekistan, Vanuatu, Vietnam, Yemen	

Architectural Works[16]
(Note: Architectural plans and drawings may also be protected as textual/graphics works.)

Date of Design	Date of Construction	Copyright Status
Prior to 1 Dec. 1990	Not constructed by 31 Dec. 2002	Protected only as plans or drawings
Prior to 1 Dec. 1990	Constructed by 1 Dec. 1990	Protected only as plans or drawings
Prior to 1 Dec. 1990	Constructed between 30 Nov. 1990 and 31 Dec. 2002	Building is protected for 70 years after death of author, or if work of corporate authorship, the shorter of 95 years from publication, or 120 years from creation[17]
From 1 Dec. 1990	Immaterial	Building is protected for 70 years after death of author, or if work of corporate authorship, the shorter of 95 years from publication, or 120 years from creation[17]

Editorial Note

January 2019 marked two important changes to the copyright duration chart. First, for the first time in 20 years, published works entered the public domain. 1923 finally arrived, and the cut-off date for the public domain has started to shift. Second, the enactment of the Orrin G. Hatch-Bob Goodlatte Music Modernization Act in 2018 radically changed the calculus for pre-1972 published sound recordings. Both of these changes are reflected in the chart.

Notes

1. This chart was first published in Peter B. Hirtle, "Recent Changes To The Copyright Law: Copyright Term Extension," Archival Outlook, January/February 1999. This version is current as of 3 January 2022. The most recent version is found at the Cornell University Library's Copyright Services page: https://guides.library.cornell.edu/copyright/publicdomain. For some explanation on how to use the chart and

complications hidden in it, see Peter B. Hirtle, "When is 1923 Going to Arrive and Other Complications of the U.S. Public Domain," Searcher (Sept 2012): http://www.infotoday.com/searcher/sep12/Hirtle—When-Is-1923-Going-to-Arrive-and-Other-Complications-of-the-U.S.-Public-Domain.shtml. The chart is based in part on Laura N. Gasaway's chart, "When Works Pass Into the Public Domain": https://web.archive.org/web/20181108140230/http:/www.unc.edu/~unclng/public-d.htm. A similar chart is found in Marie C. Malaro, *A Legal Primer On Managing Museum Collections* (3rd ed, p. 170, Washington, D.C.: Smithsonian Institution Press, 2012). Mary Minow has a useful copyright duration chart organized by year: http://www.librarylaw.com/DigitizationTable.htm. A "flow chart" for copyright duration: http://sunsteinlaw.com/practices/copyright-portfolio-development/copyright-pointers/copyright-flowchart/, and a "tree-view" chart on copyright: http://chart.copyrightdata.com/, are also available. Several U.S. copyright duration calculators are available online, including the Public Domain Sherpa: http://www.publicdomainsherpa.com/calculator.html, and the Durationator: http://www.durationator.com/ (in beta). See also Library of Congress Copyright Office, Circular 15a, Duration of Copyright: Provisions of the Law Dealing with the Length of Copyright Protection: http://www.copyright.gov/circs/circ15a.pdf. Further information on copyright duration is found in Peter B. Hirtle, Emily Hudson, and Andrew T. Kenyon, "Chapter 3, Duration and Ownership of Copyright," in *Copyright and Cultural Institutions: Guidelines for Digitization for U.S. Libraries, Archives, and Museums* (Ithaca, NY: Cornell University Library, 2009), available as a free download from Cornell eCommons: http://ecommons.cornell.edu/handle/1813/14142. Additional guidance on the public domain may be found in Melissa Levine, Richard C. Adler, and Justin Bonfiglio, "Finding the Public Domain: Copyright Review Management System Toolkit" (Ann Arbor, Michigan: Michigan Publishing, 13 June 2016): http://dx.doi.org/10.3998/crmstoolkit.14616082.0001.001, and Menesha A. Mannapperuma, Brianna L. Schofield, and Andrea K. Yankovsky, et al., "Is it in the Public Domain?" (Berkeley, CA: Samuelson Law, Technology & Public Policy Clinic at the University of California, Berkeley, School of Law, 27 May 2014): https://www.law.berkeley.edu/files/FINAL_PublicDomain_Handbook_FINAL(1).pdf.

2. Treat unpublished works registered for copyright prior to 1978 as if they had been published in the US (though note that the only formality that applied was the requirement to renew copyright after 28 years).

3. All terms of copyright run through the end of the calendar year in which they would otherwise expire, so a work enters the public domain on the first of the year following the expiration of its copyright term. For example, a book published on 15 March 1925 entered the public domain on 1 January 2021, not 16 March 2020 (1925+95=2020).

4. Unpublished works when the death date of the author is not known may still be copyrighted after 120 years, but certification from the Copyright Office that it has no record to indicate whether the person is living or died less than 70 years before is a complete defense to any action for infringement. See 17 U.S.C. § 302(e).

5. Presumption as to the author's death requires a certified report from the Copyright Office that its records disclose nothing to indicate that the author of the work is living or died less than seventy years before.

6. "Publication" was not explicitly defined in the Copyright Law before 1976, but the 1909 Act indirectly indicated that publication was when copies of the first authorized edition were placed on sale, sold, or publicly distributed by the proprietor of the copyright or under his authority.

7. Not all published works are copyrighted. Works prepared by an officer or employee of the United States Government as part of that person's official duties receive no copyright protection in the U.S. For much of the twentieth century, certain formalities had to be followed to secure copyright protection. For example, some books had to be printed in the United States to receive copyright protection, and failure to deposit copies of works with the Register of Copyright could result in the loss of copyright. The requirements that copies include a formal notice of copyright and that the copyright be renewed after twenty eight years were the most common conditions, and are specified in the chart.

8. A 1961 Copyright Office study found that fewer than 15% of all registered copyrights were renewed. For books, the figure was even lower: 7%. See Barbara Ringer, "Study No. 31: Renewal of Copyright" (1960), reprinted in Library of Congress Copyright Office. Copyright law revision: Studies prepared for the Subcommittee on Patents, Trademarks, and Copyrights of the Committee on the Judiciary, United States Senate, Eighty-sixth Congress, first [-second] session (Washington: U. S. Govt. Print. Off, 1961, p. 220). A good guide to investigating the copyright and renewal status of published work is Samuel Demas and Jennie L. Brogdon, "Determining Copyright Status for Preservation and Access: Defining Reasonable Effort," Library Resources and Technical Services 41:4 (October 1997): 323–334. See also Library of Congress Copyright Office, How to Investigate the Copyright Status of a Work, Circular 22: https://www.copyright.gov/circs/circ22.pdf. The Online Books Page FAQ, especially "How Can I Tell Whether a Book Can Go Online?": http://onlinebooks.library.upenn.edu/okbooks.html and "How Can I Tell Whether a Copyright Was Renewed?": http://onlinebooks.library.upenn.edu/renewals.html, is also very helpful.

9. The following section on foreign publications draws extensively on Stephen Fishman, "The Public Domain: How to Find Copyright-free Writings, Music, Art & More" (Berkeley: Nolo.com, 2019): http://www.nolo.com/products/the-public-domain-publ.html. It applies to works first published abroad and not subsequently published in the US within 30 days of the original foreign publication. Works that were simultaneously published abroad and in the US are treated as if they are American publications.

10. Foreign works published after 1925 are likely to be still under copyright in the US because of the Uruguay Round Agreements Act (URAA) modifying the General Agreement on Tariffs and Trade (GATT). The URAA restored copyright in foreign works that as of 1 January 1996 had fallen into the public domain in the United States because of a failure to comply with US formalities. One of the authors of the work had to be a non-U.S. citizen or resident, the work could not have been published in the United States within 30 days after its publication abroad, and the work needed to still be in copyright in the country of publication. Such works have a copyright term equivalent to that of an American work that had followed all of the formalities. For more information, see Library of Congress Copyright Office, Highlights of Copyright Amendments Contained in the Uruguay Round Agreements Act (URAA), Circular 38b: http://www.copyright.gov/circs/circ38b.pdf.

11. U.S. formalities include the requirement that a formal notice of copyright be included in the work; registration, renewal, and deposit of copies in the Copyright Office; and the manufacture of the work in the United States.

12. The differing dates is a product of the question of controversial Twin Books v. Walt Disney Co: http://caselaw.findlaw.com/us-9th-circuit/1304377.html. decision by the 9th Circuit Court of Appeals in 1996. The question at issue is the copyright status of

a work only published in a foreign language outside of the United States and without a copyright notice. It had long been assumed that failure to comply with U.S. formalities placed these works in the public domain in the United States and, as such, were subject to copyright restoration under URAA (see note 10). The court in Twin Books, however, concluded "publication without a copyright notice in a foreign country did not put the work in the public domain in the United States." According to the court, these foreign publications were in effect "unpublished" in the United States, and hence have the same copyright term as unpublished works. The decision has been harshly criticized in Nimmer on Copyright, the leading treatise on copyright, as being incompatible with previous decisions and the intent of Congress when it restored foreign copyrights. The Copyright Office as well ignores the Twin Books decision in its circular on restored copyrights. Nevertheless, the decision is currently applicable in all of the 9th Judicial Circuit (Alaska, Arizona, California, Hawaii, Idaho, Montana, Nevada, Oregon, Washington, and Guam and the Northern Mariana Islands), and it may apply in the rest of the country.

13. See Library of Congress Copyright Office, International Copyright Relations of the United States. Circular 38a: http://www.copyright.gov/circs/circ38a.pdf.

14. See 63 Fed. Reg.19,287 (1998), Library of Congress Copyright Office, Copyright Restoration of Works in Accordance With the Uruguay Round Agreements Act; List Identifying Copyrights Restored Under the Uruguay Round Agreements Act for Which Notices of Intent To Enforce Restored Copyrights Were Filed in the Copyright Office: http://www.copyright.gov/fedreg/1998/63fr19287.pdf.

15. Copyright notice requirements for sound recordings are spelled out in the Copyright Office's Circular 3, "Copyright Notice": http://www.copyright.gov/circs/circ03.pdf. Here is the exact text: The copyright notice for phonorecords embodying a sound recording is different from that for other works. Sound recordings are defined as "works that result from the fixation of a series of musical, spoken or other sounds, but not including the sounds accompanying a motion picture or other audiovisual work." Copyright in a sound recording protects the particular series of sounds fixed in the recording against unauthorized reproduction, revision, and distribution. This copyright is distinct from copyright of the musical, literary, or dramatic work that may be recorded on the phonorecord. Phonorecords may be records (such as LPs and 45s), audio tapes, cassettes, or disks. The notice should contain the following three elements appearing together on the phonorecord:

1. The symbol; and
2. The year of first publication of the sound recording; and
3. The name of the owner of copyright in the sound recording, or an abbreviation by which the name can be recognized, or a generally known alternative designation of the owner. If the producer of the sound recording is named on the phonorecord label or container and if no other name appears in conjunction with the notice, the producer's name shall be considered a part of the notice.
4. Example: 2004 X.Y.Z. Records, Inc.

16. Architectural works are defined as "the design of a building as embodied in any tangible medium of expression, including a building, architectural plans, or drawings. The work includes the overall form as well as the arrangement and composition of spaces and elements in the design, but does not include individual standard features." Architectural works were expressly included in copyright by Title VII of Pub. L. 101–650.

17. What constitutes "publication" of a building is a very interesting question. As the Copyright Office has noted, "A work is considered published when underlying copies of the building design are distributed or made available public by sale or other transfer of

ownership, or by rental. Construction of a building does not itself constitute publication registration, unless multiple copies are constructed." See its Circular 41, "Copyright Claims in Architectural Works": http://www.copyright.gov/circs/circ41.pdf.

18. If the source country's first adhered to either the Berne Treaty or the WTO after 1 January 1996, then the relevant date is the earliest date of membership. Date of membership is tracked on Wikipedia: List of Parties to International Copyright Agreements: http://en.wikipedia.org/wiki/list_of_parties_to_international_copyright_agreements.

19. Contractors and grantees are not considered government employees. Generally they create works with copyright (though the government may own that copyright). See CENDI Frequently asked Questions about Copyright: Issues Affecting the U.S. Government: https://cendi.gov/pdf/FAQ_Copyright_30jan18.pdf. The public domain status of U.S. government works applies only in the United States.

20. Thanks to Dr. Paul Goldsman and Tony Greenman for noting that the chart lacked information for foreign works created before 1978 and first published between 1978 and 2003.

APPENDIX B

Copyright Checklist: Fair Use

Name: ____________ Date: ____________ Project: ____________

Institution: ____________________ Prepared by: __________________

Purpose

Favoring Fair Use	Opposing Fair Use
☐ Teaching (including multiple copies for classroom use)	☐ Commercial activity
☐ Research	☐ Profiting from the use
☐ Scholarship	☐ Straight reproduction (copying without modification)
☐ Nonprofit educational institution	☐ Nontransformative use
☐ Criticism	☐ Entertainment
☐ Comment	☐ Bad-faith behavior
☐ News reporting	☐ Denying credit to the original author
☐ Transformative use (alters the original work in a creative manner)	
☐ Transformative use (uses the work for a purpose other than the original purpose)	
☐ Restricted access (for only students or other appropriate group)	
☐ Parody	

Nature	
Favoring Fair Use	**Opposing Fair Use**
☐ Published work	☐ Unpublished work
☐ Factual or nonfiction based	☐ Highly creative (art, music, novels, films, plays)
☐ Important to favored educational objectives	☐ Fiction
	☐ Consumable work (e.g., worksheets and standard exam forms)
Amount	
Favoring Fair Use	**Opposing Fair Use**
☐ Small quantity	☐ Large portion or whole work used beyond the favored purpose
☐ Portion used is not central or significant to entire work	☐ Portion used could interfere with a reasonable market for the use (e.g., multiple chapters from a single book)
☐ Amount is tailored to meet the educational or other favored purpose	☐ Portion used in central to work or "heart of the work"
Effect	
☐ User owns lawfully acquired or purchased copy of the original work	☐ Straight copying that is not transformative
☐ Few or modest number of copies made	☐ Portion used could interfere with a reasonable market for the use or derivatives (e.g., multiple chapters from a single book)
☐ No significant effect on the market or potential market for the copyrighted work	☐ Reasonably available licensing mechanism for the use of the copyrighted work
☐ No similar product marketed by the copyright holder	☐ Affordable permission available for using the work
☐ Lack of a reasonable licensing mechanism for the work for institutional use	☐ Numerous copies made
	☐ Posted to the internet or otherwise made widely accessible
	☐ Repeated or long-term use

References

ADA (Americans With Disabilities) National Network. n.d.-a. "Glossary of ADA Terms." ADA National Network. Accessed July 18, 2019. https://adata.org/glossary-terms.

ADA National Network. n.d.-b. "What is the Americans with Disabilities Act (ADA)?" Accessed November 12, 2019. https://adata.org/learn-about-ada.

Allen, I. Elaine, and Jeff Seaman. 2017. *Digital Learning Compass: Distance Education Enrollment Report 2017.* Babson Park: Babson Survey Research Group. https://onlinelearningsurvey.com/reports/digtiallearningcompassenrollment2017.pdf.

Amazon.com. 2021. "Amazon Music Terms of Use." Last modified September 14, 2021 https://www.amazon.com/gp/help/customer/display.html?nodeId=201380010.

American Association of Law Libraries Executive Board. 2018. "Principles and Practices for Licensing Electronic Resources." https://www.aallnet.org/wp-content/uploads/2018/05/Principles-and-Practices-for-Licensing_05.30.2018_FINALpdf.pdf.

ARL (Association of Research Libraries), Center for Social Media, School of Communication, American University, Program on Information Justice and Intellectual Property, Washington College of Law, American University. 2012. "Code of Best Practices in Fair Use for Academic and Research Libraries." https://www.arl.org/wp-content/uploads/2014/01/code-of-best-practices-fair-use.pdf.

Bazeley, Jennifer. 2018, November 2. "Purchasing Accessible E-resources: Tips for Licensing and Procurement." Presentation at the Annual Academic Library Association of Ohio Conference, Lewis Center, OH.

Big Ten Academic Alliance Libraries. n.d. "Library E-Resource Accessibility—Standardized License Language." Big Ten Academic Alliance. Accessed March 4, 2022. https://btaa.org/library/reports/library-e-resource-accessibility—standardized-license-language.

Brame, Cynthia. 2013. "Flipping the classroom." Vanderbilt University Center for Teaching. http://cft.vanderbilt.edu/guides-sub-pages/flipping-the-classroom/.

Butler, Brandon. 2015. "Transformative Teaching and Educational Fair Use after Georgia State." *Connecticut Law Review*, 48, no. 2: 473–530. https://opencommons.uconn.edu/law_review/309

Butler, Brandon, Prue Adler, and Krista Cox. 2019. The Law and Accessible Texts: Reconciling Civil Rights and Copyright. Association of Research Libraries. https://www.arl.org/resources/the-law-and-accessible-texts-reconciling-civil-rights-and-copyrights/.

Celik, Osman and Roxanne Peck. 2016. "If You Expand, They Will Come: Textbook Affordability Through Expansion of Course Reserves: The Case of UCLA Library's Course Reserves via Strategic Partnership with the Campus Independent Bookstore." *Technical Services Quarterly*, 33, no. 3: 268–278. https://doi.org/10.1080/07317131.2016.1169788.

Center for Disease Control. 2020. "Disability and Health Overview." https://www.cdc.gov/ncbddd/disabilityandhealth/disability.html#ref.

Committee on Professional Ethics. 2013–2014. "Copyright: An Interpretation of the Code of Ethics." American Library Association. https://www.ala.org/aboutala/sites/ala.org.aboutala/files/content/Section%20B%20New%20Policy%20Manual-1%20%28REVISED%2011_4_2019%29.doc

Committee on the Judiciary. 1976, September 3. *Report No. 94-1476: Copyright Law Revision*. Washington D.C.: House of Representatives.

Committee on the Judiciary. 1998, May 22. H. Rept. 105-551 - WIPO COPYRIGHT TREATIES IMPLEMENTATION AND ON-LINE COPYRIGHT INFRINGEMENT LIABILITY LIMITATION. Washington D.C.: House of Representatives. H. Rept. 105-551.

Creative Commons. n.d.-a. "About the Licenses." Accessed January 3, 2020. https://creativecommons.org/licenses/.

Creative Commons. n.d.-b. "CC0 No Rights Reserved." Accessed November 11, 2019. https://creativecommons.org/share-your-work/public-domain/cc0/.

Creative Commons. n.d.-c. "Public Domain Mark." Accessed November 11, 2019. https://creativecommons.org/share-your-work/public-domain/pdm.

Crews, Kenneth D. 2001. "The Law of Fair Use and the Illusion of Fair-Use Guidelines." *Ohio State Law Journal*, 62, no. 2: 599–702. http://hdl.handle.net/1811/70447.

Crews, Kenneth D. 2003. "Copyright and Distance Education: Making Sense of the TEACH Act." *Change: The Magazine of Higher Learning*, 35, no. 6: 34–39.

Crews, Kenneth D. 2020. *Copyright Law for Librarians and Educators: Creative Strategies & Practical Solutions*. Chicago: American Library Association.

Daines, Gary, ed. 2022. "Media Usage Guidelines." National Aeronautics and Space Administration. Last modified January 24, 2022. https://www.nasa.gov/multimedia/guidelines/index.html.

Donaldson, Robin, John Opper, and E Shen. 2019. *2018 Student Textbook and Course Materials Survey Results and Findings*. Gainesville: Florida Virtual Campus Office of Distance Learning and Student Services. https://dlss.flvc.org/documents/210036/1314923/2018+Student+Textbook+and+Co

urse+Materials+Survey+Report+—+FINAL+VERSION+—+20190308.pdf/07478d85-89c2-3742-209a-9cc5df8cd7ea.

Enis, Matt. 2018. "College Students Prefer Print for Long-Form Reading, Ebooks for Research." Library Journal. https://lj.libraryjournal.com/2018/03/technology/ebooks/college-students-prefer-print-long-form-reading-ebooks-research-lj-survey/.

Evans, Orinda, "District Court: Final Order (2020)" (2020). *Georgia State University Copyright Lawsuit*. 12. https://scholarworks.gsu.edu/univ_lib_copyrightlawsuit/12

Ferullo, Donna L. 2014. *Managing Copyright in Higher Education: A Guidebook*. Maryland: Rowman & Littlefield Publishers

Federal Communications Commission. 2019. "21st Century Communications and Video Accessibility Act (CVAA)." Last modified January 27, 2021. https://www.fcc.gov/consumers/guides/21st-century-communications-and-video-accessibility-act-cvaa.

Fry, Richard and Anthony Cilluffo. 2019. "A Rising Share of Undergraduates Are from Poor Families, Especially at Less Selective Colleges." Pew Research Center. https://www.pewsocialtrends.org/2019/05/22/a-rising-share-of-undergraduates-are-from-poor-families-especially-at-less-selective-colleges/.

Garner, Bryan A., ed. 2009. *Black's Law Dictionary*. St. Paul: West Publishing.

Goodson, Kymberly, Marlayna Christensen, Sarah Elliott, and Abigail Lowery. 2009. "Getting Buzzed in the Library: The use of Restaurant-Style Pagers for Reserves Checkout in an Academic Library." *Journal of Interlibrary Loan, Document Delivery, & Electronic Reserves*, 19, no. 2: 117–129. https://doi:10.1080/10723030902776162.

Greiner, Tony. 2012. "'All Textbooks in the Library!' An Experiment with Library Reserves." *Library Philosophy and Practice*: 838. http://digitalcommons.unl.edu/libphilprac/838.

Harris Family Center for Disability and Health Policy. n.d. "Providing Information in Alternative Formats." Western University of Health Sciences. Accessed November 27, 2018. http://hfcdhp.org/briefs/brief6a-alt-formats/#sect2.

HathiTrust Digital Library. n.d. "Our Digital Library." Accessed November 18, 2018. https://www.hathitrust.org/digital_library.

Healey, Paul D. 1995, Summer. "Chicken Little at the Reference Desk: The Myth of Librarian Liability." *Law Library Journal* 87, no. 3: 515–553.

Hickey, Daniel. 2011. "The Reuse Evangelist: Taking Ownership of Copyright Questions at Your Library." *Reference & User Services Quarterly* 51, no. 1: 9–11. www.jstor.org/stable/refuseserq.51.1.9.

Hirtle, Peter B., Emily Hudson, and Andrew T. Kenyon. 2009. *Copyright and Cultural Institutions: Guidelines for Digitizing for U.S. Libraries, Archives, and Museums*. Ithaca: Cornell University Press. https://hdl.handle.net/1813/14142.

Hodak, Brittany. (2016). "RIP VHS: World's Last VCR Will Be Made This Month." Forbes. https://www.forbes.com/sites/brittanyhodak/2016/07/23/rip-vhs-worlds-last-vcr-to-be-made-this-month/#4082d98123da.

Hoppenfeld, Jared and Wendi Arant-Kasper. 2010. "Do-It-Yourself Course Reserves: A Student-Driven Service in an Academic Library." *Journal of Interlibrary Loan, Document Delivery, & Electronic Reserves* 20: 353–361. https://doi.org/10.1080/1072303X.2010.520264.

Hornick, John F. 2003. "Copyright Law for Business People: A Handy Guide." Finnegan. https://www.finnegan.com/en/insights/articles/copyright-law-for-business-people-a-handy-guide.html.

Huber, Jared, Brian T. Yeh, and Robin Jeweler. 2006. *Copyright Exemptions for Distance Education: 17 U.S.C. § 110(2), the Technology, Education, and Copyright Harmonization Act of 2002*. Washington D.C.: Congressional Research Service.

Internet Archive. 2017. "Sonny Bono Memorial Collection." Last modified October 10, 2017. https://archive.org/details/last20?tab=about.

Jaszi, P., Carla S. Myers, Tucker Tayolr, and Andrew Wesolek. 2017. "An Interview with Peter Jaszi, Professor of Law, Faculty Director of the Glushko-Samuelson Intellectual Property Clinic." *Journal of Copyright in Education and Librarianship*, 2, no. 1: 1–8. https://doi.org/10.17161/jcel.v1i2.6970.

Jaszi, Peter, Michael Remington, October Ivins, and Sharon Dyas-Correia. 2016. "Copyright and Intellectual Property: What You Need to Know." *The Serials Librarian*, 70: 1–4, 34–43. https://doi.org/10.1080/0361526X.2016.1141624.

Leval, Pierre N. 1990. "Toward a Fair Use Standard." *Harvard Law Review*, 103, no. 5: 1105–1136. https://doi.org/10.2307/1341457.

Lewis, Elisa. 2021. "SDH Subtitles vs. Closed Captions: What's the Difference?" 3PlayMedia. Last modified January 26, 2022. https://www.3playmedia.com/blog/whats-the-difference-subtitles-for-the-deaf-and-hard-of-hearing-sdh-v-closed-captions/

Library of Congress. 1978, July 31. "Final Report of the National Commission on New Technology Uses of Copyrighted Works." http://www.digital-law-online.info/CONTU/PDF/index.html.

Lipinski, Thomas A. 2006. *The Complete Copyright Liability Handbook for Librarians and Educators*. New York: Neal-Schuman Publishers, Inc.

Ma, Jennifer. 2021. *Trends in College Pricing and Student Aid 2021*. College Board. https://research.collegeboard.org/media/pdf/trends-college-pricing-student-aid-2021.pdf.

MacKay Snowman, Ann. 2017. "Do Textbooks have a Place in the Library?" *Journal of Access Services*, 14, no. 2: 43–45. https://doi.org/10.1080/15367967.2017.1309246.

McCaslin, David. 2011. "Guest Editorial: E-reserves and the Threat to Using Persistent Links." *Journal of Access Services*, 8, no. 2: 51–55. https://doi.org/10.1080/15367967.2011.545254.

McDonald, Krista and John Burke. 2010. "On My Mind: The Case for Text books." *American Libraries*, 41, 3: 25. https://americanlibrariesmagazine.org/2010/02/17/the-case-for-textbooks/.

McElfresh, Laura Kane. 2009. "College Textbooks and Libraries: If You Reserve It, They Will Come." *Technicalities* 29, no. 6: 4–6.

McElroy, Kaelly, Dan Moore, Lori Hilterbrand, and Nicole Hindes. 2017. "Access Services Are Human Services: Collaborating to Provide Textbook Access to Students." *Journal of Access Services*, 14, no. 2: 80–91. https://doi.org/10.1080/15367967.2017.1296769.

Miami University Libraries. n.d. "Miami Libraries Set New #MoveInMiami Standards." Accessed July 9, 2019. http://www.lib.miamioh.edu/Illuminant16/moveinmiami-success.

Murphy, Molly. 2013. "Textbooks on Reserve: A Case Study." *Journal of Access Services* 10, no. 2: 145–152. https://doi.org/10.1080/15367967.2013.795429.

Myers, C. S. (2019). "Online Classrooms: Is the TEACH Act Enough?" In *Copyright Conversations: Rights Literacy in a Digital World*, edited by Sara R. Benson, 159–172. Chicago, IL: ALCTS.

Nichols, Caleb. 2019. "In Defense of Course Reserves: A Review of California Programs." *C&RL News*, 80, no. 9: 520–530. https://doi.org/10.5860/crln.80.9.520.

Office of Government-wide Policy. 2018. "Voluntary Product Accessibility Template (VPAT)." U.S. General Services Administration. Last modified April 2018. https://www.section508.gov/sell/vpat.

Paolini, Christopher. n.d. "FAQ." Paolini.net. Accessed November 17, 2018. https://www.paolini.net/faq/.

Penn (Pennsylvania) State University. 2017. "Class of 2018 Selects Libraries' Textbook Fund Among Class Gift Options." https://news.psu.edu/story/492548/2017/11/07/arts-and-entertainment/class-2018-selects-libraries-textbook-fund-among.

Perlmutter, Shira. 2021. Section 1201 rulemaking: Eighth Triennial Proceeding to Determine Exemptions to the Prohibition on Circumvention. Washington D.C.: U.S. Copyright Office. https://cdn.loc.gov/copyright/1201/2021/2021_Section_1201_Registers_Recommendation.pdf.

Peters, Mary Beth. 2004. Statement of Marybeth Peters. The Register of Copyrights before the Committee on the Judiciary. Washington D.C.: United States House of Representatives. https://www.copyright.gov/docs/regstat072204.html.

Pitts-Noggle, and Ryan Rafferty. 2017. "Investigating Textbook Reserves: A Case Study of Two Models for Reserves Collections." *College & Research Libraries* 78, no. 1: 66–79. https://doi.org/10.5860/crl.78.1.66.

Pollitz, John H., Anne Christie, and Cheryl Middleton. 2009. "Management of Library Course Reserves and the Textbook Affordability Crisis." *Journal of Access Services,* 6, no. 4: 459–484. https://doi.org/10.1080/15367960903149268.

Rainie, Lee. 2017. "About 6 in 10 Young Adults in U.S. Primarily Use Online Streaming to Watch TV." Pew Research Center. http://www.pewresearch.org/fact-tank/2017/09/13/about-6-in-10-young-adults-in-u-s-primarily-use-online-streaming-to-watch-tv/.

Register of Copyrights. 2021. *Section 1201 Rulemaking: Eighth Triennial Proceeding to Determine Exemptions to the Prohibition on Circumvention*. Washington D.C.: United States Copyright Office. https://cdn.loc.gov/copyright/1201/2021/2021_Section_1201_Registers_Recommendation.pdf.

Senate Judiciary Committee. 1998, May 11. S. Rep. No. 105-190 - THE DIGITAL MILLENNIUM COPYRIGHT ACT OF 1998. Washington D.C.: Senate. https://www.congress.gov/congressional-report/105th-congress/senate-report/190/1.

Senate Judiciary. S.Rept 94-473 1975 – Copyright Law Revision. Washington D.C.: Senate

Senate Judiciary Committee. 2001, June 5. S. Rept. 107-31 - TECHNOLOGY - TECHNOLOGY, EDUCATION AND COPYRIGHT HARMONIZATION ACT OF 2001. Washington D.C.: Senate. https://www.congress.gov/congressional-report/107th-congress/senate-report/31

Senate Judiciary Committee. 2018, June 4. S. Rep. No. 115-261 - MARRAKESH TREATY IMPLEMENTATION ACT. Washington D.C.: Senate. https://www.congress.gov/congressional-report/115th-congress/senate-report/261.

Smith, Kevin L. 2012, June. "Copyright Risk Management: Principles and Strategies for Large-Scale Digitization Projects in Special Collections." Research Library Issues: A Quarterly Report from ARL, CNI, and SPARC, no. 279: 17–23. http://publications.arl.org/rli279/.

Smith, Kevin L. 2014, May 10. "Superrights for Textbooks?" *Scholarly Communications at Duke (blog), Office of Copyright and Scholarly Communications*. May 10, 2014, https://blogs.library.duke.edu/scholcomm/2014/05/10/superrights-for-textbooks/.

Smith, Kevin L. 2015, December 1. "Swatting Three Bugs at Once." *Scholarly Communications @ Duke (blog)*. https://blogs.library.duke.edu/scholcomm/2015/12/01/swatting-three-bugs-at-once/.

Smith, Kevin L. 2018, October 20. "The GSU Copyright Case: Lather, Rinse, Repeat." Into the Open (blog). http://hdl.handle.net/1808/29907.

Smith, Kevin and Lisa Macklin. 2014. *A Framework for Analyzing Any U.S. Copyright Problem*. Duke University, Emory University, The University of North Carolina at Chapel Hill. http://hdl.handle.net/1808/22723.

Smith, Kevin and Susan Davis. 2013. "Copyright in a Digital Age: Conflict, Risk, and Reward." *The Serials Librarian* 64, no. 1-4: 57–66. https://doi.org/10.1080/0361526X.2013.759875.

Suber, Peter. (2012). *Open Access*. Boston: MIT Press, 2014.

U.S. Access Board. n.d. "Rehabilitation Act of 1973." American Association of Law Libraries. Accessed November 18, 2018. https://www.access-board.gov/the-board/laws/rehabilitation-act-of-1973#508.

U.S. Const. art. I, § 8, c8

U.S. Constitution. Art./Amend. XI

U.S. Copyright Office, Compendium of U.S. Copyright Office Practices § 101 (3d ed. 2021)

U.S. Copyright Office, Compendium of U.S. Copyright Office Practices § 312.1 (3d ed. 2021)

U.S. Copyright Office, Compendium of U.S. Copyright Office Practices § 313.2 (3d ed. 2021)

U.S. Copyright Office, Compendium of U.S. Copyright Office Practices § 313.3(B) (3d ed. 2021)

U.S. Copyright Office, Compendium of U.S. Copyright Office Practices § 503.1(B) (3d ed. 2021)

U.S. Copyright Office, Compendium of U.S. Copyright Office Practices § 508.1 (3d ed. 2021)

U.S. Copyright Office, Compendium of U.S. Copyright Office Practices § 612.2 (3d ed. 2021)

U.S. Copyright Office, Compendium of U.S. Copyright Office Practices § 703 (3d ed. 2021)

U.S. Copyright Office, Compendium of U.S. Copyright Office Practices § 802.1 (3d ed. 2021)

U.S. Copyright Office, Compendium of U.S. Copyright Office Practices § 802.2(A) (3d ed. 2021)

U.S. Copyright Office, Compendium of U.S. Copyright Office Practices § 804.1 (3d ed. 2021)

U.S. Copyright Office, Compendium of U.S. Copyright Office Practices § 806.1 (3d ed. 2021)

U.S. Copyright Office, Compendium of U.S. Copyright Office Practices § 926.1 (3d ed. 2021)

U.S. Copyright Office, Compendium of U.S. Copyright Office Practices § Glossary (3d ed. 2021)

U.S. Copyright Office, Compendium of U.S. Copyright Office Practices § Introduction (3d ed. 2021)

U.S. Copyright Office, Compendium of U.S. Copyright Office Practices § Part VIII (3d ed. 2021)

Vogels, Emily A. 2021-a. "Digital Divide Persists Even as Lower-Income Americans Make Gains in Tech Adoption." Pew Research Center. https://www.pewresearch.org/fact-tank/2021/06/22/digital-divide-persists-even-as-americans-with-lower-incomes-make-gains-in-tech-adoption/

Vogels, Emily A. 2021-b. "Some Digital Divides Persist Between Rural, Urban, and Suburban America." Pew Research Center. https://www.pewresearch.org/fact-tank/2021/08/19/some-digital-divides-persist-between-rural-urban-and-suburban-america/.

Weston, Chris, Aurelia J. Schultz, Emily M. Lanza, Michelle Choe, and Karyn Temple Claggett. 2017. Section 108 of Title 17: A Discussion Document of the Register of Copyrights. Washington D.C.: U.S. Copyright Office. https://www.copyright.gov/policy/section108/discussion-document.pdf.

Wilde, Oscar. 1915. *The Importance of Being Earnest: A Trivial Comedy for Serious People*. London: Methuen & Co. Ltd.

WIPO Copyright Treaty art. 11, Dec. 20, 1996, 2186 U.N.T.S 121.
World Blind Union. 2020. "Marrakesh Treaty Ratification and Implementation Campaign." Last modified October 19, 2020. https://worldblindunion.org/programs/marrakesh-treaty/.
World Intellectual Property Organization. n.d.-a. "What is Intellectual Property?" World Intellectual Property Organization. Accessed June 14, 2017. http://www.wipo.int/about-ip/en/.
World Intellectual Property Organization. n.d.-b. "Summary of the Marrakesh Treaty to Facilitate Access to Published Works for Persons Who Are Blind, Visually Impaired, or Otherwise Print Disabled (MVT)(2013)." World Intellectual Property Organization. Accessed November 13, 2018. https://www.wipo.int/treaties/en/ip/marrakesh/summary_marrakesh.html.

Cases

A&M Records, Inc. v. Napster, Inc., 114 F. Supp. 2d 896 (N.D. Cal. 2000)
A&M Records, Inc. v. Napster, Inc., 239 F.3d 1004 (9th Cir. 2001)
Aalmuhammed v. Lee, 202 F.3d 1227 (9th Cir. 2000)
Aalmuhammed v. Lee, (202 F.3d 1227 (9th Cir. 1999)
Allen v. Cooper, 589 US (2020)
Authors Guild, Inc. v. HathiTrust, 902 F. Supp. 2d 445 (S.D.N.Y. 2012)
Authors Guild, Inc. v. HathiTrust, 755 F.3d 87 (2d Cir. 2014)
Authors Guild v. Google, Inc., 804 F.3d 202 (2d Cir. 2015)
Bill Graham Archives v. Dorling Kindersley, Inc., F.3d 605 (2d Cir. 2006)
Bobbs-Merrill Co. v. Straus, 210 U.S. 339 (1908)
Burrow-Giles Lithographic Company v. Napoleon Sarony. 111 U.S. 53 (1884)
Cambridge Univ. Press v. Becker, 863 F. Supp. 2d 1190 (N.D. Ga. 2012)
Cambridge Univ. Press v. Patton, 769 F.3d 1232 (11th Cir. 2014)
Campbell v. Acuff-Rose Music, 510 U.S. 569 (1994)
Capitol Records LLC et al. v. ReDigi Inc. at al., 934 F. Supp. 2d 640 (S.D.N.Y. 2013)
Capitol Records LLC et al. v. ReDigi Inc. at al., 910 F.3d 649 (2d Cir. 2018)
Chamberlain Group, In. v. Skylink Technology, Inc., 381 F.3d 1178 (Fed. Cir. 2004)
Diversey v. Schmidly, 738 F.3d 1196 (10th Cir. 2013)
Feist Publications, Inc., v. Rural Telephone Service Co., 499 U.S. 340 (1991)
Florida Prepaid Post-Secondary Education Expense Board v. College Savings Bank, 527 U.S. 627 (1999)
Gershwin Pub. Corp. v. Columbia Artists Management, Inc., 443 F.2d 1159 (2d Cir. 1971)
Harper & Row v. Nation Enterprises, 471 U.S. 539 (1985)
Kirtsaeng v. John Wiley & Sons Inc., 568 U. S. 519 (2013)
Maxtone-Graham v. Burtchaell, 631 F. Supp. 1432 (S.D.N.Y. 1986)
MDY Industries, LLC v. Blizzard Entertainment, Inc., No. CV-06-2555-PHX DGC (D. Ariz. Apr. 1, 2009)
MDY Industries, LLC v. Blizzard Entertainment, Inc., 629 F.3d 928 (2010)

Morrissey v. Procter & Gamble Co., 379 F.2d 675 (1st Cir. 1967)
Seminole Tribe of Florida v. Florida, 517 U.S. 44 (1996)
Sundeman v. the Seajay Society, Inc., 142 F.3d 194 (4th Cir. 1998)
Universal City Studios, Inc. v. Corley, 273 F.3d 429 (2d Cir. 2001)
UMG (Universal Music Group) Recordings, Inc., v. Augusto, 558 F. Supp. 2d 1055 (C.D. Cal. 2008)
Wheaton and Donaldson v. Peters and Grigg, 33 U.S. 591 (1834)

Statutes

Assistive Technology Act of 2004, 29 U.S.C. § 3002
Rehabilitation Act of 1973, 29 U.S.C. § 701
The Code of Federal Regulations (C.F.R), 2 § 201.40
The Code of Federal Regulations, 2 § 201.40(b)
The Code of Federal Regulations, 2 § 201.40(b)(1)
The Code of Federal Regulations, 2 § 201.40(b)(1)(ii)
The Code of Federal Regulations, 2 § 201.40(b)(1)(ii)(A)
The Code of Federal Regulations, 2 § 201.40(b)(3)(i)
The Code of Federal Regulations, 2 § 201.40(b)(3)(ii)
The Code of Federal Regulations, 2 § 201.40(b)(3)(i)(B)
The Code of Federal Regulations, 2 § 201.40(b)(3)(i)(C)
The Code of Federal Regulations, 2 § 201.40(b)(3)(i)(D)
The Code of Federal Regulations, 2 § 202.11(b)(2)
The Code of Federal Regulations, 2 § 202.11(d)(3)(ii)
The Code of Federal Regulations, 37 § 201.14
The Code of Federal Regulations, 37 § 201.24
The Code of Federal Regulations, 37 § 201.24(b)
The Code of Federal Regulations, 37 § 201.24(c)
The Code of Federal Regulations, 37 § 201.40(b)(1)
The Code of Federal Regulations, 37 § 201.40(b)(2)(i)
The Code of Federal Regulations, 37 § 201.40(b)(2)(i)(A)
The Code of Federal Regulations, 37 § 201.40(b)(2)(i)(B)
The Code of Federal Regulations, 37 § 201.40(b)(2)(i)(C)
The Code of Federal Regulations, 37 § 201.40(b)(2)(ii)(B)
The Code of Federal Regulations, 37 § 201.40(b)(2)(ii)(C)
The Code of Federal Regulations, 37 § 201.40(b)(3)
The Code of Federal Regulations, 37 § 201.40(b)(3)(i)
The Code of Federal Regulations, 37 § 201.40(b)(3)(ii)
The Code of Federal Regulations, 37 § 201.40(b)(3)(i)(B)
The Code of Federal Regulations, 37 § 201.40(b)(3)(i)(C)
The Code of Federal Regulations, 37 § 201.40(b)(3)(i)(D)
The Code of Federal Regulations, 37 § 201.40(b)(6)
The Code of Federal Regulations, 37 § 201.40(b)(6)(ii)
The Code of Federal Regulations, 37 § 223(a)

The Code of Federal Regulations, 37 § 223(a)(5)
The Code of Federal Regulations, 37 § 223(c)
The Copyright Act of 1976, 17 U.S.C. § 101
The Copyright Act of 1976, 17 U.S.C. § 102
The Copyright Act of 1976, 17 U.S.C. § 102(a)
The Copyright Act of 1976, 17 U.S.C. § 102(a)(1)
The Copyright Act of 1976, 17 U.S.C. § 102(a)(2)
The Copyright Act of 1976, 17 U.S.C. § 102(a)(3)
The Copyright Act of 1976, 17 U.S.C. § 102(a)(4)
The Copyright Act of 1976, 17 U.S.C. § 102(a)(5)
The Copyright Act of 1976, 17 U.S.C. § 102(a)(6)
The Copyright Act of 1976, 17 U.S.C. § 102(a)(7)
The Copyright Act of 1976, 17 U.S.C. § 102(a)(8)
The Copyright Act of 1976, 17 U.S.C. § 102(b)
The Copyright Act of 1976, 17 U.S.C. § 103
The Copyright Act of 1976, 17 U.S.C. § 105(a)
The Copyright Act of 1976, 17 U.S.C. § 105(b)
The Copyright Act of 1976, 17 U.S.C. § 105(c)(1)
The Copyright Act of 1976, 17 U.S.C. § 105(c)(2)
The Copyright Act of 1976, 17 U.S.C. § 105(c)(3)
The Copyright Act of 1976, 17 U.S.C. § 106
The Copyright Act of 1976, 17 U.S.C. § 106(1)
The Copyright Act of 1976, 17 U.S.C. § 106(2)
The Copyright Act of 1976, 17 U.S.C. § 106(3)
The Copyright Act of 1976, 17 U.S.C. § 106(4)
The Copyright Act of 1976, 17 U.S.C. § 106(5)
The Copyright Act of 1976, 17 U.S.C. § 106(6)
The Copyright Act of 1976, 17 U.S.C. § 107
The Copyright Act of 1976, 17 U.S.C. § 107(1)
The Copyright Act of 1976, 17 U.S.C. § 107(2)
The Copyright Act of 1976, 17 U.S.C. § 108
The Copyright Act of 1976, 17 U.S.C. § 108(a)(1)
The Copyright Act of 1976, 17 U.S.C. § 108(a)(2)(i)
The Copyright Act of 1976, 17 U.S.C. § 108(a)(2)(ii)
The Copyright Act of 1976, 17 U.S.C. § 108(a)(3)
The Copyright Act of 1976, 17 U.S.C. § 108(b)
The Copyright Act of 1976, 17 U.S.C. § 108(b)(1)
The Copyright Act of 1976, 17 U.S.C. § 108(c)
The Copyright Act of 1976, 17 U.S.C. § 108(c)(2)
The Copyright Act of 1976, 17 U.S.C. § 108(d)
The Copyright Act of 1976, 17 U.S.C. § 108(d)(1)
The Copyright Act of 1976, 17 U.S.C. § 108(d)(2)
The Copyright Act of 1976, 17 U.S.C. § 108(e)
The Copyright Act of 1976, 17 U.S.C. § 108(e)(2)

The Copyright Act of 1976, 17 U.S.C. § 108(e)(1)
The Copyright Act of 1976, 17 U.S.C. § 108(h)(1)
The Copyright Act of 1976, 17 U.S.C. § 108(h)(2)(A)
The Copyright Act of 1976, 17 U.S.C. § 108(h)(2)(B)
The Copyright Act of 1976, 17 U.S.C. § 108(h)(2)(C)
The Copyright Act of 1976, 17 U.S.C. § 108(f)(4)
The Copyright Act of 1976, 17 U.S.C. § 108(g)
The Copyright Act of 1976, 17 U.S.C. § 108(g)(1)
The Copyright Act of 1976, 17 U.S.C. § 108(g)(2)
The Copyright Act of 1976, 17 U.S.C. § 108(i)
The Copyright Act of 1976, 17 U.S.C. § 109
The Copyright Act of 1976, 17 U.S.C. § 109(a)
The Copyright Act of 1976, 17 U.S.C. § 109(2)(b)(1)(A)
The Copyright Act of 1976, 17 U.S.C. § 110
The Copyright Act of 1976, 17 U.S.C. § 110(1)
The Copyright Act of 1976, 17 U.S.C. § 110(2)
The Copyright Act of 1976, 17 U.S.C. § 110(2)(A)
The Copyright Act of 1976, 17 U.S.C. § 110(2)(B)
The Copyright Act of 1976, 17 U.S.C. § 110(2)(C)
The Copyright Act of 1976, 17 U.S.C. § 110(2)(C)(i)
The Copyright Act of 1976, 17 U.S.C. § 110(2)(C)(ii)
The Copyright Act of 1976, 17 U.S.C. § 110(2)(D)(i)
The Copyright Act of 1976, 17 U.S.C. § 110(2)(D)(1)
The Copyright Act of 1976, 17 U.S.C. § 110(2)(D)(1)(aa)
The Copyright Act of 1976, 17 U.S.C. § 110(2)(D)(1)(bb)
The Copyright Act of 1976, 17 U.S.C. § 110(D)(i)
The Copyright Act of 1976, 17 U.S.C. § 110(2)(D)(ii)(II)
The Copyright Act of 1976, 17 U.S.C. § 110(11)
The Copyright Act of 1976, 17 U.S.C. § 110(11)(A)
The Copyright Act of 1976, 17 U.S.C. § 121
The Copyright Act of 1976, 17 U.S.C. § 121(A)(a)
The Copyright Act of 1976, 17 U.S.C. § 121(A)(b)
The Copyright Act of 1976, 17 U.S.C. § 121(A)(c)
The Copyright Act of 1976, 17 U.S.C. § 121(A)(f)(1)
The Copyright Act of 1976, 17 U.S.C. § 121(b)(1)
The Copyright Act of 1976, 17 U.S.C. § 121(b)(2)
The Copyright Act of 1976, 17 U.S.C. § 121(d)(1)
The Copyright Act of 1976, 17 U.S.C. § 121(d)(2)
The Copyright Act of 1976, 17 U.S.C. § 121(d)(3)
The Copyright Act of 1976, 17 U.S.C. § 201(a)
The Copyright Act of 1976, 17 U.S.C. § 201(b)
The Copyright Act of 1976, 17 U.S.C. § 201(c)
The Copyright Act of 1976, 17 U.S.C. § 202
The Copyright Act of 1976, 17 U.S.C. § 201(d)(1)

The Copyright Act of 1976, 17 U.S.C. § 201(d)(2)
The Copyright Act of 1976, 17 U.S.C. § 204(a)
The Copyright Act of 1976, 17 U.S.C. § 203(5)(b)
The Copyright Act of 1976, 17 U.S.C. § 302(a)
The Copyright Act of 1976, 17 U.S.C. § 302(b)
The Copyright Act of 1976, 17 U.S.C. § 302(c)
The Copyright Act of 1976, 17 U.S.C. § 302(e)
The Copyright Act of 1976, 17 U.S.C. § 305
The Copyright Act of 1976, 17 U.S.C. § 17 401(b)
The Copyright Act of 1976, 17 U.S.C. § 17 401(c)
The Copyright Act of 1976, 17 U.S.C. § 17 401(d)
The Copyright Act of 1976, 17 U.S.C. § 405
The Copyright Act of 1976, 17 U.S.C. § 408(a)
The Copyright Act of 1976, 17 U.S.C. § 501(a)
The Copyright Act of 1976, 17 U.S.C. § 504(c)(2)
The Copyright Act of 1976, 17 U.S.C. § 1201(a)(1)(A)
The Copyright Act of 1976, 17 U.S.C. § 1201(a)(3)(A)
The Copyright Act of 1976, 17 U.S.C. § 1201(a)(1)(C)
The Copyright Act of 1976, 17 U.S.C. § 1201(a)(1)(D)
The Copyright Act of 1976, 17 U.S.C. § 1502(a)
The Copyright Act of 1976, 17 U.S.C. § 1502(c)(1)
The Copyright Act of 1976, 17 U.S.C. § 1502(c)(2)
The Copyright Act of 1976, 17 U.S.C. § 1503(a)(1)(A)
The Copyright Act of 1976, 17 U.S.C. § 1502(d)(3)
The Copyright Act of 1976, 17 U.S.C. § 1504(e)(1)(D)
The Copyright Act of 1976, 17 U.S.C. § 1506(aa)
The Copyright Act of 1976, 17 U.S.C. § 1506(i)

Index

Page numbers followed by a *t* indicate tables and *f* indicate figures.

Aalmuhammed v. Lee, 100
A&M Records, Inc. v. Napster, Inc., 239–240
Accessibility, 10, 12, 59, 171
Accessible format, 10, 218, 219, 220, 221, 225, 228, 232
Accessible technology, 231
Accommodation, 173, 212, 215, 225, 228, 231, 232, 233
ADA (Americans with Disabilities Act), 212, 230
Advanced Access Content System, 174, 226
Agreement on Guidelines for Classroom Copying in Not-for-Profit Educational Institutions with Respect to Books and Periodicals, 125, 126, 134, 237
ALA (American Library Association), 169, 211
Allen v. Cooper, 251
Architectural works, 91–92, 116, 221, 268, 271, 272
Art, 60, 90, 96, 98, 106, 107, 116, 166, 270, 274
Assistive technology, 212, 216, 231
Attorney fees, awarding of, 122, 132, 249–255
Attorneys, working with, 236, 237, 243, 245–249
Attribution, 111, 129, 130, 190, 191, 272, 274
Audio description, 214, 226, 229
Audiovisual works, 3, 4, 11, 55, 60, 88, 91, 97, 114, 143, 221
Authorized entity, 217–221
Authors Guild, Inc. v. HathiTrust, 123, 124, 126, 218, 223

Berne Convention, 104, 105, 113, 171, 263, 264, 267
Bibliographic records, 45
Blackboard, 58, 163, 188
Blind, 10, 33, 61, 214, 217, 218, 223, 228
Blu-ray disc, 13, 17, 29, 34, 43, 86, 107, 150, 156, 158, 173, 174, 175, 194, 226, 228
Bobbs-Merrill Co. v. Straus, 153, 154, 156
Braille, 214, 216, 223, 230
Burrow-Giles Lithographic Company v. Sarony, 99

Cambridge Univ. Press v. Becker, 122, 125, 126, 133, 134
Cambridge Univ. Press v. Patton, 122, 123, 132, 133, 134
Campbell v. Acuff-Rose Music, 121, 122, 123, 124, 126, 127, 194, 195

Canvas, 58, 163, 188
Capitol Records LLC et al. v. ReDigi Inc. et al., 156
Captions, 226, 228, 229, 233
CASE (Copyright Alternative in Small-Claims Enforcement) Act, 255–256
Case studies: a boy, his dragon, and copyright: a review of the basics of U.S. copyright law, courtesy of Christopher Paolini, 106–108; the CASE Act, 255–256; choosing a system to administer reserve services, 58–59; circulating copies of computer programs, 150–151; circulating instructor's personal copies of works on print reserve, 153–155; copyright in state government works, 111–112; copyright notices, 86–87; digital first sale, 156–157; Georgia State e-reserves lawsuit, 132–135; how to avoid giving legal advice to patrons, 244–245; info labels on print reserve items, 30–32; making copies of works obtained through interlibrary loan available via reserve services, 145–148; organizing items on print reserve stacks, 46–47; Section 108 and limited liability for library duplication equipment, 241–242; showing reserve DVDs in the classroom, 158–160; sovereign immunity and the Copyright Remedy Clarification Act, 250–251; textbooks on reserve, 19–23; transformative uses and course reserves, 121–132; what else the TEACH Act allows to be shared, 167–168; when items fly off the shelves, 25–26
CC (Creative Commons), 189, 190–191*t*, 201, 248, 272
CD (compact disc), 3, 13, 86, 150, 172, 194, 200
Cease-and-desist letter, 248, 249
Chafee Amendment, 217
Chamberlain Group, Inc. v. Skylink Technology, Inc., 177, 178
Checklist, 131, 145, 273, 274
Choreographic works, 89, 90, 97, 98, 114, 221
Code of Best Practices in Fair Use for Academic and Research Libraries, 127, 131, 224, 225
Code of Federal Regulations (C.F.R.), 87, 151, 173, 226, 256
Collective works, 92
Compilation, 87, 92, 93, 101
Content Scramble System, 174, 206, 226
Contract, 68, 93, 103, 144, 147, 154, 155, 156, 159, 160, 176, 188, 200, 230, 239, 242
Copyright Clearance Center, 132, 191
Creativity, 84, 85, 110

Damages: actual, 249, 250, 252, 353; reduction of, 353, 354; remittance of, 251, 252; statutory, 249, 250, 252, 255, 353
De minimis, 122, 133
Derivative work, 87, 96, 107, 120, 177, 190, 214, 230, 254, 274
Digital audio transmission, 97, 98
Digital rights management, 171, 206
Digital transmission, 97, 164, 174, 226
Digitization: equipment, 58; of works, 224, 269
Disability services office, 215, 226
Display: public, 114; right of, 97, 120, 122
Distance education, 7, 55, 77; TEACH Act (Technology, Education and Copyright Harmonization Act) and, 162, 163, 165, 166, 168, 169

Distribution: accessibility considerations and, 217, 219, 220, 223; DMCA (Digital Millennium Copyright Act) and, 219; first sale doctrine and, 150, 151, 152, 154, 155, 156; legal risk and, 249, 252, 253; reproduction by libraries and archives user right and, 138, 143, 144, 146; right of, 96, 107, 120, 130; TEACH Act (Technology, Education and Copyright Harmonization Act) and, 167, 177
Diversey v. Schmidly, 120
DMCA (Digital Millennium Copyright Act): circumvention, 226; exemptions to, 217, 226, 227; history, 171; impact of court decisions, 178–179; media reserves and, 174–175; print reserves and, 173–174; rulemaking process, 173, 174, 176, 228; scope of, 176–177
Dramatic literary works, 167
Dramatic musical works, 167
Dramatic works, 89, 97, 98, 107, 114, 167, 168, 221, 271
Duplication equipment, 5, 73, 241, 242
DVD (digital video disc), 3, 6, 8, 13, 17, 29, 31, 34, 35, 42, 43, 45, 67, 69, 70, 72, 78, 86, 107, 141, 142, 145, 148, 149, 150, 155, 156, 158, 171, 173, 174, 175, 177, 194, 200, 201, 206, 226, 228, 229, 232, 241, 242, 243

eBooks (electronic books), 6, 8, 60, 68, 157, 163
Eleventh Amendment, 250
Eligible persons, 218, 218, 219, 220, 221
Equipment: photocopier, 241; scanner, 5, 73, 241
e-reserves (electronic reserve services): assessment of, 77–78; copyright policy for, 61–62; duration of access to, 73–74; linking, 68–69; making copies for, 69, 72–73; marketing of, 76–77; procedures for instructors placing items on, 62–64; processing of requests, 66–75, 75*f*; purpose of, 55; request forms, 64–66, 75; service parameters, 59; space needed to support, 58; staffing of, 56–57; storage of copies made, 74–75; submission of requests, 62–64; technology and equipment needed to support, 58–59; types of items that can be made available via, 60; types of items that cannot be made available via, 61; who can access, 129, 163–164; who can place items on, 59–60
Exclusive license, 100, 102
Exemptions: DMCA (Digital Millennium Copyright Act), 171–179; fair use doctrine, 119–135; first sale doctrine, 149–160; reproduction by libraries and archives, 137–148; TEACH Act (Technology, Education and Copyright Harmonization Act), 161–169

Face-to-face instruction, 6–7, 158, 159
Facts, 85, 94, 133
Fair use: amount being copied, 124–125; checklist, 131, 145, 273, 274; *Code of Best Practices in Fair Use for Academic and Research Libraries*, 127, 131, 224, 225; commercial use, 120–121; copyright policies and, 33, 61; *Feist Publications, Inc., v. Rural Telephone Service Co.*, 84, 85, 94, 110; misconceptions and, 33, 62, 125–126; nature of the work being copied, 123–124; noncommercial use, 120–121;

out-of-print works and, 127; potential market impact, 126–127; publication status and, 123–124; purpose of the use, 120–121; reserve services and, 36, 64, 72, 74, 83, 109, 117, 127; savings clause of section, 144–145; statute, 119; transformative use, 121–123, 273
First Amendment, 235
First sale doctrine: circulating instructor personal copies and, 153–155; computers and, 150–151; digital and, 156–157; ELUAs (end user license agreements) and, 157–158; lawfully made copy and, 151–153
Fixation, 85, 86, 91, 105, 265, 266, 271
Florida Prepaid Post-Secondary Education Expense Board v. College Savings Bank, 251
For-profit uses, 121, 162, 240
Fourteenth Amendment, 251

Gershwin Pub. Corp. v. Columbia Artists Management, Inc., 240
Good faith, 127, 131, 158, 256
Google Books, 118, 223
Government works, 111, 272
Graphical works, 60, 89, 90*t*, 214
GSU (Georgia State University), 122, 123, 125–126, 132, 133–135

Harper and Row v. Nation Enterprises, 121, 123, 124
HathiTrust Digital Library, 223
Hybrid learning, 7

ILL (interlibrary loan), 20, 32, 41, 44, 69, 70, 72, 125, 141, 145, 146, 147, 148, 168
Images, 60, 84, 91, 97, 98, 106, 107, 117*f*, 159, 161, 165, 166, 167, 177, 195, 224
Independent creation, 84
Infringement, 11, 44, 68, 86, 87, 95, 98, 103, 111, 120, 121, 132, 135, 138, 148, 150, 151–154, 161, 169, 156, 159, 176–177, 192, 194, 205, 217, 219, 220, 239–242, 244, 248–254
International agreements/law, 104–106
Intestate succession, 102
IP (intellectual property), 84, 93, 102, 162, 234, 237, 247
Item record, 45

Joint authorship, 99, 104, 114

Kirtsaeng v. John Wiley and Sons Inc., 151–153, 155

Lawfully made copies, 149, 150, 151, 152, 153, 157, 158, 159
Learning management systems, 58, 163, 168
Legal advice, avoid giving, 244–245
Liability: contributory, 239, 240; DMCA (Digital Millennium Copyright Act), 177; direct, 239; for duplication equipment, 241–242; legal, 237; limited for state institutions, 250; mitigation of, 244, 249; primary, 239; secondary, 239, 240; vicarious, 240
Librarian of Congress, 172, 176, 228
Library of Congress, 143, 146, 166, 179, 269, 270, 271, 278
License: exclusive, 100, 102; negotiation of, 144, 156, 186, 187, 191, 229–230, 242; nonexclusive, 100, 102, 103, 105, 185, 186; paying for, 149, 153, 192; tracking, 187, 192
Literary works, 88, 98, 99, 114, 116, 166
LMS (learning management system), 5, 58, 129, 163, 188, 215

Marketing services: electronic and media reserves, 76–77
Media reserve services: assessment of, 77–78; copyright policy for, 61–62; duration of access to, 73–74; linking, 68–69; making copies for, 69, 72–73; marketing of, 76–77; procedures for instructors placing items on, 62–64; processing of requests; 66–75, 75*f*; purpose of, 55; request forms, 64–66, 75; service parameters, 59; space needed to support, 58; staffing of, 56–57; storage of copies made, 74–75; submission of requests, 62–64, technology and equipment needed to support, 58–59; types of items that can be made available via, 60; types of items that cannot be made available via, 61; who can access, 129, 163–164; who can place items on, 59–60
MDY Industries, LLC v. Blizzard Entertainment, Inc., 177, 178
Moodle, 58, 163
Morrissey v. Procter & Gamble Co., 94
Motion pictures, 3, 4, 60, 91, 97, 114, 173, 174–175, 221, 226
MTIA (Marrakesh Treaty Implementation Act): changes made to, 217; making of accessible copies for reserves and, 217; print reserves, 50–51; sharing copies internationally, 219–221
Music Modernization Act, 115
Musical works: dramatic, 167; nondramatic, 167; rights in, 88, 167, 240

Noncommercial use, fair use, 120–121
Nonexclusive license, 100, 102, 103, 105, 185, 186
Non-profit use: accessibility considerations and, 218, 222; DMCA (Digital Millennium Copyright Act) and, 172; fair use, 119, 120–121, 122; first sale doctrine and, 150, 151, 158; GSU (Georgia State University) case and, 123; remittance of damages and, 251, 252, 253; reproduction by libraries and archives user right and, 138, 142, 143; TEACH Act (Technology, Education and Copyright Harmonization Act) and, 162, 165, 168

Obsolete format, 20, 137, 140, 141, 142
OGC (Office of General Counsel), 184, 236
Open access (OA), 60, 135, 188, 201, 241, 248
Originality, 84, 85, 93
Out-of-print works, 127
Ownership of copyright: considerations for, 98; exceptions to the rights of, 95; exclusive rights of, 95–98; identifying, 182; joint, 99, 100; transfer of, 102–103; works made for hire, 100–101

Pantomime, 89, 90, 97, 98, 114, 167, 168, 221
PDF (portable document format), 36, 37, 65, 73, 86, 145, 172, 188, 192, 213, 214, 216, 252
Performance: definition, 97; public, right of, 97, 102, 107, 120, 138, 151, 177; work, 89, 91, 142, 158, 159, 161, 165, 166, 167, 168, 227, 240, 253
Permissions: definition of, 181; denial of, 193; drafting, 182–185; fair use and, 194; identifying rightsholder, 182, 186–187; negotiation of, 187;

obtaining, 12, 14, 39, 57, 67, 74, 83, 110, 117, 132, 150, 153, 156, 181, 194, 202, 206, 221, 236, 239, 248, 256; paying for, 5, 192; seeking, 87, 103, 155, 191, 274; terms of, 74; tracking of, 192
Personal copies, circulation of, 21, 22, 34, 35, 43, 44, 45, 49
Phonorecord, 85, 86, 87, 88, 96, 97, 113, 114, 119, 137, 138, 139, 140, 142, 144, 145, 146, 149, 150, 153, 155, 157, 168, 217, 218, 219, 220, 223, 227, 241, 250, 251, 252, 253, 271
Photocopier, 241
Photocopies, 14, 17, 18, 35, 44, 86, 130, 183, 200, 241
Photocopying, 44, 145, 146, 155, 201, 207, 242
Photographs, 90, 111, 139, 166, 221, 222, 251
Pictorial works, 90*t*, 92, 100, 219
Policies: communicating, 34, 35, 38, 50, 63, 64, 76; copyright, 210, 243, 245, 246; development of, 11, 24, 26, 27, 28, 29, 60, 129, 230, 243, 247; electronic reserve copyright policy, 61–62; enforcement of, 31, 38, 39, 40 41, 42, 67, 69, 71; institutional, 162, 163, 169, 220, 225; media reserve copyright policy, 61–62; print reserve copyright policy, 33–34, 52; revision of, 246
Premises, 140, 142, 145, 174, 241
Print reserve services: assessing overdue fines, 28–29; assessment of, 51–52; circulating instructor copies, 43–44; copyright policy for, 33–34; duration of circulation, 24–25; housing of, 15–16; ILS processing of, 45; labels for, 30–31; marketing of, 50–51; number of copies circulated, 24; organization of on stacks, 46–47; photocopies and, 17, 18, 44; procedures for instructors placing items on, 34–35; processing of requests, 38–45, 46*f*, 47–49; purpose of, 13; removal of items from, 47–49; renewal of, 28; replacement of, 29–30; request forms, 35–37, 38, 49; staffing of, 14–15; service parameters, 17; submission of requests, 17, 37–38; technology and equipment needed to support, 16–17; turnover of, 32–33; types of items that can be circulated via, 17, 18–19; types of items that cannot be circulated via, 23–24; who can borrow, 26–27; who can place items on, 17
Private study, copies for, 146, 147
Public display, right of, 97, 114, 120, 122
Public domain: reserves copyright workflow, 199–205; works in, 95, 109, 110–118, 241, 254, 259–271
Public Domain Mark, Creative Commons, 189, 191*t*
Public performance, right of, 97, 102, 107, 120, 138, 151, 177
Publication: agreements, 201, 206; definition of, 138; determining the status of, 113

Quoting, 121, 122, 131, 177

Recommended resources, 95, 101, 117, 143, 237, 238, 246
Registrar of copyrights, 143, 172, 175
Registration of copyright, 86, 105, 114, 260, 266, 270, 272
Remediation, 229, 231
Remedy, 103, 172, 177, 249, 250
Reproduction: fair use and, 119, 120, 122; right of, 96, 107
Reproduction by libraries and archives (Section 108) user right:

contractual limitations and, 144; electronic and media reserve applications of, 140; fair use savings clause and, 144; print reserve application of, 139–140, 141, 143; published works and, 140–141, 142, 143; qualified works, 143–144; qualifying libraries 137–138
Reserve services (generally): assessing instructor need for, 5–8; assessing student need for, 8–10; evaluating the library's ability to offer, 10–11; relationship between instructor and student needs for, 12*f*; types, 3–4
Rights granted to creators of copyrightable works: adaptation, 96; public distribution, 96; public performance, 96–98; public transmission, 98; reproduction, 96

SCOTUS (Supreme Court of the United States), 84, 111, 121, 122, 123, 151, 152, 153, 154, 155, 157, 178, 194, 251
Screen capture, 175
Sculptural works, 90*t*
Seminole Tribe of Florida v. Florida, 251
Sounds recordings, and reserves, 3, 4, 6, 11, 13, 34, 36, 63, 73; definition of, 91; duration of protection, 115, 264–265, 268, 271; first sale doctrine and, 150; making of accessible copies and, 221, 227; rights in, 96, 97, 98, 166; TEACH Act (Technology, Education and Copyright Harmonization Act) and, 168
Sovereign Immunity, 250–251
Special collections, 23, 24, 60
State law, 115, 154, 212, 240
Statutory damages, 249, 250, 251, 252, 235, 255
Sundeman v. the Seajay Society, Inc., 122

TA (teaching assistants), 17, 59, 164
Tangible medium of expression, 84, 85, 91, 95, 106, 271
TEACH (Technology, Education and Copyright Harmonization) Act: content that cannot be made available under, 168; displays of works under, 166–167; institutional requirements, 162–163; instructor requirements, 165; performances of works under, 165–166; technology requirements, 163–164
Technology, 4, 7, 9, 11, 13, 16–17, 35, 52, 56, 58, 73, 78, 88, 141, 175, 212, 214, 216, 231
Termination of transfer, 103–104
Textbooks, 19–23
TPM (technical protection measures), 171, 172, 175, 176, 226, 227, 230
Transfer of copyright: exclusive, 102–103; nonexclusive, 102; termination of, 103–104
Transformative use, 121–123, 273
Triennial rulemaking process, 173, 174, 176, 228

Universal City Studios, Inc. v. Corley, 177
Universal Music Group Recordings, Inc., v. Augusto, 154
Unpublished: definition of, 139; fair use determinations, 133; form, 112; literary works, 221; manuscripts, 122; plans, 92, 116; reproduction by libraries and archives user right, 138, 139, 140, 142; works, 104, 112, 113, 114, 124, 259, 260, 263, 264, 269, 271, 274
U.S. Constitution, copyright clause, 84, 96, 108, 120, 133, 210
U.S. Copyright Act, 84, 88, 95, 104, 112, 113, 116, 127, 146, 152, 223
U.S. Courts of Appeals, geographic boundaries, 178*f*

USCO (U.S. Copyright Office), 84, 112, 143, 176, 182, 228, 238

VHS (video home system), 13, 17, 86, 141
Vicarious infringement, 240
Vicarious liability, 239, 240
VPAT (Voluntary Product Accessibility Template), 215, 229, 230, 241

WCAG (Web Content Accessibility Guidelines), 213, 230
Wheaton and Donaldson v. Peters and Grigg, 111
Workflow: copyright, 181; copyright for electronic and media reserves, 202, 205–207, 208*f*, 209*f*; copyright for print reserves, 199, 200–202, 203*f*, 204*f*; electronic and media reserves processing, 59, 67, 74, 75*f*; fair use, 130; print reserves processing, for, 39, 45, 46*f*; Section 108, 145
Works: architectural, 91–92, 116, 221, 268, 271, 272; audiovisual, 3, 4, 11, 55, 60, 88, 91, 97, 114, 143, 221; choreographic, 89, 90, 97, 98, 114, 221; collective, 92; derivative, 87, 96, 107, 120, 177, 190, 214, 230, 254, 274; determining the copyright status of, 109–118, 260–272; fixation of, 85, 86, 91, 105, 265, 266, 271; graphic, 60, 89, 214; lawfully made copies, 149, 150, 151, 152, 153, 157, 158, 159; literary, 88, 98, 99, 114, 116, 166; made for hire, 100, 101, 103, 104, 114, 115, 182, 201, 206, 260, 265; not eligible for copyright protection, 93–95, 99, 110, 236; out of print, 127; published, 111, 113, 123, 137, 138, 140–142, 213, 217, 260–272; unpublished, 104, 112, 113, 114, 124, 259, 260, 263, 264, 269, 271, 274
Works made for hire, 100, 101, 103, 104, 114, 115, 182, 201, 206, 260, 265
WIPO (World Intellectual Property Organization), 84, 105, 171, 217, 220

About the Author

Carla S. Myers serves as associate professor and coordinator of scholarly communications for the Miami University Libraries, Ohio. Her professional presentations and publications focus on fair use, copyright in the classroom, and library copyright issues. She is a recipient of the Robert L. Oakley Memorial Scholarship, which is sponsored by the American Library Association and supports research and advanced study for librarians who are interested and active in the fields of intellectual property, public policy, and copyright and their impacts on libraries and the ways libraries serve their communities. She has a Bachelor of Arts in psychology from the University of Akron, Ohio, and a Masters of Library and Information Science from Kent State University, Ohio.

Milton Keynes UK
Ingram Content Group UK Ltd.
UKHW020255121223
434216UK00007B/188

9 781440 862038